Access to Academics
Planning Instruction for K–12 Classrooms with ELLs

Joy Egbert

Washington State University

Gisela Ernst-Slavit

Washington State University

PEARS

Boston • Columbus • Indianapolis • New York • San Francisco • Upper Saddle River
Amsterdam • Cape Town • Dubai • London • Madrid • Milan • Munich • Paris • Montreal • Toronto
Delhi • Mexico City • Sao Paulo • Sydney • Hong Kong • Seoul • Singapore • Taipei • Tokyo

Editor-in-Chief: Aurora Martínez Ramos
Series Editorial Assistant: Meagan French
Director of Marketing: Chris Flynn
Marketing Manager: Danae April
Production Editor: Cynthia Parsons
Editorial Production Service: TexTech International
Manufacturing Buyer: Meagan Cochran
Electronic Composition: TexTech International
Interior Design: Debbie Schneck
Cover Designer: Elena Sidorova

*For Princess and Super Pickle.
Yes, you can play on the computer now.*
—J. E.

*To Dave, Max, and Arthur,
who are there for me every day in every way.
Gracias.*
—G. E. S.

For related titles and support materials, visit our online catalog at www.pearsonhighered.com.

Between the time website information is gathered and then published, it is not unusual for some sites to have closed. Also, the transcription of URLs can result in typographical errors. The publisher would appreciate notification where these errors occur so that they may be corrected in subsequent editions.

Library of Congress Cataloging-in-Publication Data

Egbert, Joy.
   Access to academics : planning instruction for k-12 classrooms with ELLs / J. Egbert and G. Ernst-Slavit.
      p.   cm.
   Includes bibliographical references and index.
   ISBN-13: 978-0-13-815676-3
   ISBN-10: 0-13-815676-X
   1.   English language—Study and teaching—Foreign speakers.   2.   Language arts—Correlation with content subjects.   3.   Language acquisition.   4.   Education, Bilingual.   5.   Mainstreaming in education.   I.   Ernst-Slavit, Gisela   II.   Title.
   PE1128.A2E36 2010
   428.2'4—dc22

                                                                                          2010008861

Printed in the United States of America

Credits appear on the appropriate pages, which constitutes an extension of the copyright page.

17

www.pearsonhighered.com

ISBN-10: 013815676X
ISBN-13: 9780138156763

contents

Preface   **x**

part one

Understanding the Roles of Language and Content   **1**

chapter **1** *Academic Success: Learning the Language of School*   **2**

Key Issues   2
The Language of School   4
  Social Language   6
    Everyday Aspects of Social Language   6   ● Intercultural Aspects of Social Language   7   ● Instructional Aspects of Social Language   8
  Academic Language   8
    Vocabulary   9   ● Grammar/Syntax   9   ● Discourse   9
  A Comparison of Social and Academic Languages   11
  The BICS and CALP Distinction   12
    Critiques of the BICS and CALP Distinction   15   ● Connections Between the BICS/CALP Distinction and the Language of School   16
  Conclusion   17
  Extensions   17
    For Reflection   17   ● For Action   18

chapter **2** *Language Proficiency and Communicative Competence*   **19**

Key Issues   19
Language Proficiency   20
  Language Domains   21

English Language Proficiency   22   ●   English Language
Proficiency Levels   23   ●   CAN DO Descriptors   28

Communicative Competence   28
Elements of Communicative Competence   30   ●   The Role of
Native Languages and Cultures   32
Approaches for Using the Native Language in the Classroom   33

Conclusion   35

Extensions   35
For Reflection   35   ●   For Action   35

part two
Components of Effective Lesson Design   37

chapter 3   *Assessing Student Strengths and Needs*   38

Key Issues   38

Background   39

Understanding Strengths and Needs   41
Collecting General Information   41   ●   Gathering Information on
Learners' Language Backgrounds   43   ●   Understanding
Educational/Academic Background   45   ●   Discovering Content
Background and Knowledge   46   ●   Exploring Cultural
Background   48

Guidelines for Understanding Student Strengths and
Needs   51
Guideline 1: Model the Techniques   51   ●   Guideline 2: Try Not
to Assume   51   ●   Guideline 3: Embrace Variety   51

Conclusion   52

Extensions   53
For Reflection   53   ●   For Action   53

chapter 4   *Writing and Teaching to*
Language Objectives   54

Key Issues   54

Background   55

Understanding Objectives   56
   Content Objectives   56   ●   Language Objectives   57
    Constructing Language Objectives   58

Teaching to the Language Objectives   62
   Guideline 1: Integrate Language and Content   62   ●   Guideline 2:
   Use Pedagogically Sound Techniques   63   ●   Guideline 3: Break
   Down the Language   63

Conclusion   64
Extensions   65
   For Reflection   65   ●   For Action   65

chapter 5   *Connecting to Students' Lives*   66

Key Issues   66
Background   68
Understanding Connections   68
   Making Personal Connections   69   ●   Making Academic
   Connections   71

Building Background knowledge   72
   Integrating Connections   74

Guidelines for Making Connections   76
   Guideline 1: Be Deliberate   76   ●   Guideline 2: Help Students
   Transfer Connections Back to Their Lives   76   ●   Guideline 3:
   Consider Culture   76

Conclusion   76
Extensions   78
   For Reflection   78   ●   For Action   78

chapter 6   *Designing Engaging Tasks*   79

Key Issues   79
Background   80
Understanding Engagement and Tasks   80
   Engagement   80   ●   Elements of Tasks   81
    Elements of Task Process   82   ●   *Elements of Task Product   84*

Pedagogical Connections   85
   Techniques for Making Pedagogical Connections   85

Guidelines for Task Design   85
  Guideline 1: Give Students a Reason to Listen   87 ●
  Guideline 2: Do Not Do What Students Can Do   87

Conclusion   88

Extensions   88
  For Reflection   88 ● For Action   89

chapter 7   *Assessing Tasks, Lessons, and Students*   **90**

Key Issues   90

Background   91

Understanding Assessment   91
  Purposes of Assessment   92

Assessing Student Process and Product   94
  Adapting Traditional Classroom Assessments   94 ●   Student
  Roles in Alternative Assessments   95

Lesson Examples   96

Homework   96

Additional Guidelines for Assessment   99
  Guideline 1: Be Transparent   99   ●   Guideline 2: Reconsider
  Grades   99

Assessing the Lesson   100

Conclusion   102

Extensions   102
  For Reflection   102 ●   For Action   103

part three
Designing Lessons for Academic Success   **105**

chapter 8   *Unlocking the Language of Science*   **106**

Key Issues   106

Science Education: A Focus on Inquiry   107

The Specialized Language of Science   108
  Vocabulary   110 ●   Grammatical Features   113 ●
  Discourse   113

Strategies for Learning and Talking Science   114

Learning the Language of Scientific Inquiry   114   •

Compare and Contrast   114   •   Cause and Effect   116   •

Teaching Greek and Latin Roots   117

Conclusion   119

Extensions   120

For Reflection   120   •   For Action   120

chapter **9**   *Unlocking the Language of*
Mathematics   **121**

Key Issues   121

Mathematics Reform: "The New Math"   123

The Specialized Language of Mathematics   124

Vocabulary   125   •   Grammatical Features   128   •

Mathematical Discourse   128

Teaching Strategies for Learning and Talking Mathematics   130

Use a Variety of Instructional Formats and Supports   130   •

Introduce New Vocabulary in a Thoughtful and Integrated

Manner   131   •   Identify and Highlight Key Words with Multiple

Meanings   131   •   Modify Your Speech   131   •   Use Preview

and Review   132   •   Search for Cognates: Validating Students'

Languages and Cultures   133   •   Use Cooperative Learning and

Promote Opportunities for Interaction   134   •   Teach

Organizational and Study Skills   134   •   Create an Atmosphere

for Risk Taking and Making Mistakes   135

Conclusion   136

Extensions   136

For Reflection   136   •   For Action   136

chapter **10**   *Unlocking the Language of English*
Language Arts   **137**

Key Issues   137

English Language Arts: Preparing Students for the Literacy

Demands of Today and Tomorrow   139

Clarification: Six Language Arts or Four Language

Domains?   139   •   Multiple Literacies   140

Effective Literacy Practices for ELLs in the Elementary
Grades   141

Key Elements for Improving Literacy for Elementary English
Language Learners   141

*Theoretical Orientation   141   •   Language-Rich
Environment   141   •   Meaningful Literacy   141   •
Culturally Relevant Literacy Practices   141   •   Additive
Perspective on Language   142   •   Emphasis on Academic
Language   142*

Prereading Strategies   142   •   Reading Strategies for
Beginning Readers   143   •   Reading Strategies for
Intermediate Readers   143   •   Key Elements for Improving
Adolescent Literacy   145   •   Effective Reading Instruction
for ELLs   146   •   Effective Writing Instruction for ELLs   147

The Language of English Language Arts   149

Vocabulary   150

Vocabulary Teaching Strategies   150

Grammatical Features   152   •   Language Functions   154   •
Discourse   156

Conclusion   157

Extensions   157

For Reflection   157   •   For Action   158

chapter **11**   *Unlocking the Language of Social Studies*   **159**

Key Issues   159

About the Field of Social Studies   161

The Specialized Language of Social Studies   163

Vocabulary   165   •   Grammatical Features   167   •
Discourse   169

*1. Difficulties Presented by Social Studies Textbooks and
Materials   169   •   2. Students Need to Access and Produce
Different Kinds of Written Genres   170*

Strategies for Teaching and Learning Social Studies   171

*1. Developing Socially Supportive Classrooms   171   •
2. Explicit Teaching of Academic Skills   173   •   3. Reducing
Cognitive Load and Increasing Accessibility of Complex Content
Knowledge   175*

Conclusion   176

Extensions   177

    For Reflection   177   ●   For Action   178

chapter **12** *Putting It All Together*   **179**

Key Issues   179

Background   180

Understanding the Whole   180

Lesson Examples   180

Creating a New Lesson   180

    Step 1: Find and Create the Learning Targets   180 ●
    Step 2: Make Initial Connections   181 ● *Step 3: Create*
    Engaging Tasks   182 ● *Step 4: Assessment   182*

Adapting Lessons   182

    Adaptation 1   184 ● *Adaptation 2   186* ●
    Adaptation 3   188

Guidelines for Creating and Adapting Lessons   190

    Guideline 1: Do Not Reinvent the Wheel   190 ●
    Guideline 2: Share   191

Conclusion   191

Extensions   191

    For Reflection   191 ● For Action   192

Appendix   *193*

References   *199*

Index   *205*

Many excellent methods texts deal with everything from second language acquisition to language policy, to general teaching methods, but there is a clear lack of appropriate resources that *directly* address planning lessons for K–12 mainstream classrooms with diverse learners such as English language learners (ELLs). Methods books consistently tell readers to "make learning engaging" or "teach to your language objectives," but they rarely explain *how* to engage language learners or to *create* objectives, let alone teach to them. As teacher educators, we have struggled with this oversight for years, cobbling together resources and developing activities to help ground the ideas in the methods books we use for our students. Colleagues have asked for materials and information to help their teacher education students and professional development participants learn the specifics of these concepts, too. This text is an answer to this gap in the literature.

Access to Academics: Planning Instruction for K–12 Classrooms with ELLs takes a different look at language than most other texts—it addresses language as something students must use constantly, in a variety of school venues, and in different ways depending on the context. The text shows language as vital to content access and thereby academic achievement but, more important, it also provides step-by-step instructions explaining how to help students acquire the language they need. We assume a level of familiarity on the part of readers with basic lesson planning and other facets of instruction, but knowledge of these topics can also be gained in tandem with this text. Therefore, our audience includes both pre-service and in-service teachers and others interested in better serving the needs of all learners.

Although our main emphasis is on English language learners (ELLs), the term *diverse learners* used throughout the text also encompasses the great variety in any classroom of student backgrounds, abilities, needs, and interests. Thus, the suggestions included in this text are important for every content-area teacher.

We do not mean this text to be prescriptive, although to some readers it may sound as if we do. In fact, we recognize that teachers are the ultimate decision makers when it comes to instruction, and our goal is to help teachers think about issues in ways that they may not have previously considered. We hope that this text will provide points for discussion and action. This text is not intended as a methods text; many excellent methods texts are already on the market. Instead, our intent is for it to *accompany* every methods text, to take the "big ideas" from the more general texts and make them practical and doable. Our text can be effective on its own, or it may act as a companion to general methods texts such as Peregoy and Boyle (2004) or Echevarria, Vogt, and Short's (2008) Sheltered Instruction Observation Protocol (SIOP) texts, from which we draw some of our inspiration.

Overview of the Text

Part One of *Access to Academics,* "Understanding the Roles of Language and Content," explains the elements of language and how and why aspects of language are crucial for school achievement. The two chapters in Part One set the foundation for the rest of the text by describing the importance of language to academic success, especially in relation to content learning. Although the focus of these chapters is on English language learners, they also make the point that an instructional emphasis on language is essential for all students.

Part Two, "Components of Effective Lesson Design," applies the ideas from Chapters 1 and 2 to help readers understand specifically how to assist learners in accessing language and content. An emphasis on gathering student information in Chapter 3 underscores the detailed guidelines in Chapters 4–7. These four chapters address central lesson components, including lesson objectives, connections to students' lives, engaging tasks, and appropriate assessments. These components lead to the content-specific lessons and guidelines in Part Three.

Part Three, "Designing Lessons for Academic Success," demonstrates how the concepts in Parts One and Two of the book come together to form coherent plans for helping learners access academic language and content. It focuses on the genres of different content areas and includes additional strategies for integrating language and content. Chapters present specific standards-based examples from math, science, language arts, and social studies.

The final chapter in the book, Chapter 12, "Pulling It All Together," provides complete lessons and integrates the components and guidelines from the rest of the text. The lessons include discussion of how they help learners from diverse backgrounds with different needs succeed in mainstream classrooms.

Acknowledgments

We are grateful for the detailed professional help of the reviewers, whose comments helped us make this text more accessible to our readers: Lisa DeMaagd, Aquinas College; Kimberley Kreicker, Emporia State University; Renee Rubin, University of Texas at Brownsville; and Brian Whitney, Boise School District. In addition, we gratefully acknowledge Kelly Chen and Tomás Flores for permission to use their poems and the National Middle School Association for permission to use information from the following previously published article: Slavit, D., & Ernst-Slavit, G. (2007). Teaching mathematics and English to English language learners simultaneously. *Middle School Journal, 39*(2), 4–11.

We would also like to thank Meagan French, editorial assistant, for her patience and support, and Aurora Martinez, editor-in-chief, for seeing the worth in our ideas. Special thanks to Tamara Nelson and David Slavit, for their thoughtful feedback on the science and mathematics chapters, and to doctoral student Michele Mason, for her assistance, insight, and support throughout the many phases of the manuscript. Others who helped in the preparation of this book include Yi (Tanya) Chen, Allison Yang, Tom Salsbury, and the administration at Franklin Elementary School in Pullman, Washington, Mary Roe, and Jamie and David Jessup. In addition, our heartfelt thanks go to the many teachers who, over the years, have opened their classrooms and shared their many accomplishments and successes as well as their troubles and tribulations, our teacher education students who worked with us and showed us the way, and our ESL students who motivate us to be better.

about the authors

Joy Egbert, PhD, is Professor of ESL and Education Technology at Washington State University, Pullman. She is an award-winning teacher, materials developer, and researcher. In addition to many other publications, she is the author of *Supporting Learning with Technology: Essentials of Classroom Practice* (Pearson, 2009), *CALL Essentials* (TESOL, Inc, 2005), and seven other books for ESL and technology-using teachers.

Gisela Ernst-Slavit, Ph.D., is a professor of ESL and Education at Washington State University, Vancouver. She investigates language and education in culturally and linguistically diverse settings using ethnographic and sociolinguistic perspectives. She teaches courses in ESL methods, sociolinguistics, research on second language teaching and learning, and critical issues for Latino students.

part one

Understanding the Roles of
Language and Content

Chinadoll

Torn between two cultures
Town between two worlds
Into a sea of Barbies
A little Chinadoll is hurled

I'm lucky to be in America
The land of the brave and the free
Many children around the world
Don't have it as good as me

Our parents bring us here
To the land of opportunity
To learn everything there is to learn
And be the best that we can be

Mommy tells me that good Chinese girls
Are quiet and polite
And that good Chinese girls study
All day and every night

But I'm not a perfect student
Sometimes I'm too loud
It's hard to live up to their expectations
It's impossible to make them proud

I don't think I'm growing up
Exactly how they planned
They ask, "Why do you act so American?
You're CHINESE, don't you understand?!"

And the other Asian kids
Say the same kind of stuff
Years of prejudice and pain
Have made them cold and tough

"Don't try to act white,
You'll never be like them
Different blood flows through your veins
From a different place you stem."

I don't know how I'm supposed to "act"
American or Chinese
There are too many voices yelling
Too many people I can't please

"Be proud to be American!"
"Shout out Asian Pride!"
It's hard to suppress the screaming
Building up inside

Sometimes I wonder
If somebody might
Flick a little switch
And turn off all the lights

People won't be so quick to judge me
If my color they can't see
And maybe for a little while
I could just be me.

By Kelly Chen, used with permission.

• *Reflect on the content of Kelly's poem as you read the chapters in Part One.*
How does the content of her poem relate to the ideas in the chapters?

chapter 1

Academic Success: Learning the Language of School

● Key Issues ●

1. The language of school is a distinct and multifaceted type of English.

2. The language of school includes both social and academic language.

3. Social language is the language used mostly in everyday, casual interactions.

4. Specific linguistic features associated with different content areas characterize academic language.

5. The basic interpersonal communicative skills (BICS) and cognitive academic language proficiency (CALP) distinction highlights some of the differences between social and academic language.

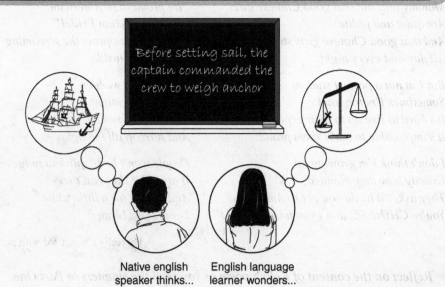

Before setting sail, the captain commanded the crew to weigh anchor

Native english speaker thinks...

English language learner wonders...

Stop and Think

History class • Prior to continuing to read this chapter, think about what the cartoon on the previous page implies about language learning and language learners.

Even before children begin their formal schooling, they have experienced sounds, languages, concepts, people, places, and ways of doing things. For some children, going to school for the first time means learning to follow directions, taking turns, cleaning up their space, forming a line, and sharing the attention of one adult with about 20 other children. For other students, particularly **English language learners** (ELLs), the learning curve is steeper, because they have to learn in a language that they have not yet mastered in the context of an unfamiliar culture. As the chapter-opening cartoon illustrates, an idiomatic expression used by a history teacher can leave an English language learner confused not only about the meaning of a particular term or phrase but also about the gist of the entire narrative.

> *English Language Learners* Other labels and acronyms used to describe students who are learning English as a second, third, or additional language include: limited English proficient (LEP) student, English as a second language (ESL) learner, second language learner, non-English speaker (NES), non-native speaker (NNS), and limited English speaker (LES), among others.

However, words and phrases are only one aspect of what ELLs students have to learn. As the list below illustrates, students need to acquire many other pieces of knowledge in order to navigate the schooling process successfully. For example, during the first days of school, students need to learn about each of the following:

- **The school bus:** when and where to get on and off, how long the ride is, what rules apply while riding, meeting unknown students of many ages, leaving home.
- **School supplies:** getting a backpack or bag, bringing supplies to school.
- **New routines:** carrying papers back and forth to school, what to do if parents do not meet the bus, completing homework by a deadline.
- **School bells:** recess, fire drills, schedules.
- **The people and the school:** the names and titles of people, rules for hallways, location of their homeroom or classroom and other places, for example, the library, music room, gymnasium, cafeteria, nurse's room, etc.
- **Classroom rules and procedures:** when and where to talk, sharpen pencils, ask for help, offer an answer, turn in homework, etc.
- **Lunch procedures:** "hot" or "cold" lunch, where to obtain codes or tickets for hot lunches.
- **Recess routines:** rules, length of time for recess, equipment (balls, slide, swings).

- **Academic content:** life cycle of a frog (science), addition (mathematics), the founding of the United States (social studies), poetry (language arts).

As most readers will realize, this is an extensive but not exhaustive list because there are many other aspects of schooling that students need to learn in order to fully participate in and benefit from their educational experiences. To ELL students with prior or interrupted education in their countries of origin, these extra and often unfamiliar aspects of schooling can add layers of anxiety and confusion to their load of what to learn—sources of concern not experienced by children familiar with the U.S. school system and culture.

Stop and Do

What students need to learn • What else do students need to learn the first few days of school? Add your own ideas to the list above.

The Language of School

The language of school is a "distinct, multifaceted type of English" primarily used in school settings (Gottlieb, Katz, & Ernst-Slavit, 2009, p. 10). It is characterized by a broad range of language competencies that English language learners must learn in order to fully participate in classroom activities and function as accepted and valued members of content-centered communities (Gottlieb et al., 2009; also see Chapter 2 in this text for more discussion of these competencies). As students develop competence in using everyday, **social** English to interact, they must also acquire the **academic** language associated with each specific content area (see Chapters 8–11). As Figure 1.1 depicts, the language of school is comprised of both social and academic language **proficiencies**.

In addition to having many other functions, such as social networking and socializing students into classroom norms and societal expectations, school is one context in which children learn language. According to Halliday (1993), students learn the use of language, through language, and about language. These three aspects and pertinent examples are presented in Figure 1.2.

FIGURE 1.1

The Language of School

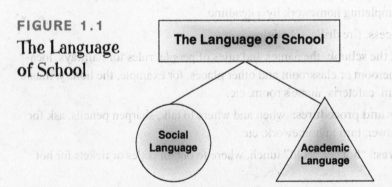

FIGURE 1.2 Types of Language Learning in School

Language Learning	General Examples	School-based Example(s)
1. The **use** of language	How to: ● listen ● speak ● read ● write in order to reach goals ● registers or specialized varieties of language	**Ways of interacting:** "Mrs. Pérez, I need help with my biology assignment." **Different registers:** "Adopt one of the two sides and prepare a statement to support your decision."
2. **Through** language	Learning all about the world inside and outside the classroom	**Expectations:** ● **Academic:** "When answering the math story problem, show all of your work, not just the final answer." ● **Behavioral:** "Do not run in the hallways," "No talking during a test," "Eyes on your own paper."
3. **About** language	● What are the differences among languages ● Historical aspects of language ● Cultural influences on language	**Genres of printed materials:** autobiographies, diaries, dictionaries, encyclopedias, fantasy, letters, textbooks **Parts of speech:** subject, verb, object; noun, adjective, adverb

To fully participate in school, English language learners need to develop all of the specific **registers** required to benefit from every aspect of schooling. For example, the language you use with your friends during a ballgame might be very different from that you use during a job interview or used by an auctioneer at an estate sale. There are also different written registers of English. The following three samples have been taken from different sections of a local newspaper. (1) "Standard on every 2010 MKT is Lincoln's signature design—complete with a split waterfall grille, a beveled chamfer along the vehicle's shoulder line, a flowing cantrail that frames the greenhouse and full-width horizontal taillamps that span the subtly curved weight-saving magnesium liftgate that adds visual character while protecting generous rear cargo space." (2) "Pinch-hitter Mike Sweeney kept the ninth inning alive

Register In the study of language, a register is a variety of a language used for a specific purpose or in a particular social context.

with a two-out double to deep right-center field. Ichiro then jumped on the first pitch from Rivera for his 10th homer of the season and second straight day with a game-winning hit." (3) "Plaintiff alleged that defendant did hit, beat, pummel, cuff, and mutilate plaintiff, and did damage and/or destroy valuable camping equipment belonging to plaintiff."Awareness of different registers is important because it allows us to predict what type of language is expected according to the context or social situation. In schools and classrooms, this awareness allows students to participate appropriately in conversations with others whether they take place in the gym, in the science lab, or during a high-stakes standardized test. Registers include social language, used to interact in the classroom and school settings, and academic language needed to obtain, process, and construct meaning, and provide content-area information. The following pages reveal that social and academic languages are very distinct; however, both types of language are very much needed in the context of school.

Stop and Think

Before reading further, try to predict what the important differences between social language and academic language might be based on your experiences and current understanding of language.

Social Language

Social language is the language used in everyday, casual interactions. It is the language used at the grocery store, when ordering a pizza by telephone, or when chatting with family and friends. It is generally accepted that English language learners can reach a functional (but not necessarily fluent) level of social language competence in approximately two years (Cummins, 2005).

Stop and Do

Social Language • Brainstorm a list of ways students might use social language in a day. Include as many examples as you can.

While social language is the speech used most often during recess, in the hallway, and outside school, it is also relied on heavily in the classroom. Simply stated, social language provides a foundation on which academic language and literacy can flourish. Figure 1.3 depicts three important aspects of social language that deserve attention: everyday, intercultural, and instructional.

While distinctions among these three aspects of social language are not precise, a description of each aspect of social language is discussed below. Figure 1.4 contains pertinent examples.

Everyday Aspects of Social Language The kind of language used in the cafeteria, at recess, or with friends at home is very much needed in the classroom. For English language learners to participate successfully in classroom activities, they must learn how to ask where to find the cafeteria, how to check out a book, and where to wait for the bus.

FIGURE 1.3

Social Language

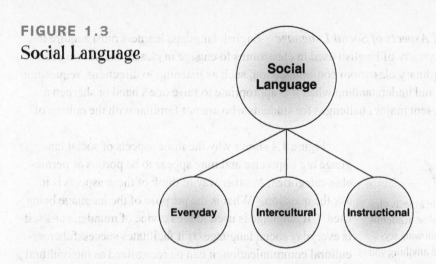

FIGURE 1.4   Aspects of Social Language

Social Language	Examples
Everyday	"This is a great book! You should read it." "I left my lunch on the bus." "Will you teach me how to play kickball?"
Intercultural	"Please, sit down criss-cross applesauce." "When is your family carving pumpkins?" "What is henna? I thought that was just brown writing on your hands."
Instructional	"Please take out a piece of paper and a pencil." "You may sharpen your pencils before school, after recess, and during snack time." "You may now take out your books."

Intercultural Aspects of Social Language   As U.S. school populations become increasingly diverse, English language learners must also learn how to interact appropriately and effectively in cross-cultural situations. Consider, for example, the common command, "Eyes here, please." This phrase may be linguistically challenging for a newcomer, and it may also be culturally uncomfortable. Students from some cultures are taught to look down out of respect when an adult speaks to them. Expecting or forcing English language learners to transgress their families' cultural norms and values can lead to increased stress and conflict between the home and school.

Instructional Aspects of Social Language English language learners must acquire the nontechnical variety of English used in classrooms to engage in classroom learning routines. Even ordinary classroom communication, such as listening to directions, requesting clarification, and understanding when it is appropriate to raise one's hand or sharpen a pencil can present major challenges for students who are not familiar with the culture of the school.

Figure 1.4 shows why the three aspects of social language are imprecise and may appear to be porous or permeable categories. Another way to think of these aspects is to ask the question, "What is the purpose of the language being used?" If language is used in the service of mundane tasks, it is everyday social language. If it facilitates successful cross-cultural communication, it can be recognized as intercultural language. If social language is used to accomplish educational tasks, it is probably instructional in nature.

Stop and Do

Academic language • List the aspects of language that you think comprise academic language. After reading the following section, recheck your list and add anything you may have missed.

Academic Language

When many educators think about the term **academic language**, the vocabulary specific to certain content areas immediately comes to mind. Unquestionably, vocabulary is one component, but as Figure 1.5 illustrates, academic language is comprised of more than words or short phrases.

Academic language includes multiple, dynamic, and interrelated competences (Scarcella, 2003). It also requires the use of a wide range of specific **vocabulary** items, **grammar and syntax** constructions, and **discourse** features. Figure 1.6 presents descriptions and examples

FIGURE 1.5
Academic Language

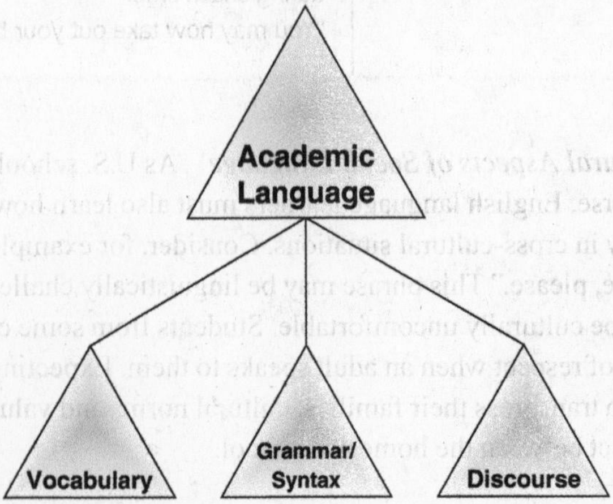

FIGURE 1.6 Dimensions of Academic Language

Aspects of Academic Language	Description	Examples
Vocabulary	Individual words or short phrases	Constitution, essay, microscope, symmetry
Grammar	Syntax, mechanics, sentence and paragraph structure	Punctuation, subject–verb agreement, topic sentence
Discourse	Cohesion and coherence in texts and across genres	Lab reports, development of theme, ellipsis, word problems

of the different aspects of academic language. The following discussion of different aspects of academic language—vocabulary, grammar, and discourse—includes examples organized by content area.

Vocabulary   Vocabulary consists of words and phrases, including (1) **general academic vocabulary** that students may encounter in a variety of content areas, (2) **specialized academic vocabulary** that is specific to a content area, and (3) **technical academic vocabulary** necessary for discussing particular topics within a content area. Figure 1.7 displays examples of these vocabulary types categorized by content area.

Grammar/Syntax   In addition to vocabulary, each content area often has unique ways of organizing and presenting language at the sentence level. The complexity of these language structures may be recognized more easily in written form, such as those found in school content-area textbooks. Figure 1.8 provides examples of particular syntactic features that have unique uses in particular disciplines.

Discourse   Oral or written language is also organized in larger forms, such as paragraphs, thesis papers, or speeches. Discourse refers to these larger bodies of language and how they are both coherent and cohesive. Forms of discourse are categorized into genres, such as those displayed in Figure 1.9. Readers may look at the lists in Figure 1.9 and wonder why an item such as "speeches" was included in social studies but not in language arts. The lists in the figure are not exhaustive nor are the content-area categories exclusive.

RESOURCES

General Academic Vocabulary • Lists of general academic vocabulary can be found in publications and on websites from school districts, learning centers, and publishing companies. See, for example, http://www.u-46.org/roadmap/dyncat.cfm?catid=246Fo, http://esl.fis.edu/vocab/index-a.htm, and http://simple.wiktionary.org/wiki/Wiktionary:Academic_word_list.

FIGURE 1.7   Types and Examples of Vocabulary

	General Academic Vocabulary	Specialized Academic Vocabulary	Technical Academic Vocabulary
Language arts	**Mechanics:** capital letter, lowercase letter, spelling, punctuation	**Parts of a story:** title, characters, setting, plot, antagonist	**Genre specific:** haiku, kigo word
Mathematics	**Numbers:** cardinal (1, 2, 3); ordinal (1st, 2nd, 3rd) **Names of symbols:** +, −, =, <, >	**Significance of words in math:** about, by, in all, less than, altogether, no more than	**Geometry specific:** radius, diameter, pi, circumference
Science	**Inquiry:** assumptions, reasoning, construct explanations	**Parts of a cell:** nucleus, cell wall, endoplasmic reticulum, mitochondria, ribosomes	**Cell division:** mitosis, prophase, metaphase, anaphase, telophase
Social studies	**Continents:** Africa, Antarctica, Asia, Europe, North America, South America, Australia	**Forms of government:** democracy, monarchy, republic, theocracy	**Associated with English monarchy:** divine right of kings, Magna Carta, Parliament

FIGURE 1.8   Examples of Grammatical/Syntactic Features
by Content Area

Content Areas	Examples of Grammatical Features
Language arts	Sensory imagery, alliteration, hyperbole, onomatopoeia, simile
Mathematics	Formulas, significance of prepositions (e.g., *divided by* versus *divided into*), logical connectors, comparative structures
Science	Passive voice, grammatical metaphor, syntactic ambiguity, complex noun phrases
Social studies	Multiple forms of past tense, sequence words, causative signals, historical present

Source: Adapted from *Paper to practice: Using the TESOL English language proficiency standards in PreK-12 Classrooms* by Gottlieb, M., Katz, A., and Ernst-Slavit, G. Copyright 2009 by Teachers of English to Speakers of Other Languages, Inc. (TESOL). Reprinted with permission.

FIGURE 1.9 Examples of Discourse Across Content Areas

Content Areas	Examples of Discourse
Language arts	Autobiographies, plays, scripts, persuasive writing, editorials, newspaper articles
Mathematics	Story problems, graphs, proofs
Science	Lab directions, lab reports, writing in classroom science journals and notebooks
Social studies	Historical diaries, media reports, speeches, folktales from around the world

It is important to emphasize that academic language involves more than terms, conventions, and genres. In other words, the teaching and learning of academic language requires *more* than learning a variety of linguistic components. It involves cultural knowledge about ways of being in the world, ways of acting, thinking, interacting, valuing, believing, speaking, and sometimes writing and reading, connected to particular identities and social roles (Gee, 1992, p. 73).

While this book offers compartmentalized information regarding specific aspects of language, it also acknowledges the importance of considering a host of other factors that will enhance, challenge, or override the teaching, learning, and assessment processes of academic discourses (see Chapters 2 and 3). Bartolomé (1998) warns educators of the dangers of not acknowledging that some students from minority cultural, linguistic, and racial groups might have limited access to academic discourses. For these students, school might be the only setting where they have the opportunity to encounter and acquire the language of school, which may affect the length of time needed to become proficient users of academic language.

A Comparison of Social and Academic Languages

While English language learners may become competent social language users in one or two years, it takes a minimum of five to seven years of **"sustained institutional support** for students to access and gain command of the academic registers needed for success in school" (Cummins, 2005; as referenced in Gottlieb et al., 2009, p. 18). Figure 1.10 illustrates how terms, phrases, and sentences can take different forms when they are used within academic settings.

FIGURE 1.10   A Comparison of Social and Academic Language

Social Language	Academic Language
The rocket took off late.	The launch of Apollo 13 was delayed.
Live	Survive
Can I eat this mushroom?	Is this mushroom edible?
The country didn't have any money.	Government funds were depleted.
This is right.	This answer is appropriate.
Without purpose	Desultory
The same	Equal

RESOURCES

Academic Language • For additional information on how to teach specific content-area academic language, see Chapters 2, 8, 9, 10, and 11 in this text.

To achieve academic success, students must also understand and produce **academic language**. Also referred to as **academic English** or **content-specific** language, academic language is a variety or register of English that is very different from social language. It varies by content area and often involves difficult vocabulary incorporated into texts densely packed with meaning (Bailey, 2006; Scarcella, 2003; Schleppegrell, 2004; also see Chapters 8–11 in this text).

Robin Scarcella and Russell Rumberger (2000) identify five main differences between social and academic language (see Figure 1.11). As suggested by Scarcella and Rumberger (2000), there are many differences between social and academic languages. For students to succeed in the content areas, they need to rely on a broad base of language, content, and background knowledge; access information with fewer contextual clues; produce accurate oral and written texts; utilize higher-order thinking skills; and access and communicate information via oral and written texts. These requirements are challenging for all students, but more so for those learning English as a second language.

The BICS and CALP Distinction

Within the discussion of academic and social languages, we must refer to the influential work of Canadian linguist Jim Cummins who, in 1984, coined two acronyms commonly referred to in second language education: basic interpersonal communication skills

FIGURE 1.11   Differences Between Social and Academic Language

Aspect of Proficiency	Social Language	Academic Language
Language domains	Relies on listening and speaking.	Relies on reading and writing.
Accuracy	Minor errors are acceptable.	Requires a high standard of accuracy in grammar and vocabulary.
Language functions	Relies primarily on narrative.	More complex, such as persuading, arguing, interpreting, hypothesizing, etc.
Cognitive demands	Often less demanding and highly contextualized.	More demanding; must rely on prior knowledge of words, grammar, and conventions.
Range of knowledge	Requires smaller vocabulary.	Requires knowledge of over 20,000 word forms.

(BICS) and cognitive academic language proficiency (CALP) (Cummins, 1984). This model proposes an explanation of why young ELL students who are fluent in social English may have difficulties in academic contexts. The distinction Cummins draws between BICS and CALP is akin to the difference between everyday (playground, hallway) and more formal (classroom, academic) language.

While BICS refers to the development of conversational language, CALP refers to the academic dimension of language necessary for school success. For example, BICS would be used for talking with a peer during lunch, but CALP would be used to provide a summary of Tolstoy's *War and Peace*, to write a report on photosynthesis, or to take a content-area test. These academic tasks often have little contextual support or clues that can help students construct meaning. Cummins argued that students who have not developed CALP in either their native or second language suffer a real academic disadvantage. Figure 1.12 depicts BICS and CALP along two continua, which form a grid.

Activities above the horizontal continuum (quadrants A and C) fall into the category of BICS; that is, they do not involve a high degree of cognitive challenge and they generally take place in highly contextualized environments. On the other hand, activities below the horizontal continuum (quadrants B and D) are more abstract and cognitively demanding.

The left side (quadrants A and B) of the figure includes activities supported by contextual clues that aid understanding. For example, if third-graders are studying objects in space as part of a unit on the solar system, it would be helpful to use planet models or

FIGURE 1.12 Cummins' Quadrants

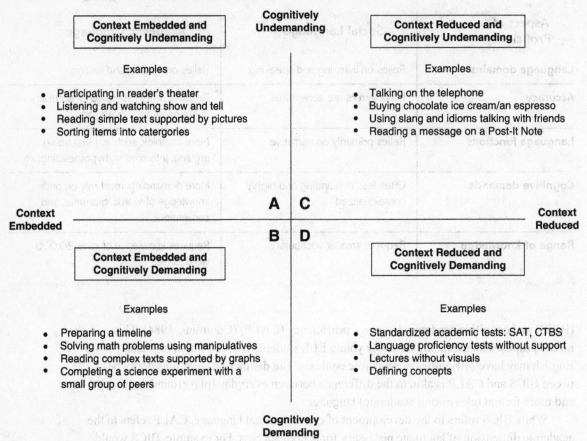

```
┌─────────────────────────────┐    Cognitively        ┌─────────────────────────────┐
│   Context Embedded and      │   Undemanding         │   Context Reduced and       │
│   Cognitively Undemanding   │                       │   Cognitively Undemanding   │
└─────────────────────────────┘                       └─────────────────────────────┘

            Examples                                            Examples

  • Participating in reader's theater              • Talking on the telephone
  • Listening and watching show and tell           • Buying chocolate ice cream/an espresso
  • Reading simple text supported by pictures      • Using slang and idioms talking with friends
  • Sorting items into catergories                 • Reading a message on a Post-It Note
```

Context Embedded ————————————— **A | C** ————————————— Context Reduced

                                                               B | D

```
┌─────────────────────────────┐                       ┌─────────────────────────────┐
│   Context Embedded and      │                       │   Context Reduced and       │
│   Cognitively Demanding     │                       │   Cognitively Demanding     │
└─────────────────────────────┘                       └─────────────────────────────┘

            Examples                                            Examples

  • Preparing a timeline                           • Standardized academic tests: SAT, CTBS
  • Solving math problems using manipulatives      • Language proficiency tests without support
  • Reading complex texts supported by graphs      • Lectures without visuals
  • Completing a science experiment with a         • Defining concepts
    small group of peers
```

Cognitively
Demanding

Source: Adapted from Cummins, 1981.

cutouts to visualize the processes and interactions of Earth's systems and other objects in space.

    Activities on the right side (quadrants C and D) are not aided by contextual clues beyond those embedded in the language. Continuing with the example of third-graders studying objects in space, one alternate way for these students to explore objects in space is by reading from a science text with no illustrations.

    This framework suggests that, in classrooms where there is a high level of student success, instruction often takes place in quadrant B, where activities challenge students academically and are often scaffolded by the use of supports to enhance understanding. However, it is imperative for educators to prepare students to manipulate language in Quadrant D because most of the standardized and nonstandardized assessments currently fall in this quadrant. In other words, most high-stakes tests require students to perform at high levels of cognitive activity and will have little or no additional contextual support beyond linguistic cues.

Stop and Think

BICS and CALP • Cummins's framework has been used to ground both language learning research and teaching. Pause and think critically about this framework. Do you have any questions about its development or use?

Critiques of the BICS and CALP Distinction

While Cummins's BICS and CALP framework has been useful in educational settings by putting forward a construct that brings attention to the development of academic English, it has also received some criticism from researchers and scholars in the field. We offer a brief review of some of the major criticisms regarding the BICS/CALP distinction.

First, some authors believe that "decontextualized language" does not exist. Cummins defines CALP as "decontextualized" language, that is, language that has been stripped of social context. For many (see, for example, Bartolomé, 1998; Gee, 1990), language is always contextualized. No text, oral or written, ever exists independently from a context because words, symbols, and phrases rely chiefly on linguistic and textual cues as well as on cultural understandings. For example, the term *quadrilateral* comes from the Latin *quadri* ("four") and *latus* ("side"). To understand this term, you need to have an understanding of Latin terminology or knowledge of mathematical terms, or you must know about the famous four fortresses supporting each other during the Austrian rule of northern Italy. Yet the term itself holds linguistic clues.

Terms from everyday language may have additional clues beyond linguistic aspects. The following example takes place in a high school cafeteria. Alicia asks Misha, "Have you seen Matt? Two minutes ago he was sitting at that maroon table in the corner" (she points to a specific table). In this case, there are a variety of clues that aid understanding, including pointing, verbally signaling a location (e.g., in the corner), indicating a time (two minutes ago), and describing a characteristic of the table where Matt was sitting (maroon). Even if Misha does not know the meaning of *maroon,* other clues will help his understanding.

A second criticism of the BICS/CALP distinction is that it does not provide educators with sufficient information about the diverse aspects of CALP and how to help students acquire it (Scarcella, 2003). In other words, educators can benefit from having explicit information about the diverse aspects of CALP. Without additional information, many educators equate CALP with vocabulary alone.

Finally, other critics challenge the notion that students acquire BICS in two years and CALP in seven years (e.g., Scarcella, 2003). On the contrary, many learners who are not exposed to academic English speakers in their homes, neighborhoods, and schools do not acquire academic language within this relatively short time period. For several years, McSwan and Rolstad (2006; 2005), Edelsky (2006), and Edelsky and others (1983) have questioned the BICS/CALP distinction because it promotes deficit thinking: it focuses on the low cognitive/academic skills of students. Instead, or in addition, educators are encouraged to consider the skills, abilities, and funds of knowledge students bring with them from their families, cultures, and native countries.

In sum, while the BICS and CALP distinction has made an enormous contribution to our understanding of the differences between social and academic language in classrooms, it has also received some criticisms. In the following section, we explain how Cummins's BICS and CALP distinction relates to the language of school approach discussed in this text.

Connections Between the BICS/CALP Distinction and the Language of School

Although there are obvious similarities between Cummins's BICS/CALP distinction and how we discuss the language of school, for example by looking at social and academic language, there are fundamental differences. First, we define academic language as a complex type of discourse that necessitates the use of multiple and interrelated competencies, including a broad range of discrete skills (e.g., reading, understanding vocabulary). Educators need to help ELLs students learn these competencies and skills beginning in primary school.

Second, we view social language as the foundation on which academic language is built, not as separate but as symbiotic processes in which these different types of languages are always developing and changing. For example, while we have highlighted the intercultural dimension of social language and explicitly identified specific syntactic features of academic language, we acknowledge the intercultural nature of academic language as well as the grammatical rules that govern face-to-face interactions. In other words, social language has specific vocabulary, syntactic features, and discourse just as academic language does. At the present time, however, we focus on academic language because of its crucial link to academic achievement.

Third, social language is not only the language of the playground; it is much needed in the classroom. Take, for example, the daily routines a fifth-grade teacher engages in with his students at the beginning of the day by checking in, going over the calendar, and giving a two-minute daily homophone sprint. Likewise, social language is used by a math teacher who at the end of her math class tries to extend the content of her lesson by connecting it with students' everyday experiences, as suggested by Core-Plus Mathematics (Coxford, Fey, Hirsch, Schoen, Hart, et al., 2001), which is a reform-oriented curriculum.

Finally, language provides some of its own context. What is often decontextualized from students' backgrounds and experiences are many of the activities that students are asked to do in a language that they have not yet mastered. These activities may include topics that are completely removed from their past and present lives and possibly irrelevant for their future.

Conclusion

The language of school is a distinct and complex type of English used in classrooms and schools. It involves different kinds of registers. On the one hand, we have social language, that is, the language used in everyday, casual interactions (e.g., playground, neighborhood). Academic language, on the other hand, is the language needed to succeed in the content areas. It includes not only vocabulary but also distinct grammatical and discourse features that may be specific to each discipline.

Educators often use simplified texts (both oral and written) with their English language learners as a way of making the content accessible for students. This practice, however, might deprive students of opportunities to be exposed to and learn the specific, connected discourse that characterizes the language of a content area. In addition, simplified texts might not provide students with the necessary information required to understand the material and to successfully demonstrate understanding of the topic at hand. For English language learners to succeed in school, they need to become skilled users of social and academic language features for each content area. Chapter 2 discusses the factors that influence how students acquire these language features and how they affect school success for ELLs.

> ### Stop and Think
>
> **History Class** • Look back at the chapter-opening cartoon and your reply to the Stop and Think feature following it. How does your answer about the cartoon's meaning change as a result of reading this chapter?

• Extensions •

For Reflection

1. *Reflect on student opportunities.* List all the ways you promote academic language in your classroom (or could do so if you are not currently teaching). Do English language learners have a variety of opportunities to hear, read, and use academic language?

2. *Reflect on word meanings.* List some everyday words, such as *table, tree,* and *column,* that have additional specific meanings in a content area. What are some activities that can be used in a classroom that allow students to practice and use those terms within an academic context?

For Action

1. *Compare social and academic language.* Stop by the playground, or anywhere students are socializing informally, and note the language they use (vocabulary, grammar, and discourse). Then observe a classroom with children of the same age and also observe their language. Describe the differences that you notice and explain what these differences imply for language learning.

2. *List discourses that are required by the standards.* Find the standards for your grade level and/or content area. List the different discourses that students are required to know and use. Discuss how these differences might be described and presented to students effectively.

chapter 2

Language Proficiency and Communicative Competence

• Key Issues •

1. Language proficiency is multidimensional and entails linguistic, cognitive, and sociocultural factors.

2. As students learn a second language, they progress at different rates along a continuum of predictable stages.

3. CAN DO Descriptors depict what students can do with language at different levels of language proficiency.

4. Communicative competence involves more than linguistic or grammatical competence.

5. Native languages, cultures, and life experiences are resources to be tapped and provide a solid foundation for learning language and content.

As you read the scenario below, think about English language learners (ELLs) you may know. What are their language proficiency levels? How is instruction planned to address their different content and language needs? Reflect on how knowledge of their English language proficiency might help teachers better address their unique needs and tap their strengths.

Marc Brown's head was swimming: state content standards, national content standards, state English language development standards, Teachers of English to Speakers of Other Languages, Inc. (TESOL) English language proficiency standards, district mandates, mandatory curriculum. It was becoming overwhelming to try to fit all of the different and sometimes conflicting objectives together into a coherent lesson.

"How can I possibly teach all of this? Why do I have to worry about English language development standards anyway?" moaned Marc to himself. "That's the English department's job—or the ELL teacher's job—not mine! I teach history!"

Suddenly the picture of a bumbling juggler (with himself in the lead role) trying to add one more item to his routine sprang into his mind. Like many other teachers, Marc was a creative guy with a passion for teaching. Sure, stress affected his ability to be creative, but he refused to give up, drawing courage, strength, and inspiration from the memory of the smiling and inquisitive faces of Roman, Marina, Yelena, Augusto, Faridah, and Kumar. Marc turned once again to the history and English language proficiency standards spread out before him. Each one of his ELL students was a unique individual with specific strengths and weaknesses in both language and content. These diverse needs made lesson planning challenging, but his ELL kids were counting on him to find a way to communicate with them. Marc was determined to do just that.

Stop and Think

Think about the ELLs you know. What information do you already have that would help to inform the strategies you can use to meet their instructional needs? What information do you still need to obtain?

RESOURCES

Pronouncing foreign names • To assist you with the pronunciation of many foreign names, visit hearnames.com. Many names are available with audio files by native speakers. Go to **http:// www.hearnames.com**.

Language Proficiency

Language proficiency can be defined as the ability to use language accurately and appropriately in its oral and written forms in a variety of settings (Cloud, Genesee, & Hamayan, 2000). Kern (2000) developed a broad conceptual framework for understanding language proficiency that includes three dimensions of academic literacy: linguistic, cognitive, and sociocultural. To be proficient in a language requires knowledge and skills using the linguistic components. It also requires background knowledge, critical thinking, and metacognitive skills, as well as understanding and applying cultural nuances, beliefs, and practices in context. Finally, being proficient in a language requires skill in using appropriately the four language domains—listening, speaking, reading, and writing—for a variety of purposes, in a variety of situations, with a variety of audiences.

Language Domains

There are four **language domains**: listening, speaking, reading, and writing. Although these four domains are interrelated, they can develop at different rates and independently of one another. These four domains can be classified as receptive or productive skills and as oral or written. The matrix below depicts the four language domains.

Language Domains In language teaching, particularly foreign language teaching, the four language domains of listening, speaking, reading, and writing have also been called the four language skills. This text uses *language domain* because this term reflects the complexity involved in each of the four language domains.

	Receptive	Productive
Oral	Listening	Speaking
Written	Reading	Writing

Receptive Language refers to the information someone *receives* through listening or reading activities.

- **Listening.** English language learners process, understand, and respond to spoken language from a variety of speakers for a range of purposes in a variety of situations. Listening, however, is not a passive skill; it requires the active pursuit of meaning.
- **Reading.** English language learners process, interpret, and evaluate written words, symbols, and other visual cues used in texts to convey meaning. Learning to read in a second language may be hindered or enhanced by students' levels of literacy in their native languages. Students who have strong reading foundations in their first languages bring with them literacy skills that can typically be transferred to the process of learning to read in English.

Productive Language refers to the information *produced* to convey meaning. The very nature of productive language implies an audience, although not always an immediate audience, as in the case of writing a book review or an e-mail.

- **Speaking.** English language learners engage in oral communication in a variety of situations for a variety of purposes and audiences in a wide array of social, cultural, and academic contexts. Contextual roles for getting and keeping the floor, turn taking, and the way in which children converse with adults are only a few examples.

- **Writing.** English language learners engage in written communication in a variety of forms for a variety of purposes and audiences. These forms include expressing meaning through drawing, symbols, and/or text. ELLs may come with writing styles and usages that are influenced by their home cultures.

Understanding the different demands of each language domain aids educators in addressing the language learning needs of their English language learners. Note that proficiency in a language may vary across the four basic language skills. For example, think about the times we have heard an adult language learner say, "I can read German, but I can't speak it at all." Likewise, some ELLs may have stronger listening and speaking skills, while others might be strong writers but not as strong when it comes to speaking. When assessing the proficiency levels of ELLs, it is important to take into account individual students' performances in each domain.

Stop and Think

Marc Brown has learned that his sixth-grade ELL student, Faridah, scored at a Level 2 on the state's English language proficiency (ELP) exam. This information provides an incomplete and misleading picture, however, of Faridah's needs and abilities. To address her language needs effectively, to understand the impact of her language proficiencies in the content areas, and to build on her language strengths, Marc must uncover Faridah's individual scores in every language domain and in combinations of domains.

Faridah's cumulative file holds a copy of the state's language proficiency test, which she completed the previous spring. Here are the scores (on a scale from 1 to 4, with 4 being advanced proficiency):

Listening: 3   Reading: 2

Speaking: 1   Writing: 2

Marc felt some degree of success at locating the language proficiency information, but he still wondered what to do next. How are these scores helpful? What do they mean in the real-life context of the busy classroom?

English Language Proficiency

As students learn a second, third, or fourth language, they move along a continuum of predictable stages. Careful observation of and interaction with individual students aids educators in identifying each student's level of language proficiency. This information is pivotal when planning appropriate instruction for ELLs.

The *PreK–12 English Language Proficiency Standards* (TESOL, 2006), developed by Teachers of English to Speakers of Other Languages (TESOL), provides a guide for teaching content across the four language domains.

TESOL's five preK–12 English language proficiency standards (see Figure 2.1) can guide teachers in helping ELLs become proficient in English while, at the same time, achieving in the content areas.

RESOURCES

For additional information about the *PreK–12 English Language Proficiency Standards* (TESOL, 2006), visit the Teachers to Speakers of Other Languages (TESOL) website. Go to http://iweb.tesol.org/Purchase/ProductDetail.aspx?Product_code=318.

English Language Proficiency Levels

Students progress through the stages of language proficiency at different rates: some acquire nativelike competency in seven years, some may take 10 years, while others may never reach that level. Most students learning a second language follow a similar route; that is, certain linguistic forms and rules are acquired early, whereas others tend to be acquired late, as illustrated in Figure 2.2. In other words, while most students follow the same path in learning English, their pace and rate is different depending on a variety of factors, such as familiarity with the Latin alphabet, competence in the native language,

FIGURE 2.1   PreK–12 English Language Proficiency Standards

Standard 1	English language learners **communicate** for **social, intercultural,** and **instructional** purposes within the school setting.
Standard 2	English language learners **communicate** information, ideas, and concepts necessary for academic success in the area of **language arts.**
Standard 3	English language learners **communicate** information, ideas, and concepts necessary for academic success in the area of **mathematics.**
Standard 4	English language learners **communicate** information, ideas, and concepts necessary for academic success in the area of **science.**
Standard 5	English language learners **communicate** information, ideas, and concepts necessary for academic success in the area of **social studies.**

Source: PreK–12 English Language Proficiency Standards by TESOL. Copyright 2006 by Teachers of English to Speakers of Other Languages, Inc. (TESOL). Reprinted with permission.

FIGURE 2.2 Acquisition of English Features

Typical Stages in the Acquisition of Negation

(1) "no want pizza"

(2) "me no want pizza"

(3) "I don't want pizza"

Linguistic Features Acquired in the Early Stages

-/s/ plural	"Max has many books."
-ing verb ending	"Emily is playing ball."
active sentences	"Arthur built a big tower with blocks."

Linguistic Features Acquired in the Later Stages

-/s/ possessive	"That is Maddie's coat."
-/s/ third person singular	"Sasha plays with Leia."
passive sentences	"A big tower with blocks was built by Lorca."

RESOURCES

For examples of state English language proficiency standards for K–12 education, see the website for the state of California at http://www.cde.ca.gov/be/st/ss/documents/englangdevstnd.pdf; Illinois at http://www.isbe.net/bilingual/htmls/elp_standards.htm; Pennsylvania at http://www.pde.state.pa.us/esl/cwp/view.asp?a=3&Q=110015&eslNav=I6449I&eslNav=I6449I; and Washington at http://www.k12.wa.us/MigrantBilingual/ELD.aspx.

age, previous schooling experiences, aptitude, motivation, personality, and other social and psychological factors.

While many states have developed their own sets of standards and may use three or four stages instead of five or apply different labels for the stages (e.g., beginning, early intermediate, intermediate, early advanced, and advanced), the English language proficiency (ELP) standards developed by TESOL are intended to highlight and provide a model of the process of language acquisition that can be adapted by districts and states within the context of their own language leveling system (see Figure 2.3).

The language proficiency levels are not necessarily connected to cognitive functioning. Often students may be able to process advanced cognitive tasks and yet not be able to express those understandings in the second language. For example, Level 1 or Level 2 English language learners can still analyze and classify information if it is presented in small chunks and supported visually.

FIGURE 2.3   Levels of Language Proficiency

Stages of English Language Proficiency (ELP)

LEVEL 1: STARTING

Speaking/Listening

At this level, students . . .

- initially have limited or no understanding of English.
- rarely use English for communication.
- respond nonverbally to simple commands, statements, and questions.
- begin to imitate the verbalizations of others by using single words or simple phrases.
- often pass through a silent period, during which time the student may not speak English.
- begin to use English spontaneously.

Reading/Writing

At the earliest stage, learners . . .

- construct meaning from text primarily through nonprint features (e.g., illustrations, graphs, maps, tables).
- gradually construct meaning from the words themselves.
- are able to generate simple texts that reflect their knowledge level of syntax.

Student-produced texts may include unconventional features such as . . .

- invented spelling
- grammatical inaccuracies
- pictorial representations
- words in the first language (L1)
- surface features and rhetorical patterns of the native language (such as replication of ways of structuring text from native culture and language)

LEVEL 2: EMERGING

Speaking/Listening

At this level, students . . .

- understand phrases and short sentences using familiar vocabulary.
- communicate limited information in everyday and routine situations by using memorized phrases, groups of words, and formulas.
- use selected simple structures correctly but still systematically make basic errors.
- begin to use general academic vocabulary and familiar everyday expressions.

(continued)

FIGURE 2.3 continued

Reading/Writing

Reading and writing proficiency may vary depending on students' . . .

- literacy development in their native language.
- familiarity with the Latin alphabet.

At this level, students

- read words and phrases.
- locate specific, predictable information in simple everyday or environmental print.
- approximate the spelling of words.
- write for themselves to express their own personality and personal thoughts.

Errors in writing are present and often hinder communication.

LEVEL 3: DEVELOPING

Speaking/Listening

At this level, students . . .

- understand more complex speech.
- still may require some repetition or a slower rate of speech.
- acquire a vocabulary of stock words and phrases covering many daily situations.
- use English spontaneously.
- may have difficulty expressing all their thoughts due to a restricted vocabulary and a limited command of language structure.
- speak in simple sentences that are comprehensible and appropriate but are frequently marked by grammatical errors.
- may understand and use some specialized academic vocabulary.
- still have some trouble comprehending and producing complex structures and academic language.

Reading/Writing

Proficiency in reading may vary considerably depending on learners' familiarity and prior experience with . . .

- themes, concepts, genre, characters, and so on.

Students are most successful constructing meaning from texts for which they have background knowledge on which to build.

In writing, they are able to generate . . .

- increasingly complex texts.
- a wider variety of texts.
- more coherent texts than beginners.
- texts still containing a considerable number of unconventional features.

FIGURE 2.3 continued

LEVEL 4: EXPANDING

Speaking/Listening

At this level, students . . .

- possess language skills that are generally adequate for most day-to-day communication needs.
- occasionally make structural and lexical errors.
- may have difficulty understanding and using some idioms, figures of speech, and words with multiple meanings.
- communicate in English in new or unfamiliar settings.
- have occasional difficulty with complex structures and abstract academic concepts.

Reading/Writing

Students at this level . . .

- may read with considerable fluency.
- are able to locate and identify specific facts within the text.
- may not understand texts in which the concepts are presented in isolation and without contextualized support, the sentence structure is complex, or the vocabulary is abstract or has multiple meanings.
- encounter more difficulty with grade-level literacy than with oral language.
- may read independently but may have occasional comprehension problems, especially when processing grade-level information.
- may produce texts independently for personal and academic purposes.
- produce texts that approximate the writing of the structures, vocabulary, and overall organization of native speakers of English.
- make errors in one or more domains that generally do not interfere with communication.

LEVEL 5: BRIDGING

Reading/Writing

Students . . .

- are able to work with grade-level material with some modification.
- have a good command of technical and academic vocabulary as well as idiomatic expressions and colloquialisms.
- can produce clear, smoothly flowing, well-structured texts of differing lengths and degrees of linguistic complexity.
- make minimal errors that are difficult to spot or are generally corrected when they occur.

RESOURCES

The Council of Europe developed their 2001 *Common European Framework of Reference for Languages: Learning, Teaching, Assessment* to describe achievements of all learners of foreign languages in Europe. The document considers six levels of language proficiency. Go to http://www.coe.int/T/DG4/Portfolio/?L=E&M=/main_pages/levels.html. The American Council of Teachers of Foreign Languages (ACTFL) currently uses five levels of language proficiency. Go to http://www.actfl.org/i4a/pages/index.cfm?pageid=4236.

CAN DO Descriptors

The CAN DO Descriptors developed by the World-Class Instructional Design and Assessment (WIDA) consortium (2009) provide a starting point for planning and implementing instruction. They define levels of ability in terms of what language learners typically can do with the language at different language proficiency levels. Each proficiency level has sets of descriptors relating to separate language domains: listening, reading, writing, and speaking. Figure 2.4 presents a sample of CAN DO Descriptors for the language domains of reading and writing for grades 3 through 5. The WIDA CAN DO Descriptors are organized by grade-level clusters (preK–kindergarten, Grades 1–2, Grades 3–5, Grades 6–8, and Grades 9–12).

RESOURCES

For expanded CAN DO Descriptors across grade-level clusters, see http://www.wida.us/standards/CAN_DOs/index.aspx.

Stop and Think

Take a moment to recall the information Marc Brown collected about Faridah's English language proficiency test scores:

Listening: 3   Reading 2
Speaking: 1   Writing 2

Using the information presented in the preceding section, answer the following questions.

1. What are Faridah's strengths?
2. How does this information help Marc plan instruction for Faridah?
3. What can Marc reasonably expect Faridah to understand and do in his ancient history class?
4. Is that all there is to learning a language?

Communicative Competence

Pike (1982) notes that "[l]anguage is not merely a set of unrelated sounds, clauses, rules, and meanings; it is a total coherent system of these integrating with each other, and with behavior, context, universe of discourse, and observer perspective" (p. 44). As early as the

FIGURE 2.4 CAN DO Descriptors for Reading and Writing, Grades 3–5

Level 1	Level 2	Level 3	Level 4	Level 5
Reading				
• Match icons or diagrams with words/concepts. • Identify cognates from first language, as applicable. • Make sound/symbol/word relations. • Match illustrated words/phrases in differing contexts (e.g., on the board, in a book).	• Identify facts and explicit messages from illustrated text. • Find changes to root words in context. • Identify elements of story grammar (e.g., characters, setting). • Follow visually supported written directions (e.g., "Draw a star in the sky").	• Interpret information or data from charts and graphs. • Identify main ideas and some details. • Sequence events in stories or content-based processes. • Use context clues and illustrations to determine meaning of words/phrases.	• Classify features of various genres of text (e.g., "and they lived happily ever after"—fairy tales). • Match graphic organizers to different texts (e.g., compare/contrast with Venn diagram). • Find details that support main ideas. • Differentiate between fact and opinion in narrative and expository text.	• Summarize information from multiple related sources. • Answer analytical questions about grade-level text. • Identify, explain, and give examples of figures of speech. • Draw conclusions from explicit and implicit text at or near grade level.
Writing				
• Label objects, pictures, or diagrams from word/phrase banks. • Communicate ideas by drawing. • Copy words, phrases, and short sentences. • Answer oral questions with single words.	• Make lists from labels or with peers. • Complete/produce sentences from word/phrase banks or walls. • Fill in graphic organizers, charts, and tables. • Make comparisons using real-life or visually supported materials.	• Produce simple expository or narrative text. • String related sentences together. • Compare/contrast content-based information. • Describe events, people, processes, procedures.	• Take notes using graphic organizers. • Summarize content-based information. • Author multiple forms of writing (e.g., expository, narrative, persuasive) from models. • Explain strategies or use of information in solving problems.	• Produce extended responses or original text approaching grade level. • Apply content-based information to new contexts. • Connect or integrate personal experiences with literature/content. • Create grade-level stories or reports.

Source: Reprinted with permission. WIDA CAN DO Descriptors © 2008 Board of Regents of the University of Wisconsin System, on behalf of the WIDA Consortium, www.wida.us.

1970s, Dell Hymes (1972) put forward a notion of linguistic competence to mean more than mastery of formal linguistic systems. Communication is not only about oral and written language. When we speak, our speech is often accompanied by nonverbal communication such as facial expressions, gestures, body movement, and sighs. The way we stand, the distance between us and our listeners, the looks on our faces, and our tone of voice all influence the manner and content of our communication.

While the ability to correctly form words, sentences, paragraphs, and larger bodies of text is an important expectation by schools and educators, the area of **communicative competence** can sometimes be overlooked. Briefly, the idea of communicative competence is the communicator's comprehensive knowledge and appropriate application of particular language in a specific context. This knowledge helps the communicator know what to communicate and, more important, how, when, and where to communicate something. For example, the following exchange between a principal and her middle school Honduran student includes appropriate grammatical features but much more information than needed:

Stop and Think

1. Can you recall any conversations with ELL students and/or their families that are similar to the example involving Antonio?

2. What did you find inappropriate in the example(s) that you recalled?

3. Why was that instance from your student (or from his or her family member) inappropriate? By whose standards?

Principal: Antonio, you've been absent for two days. Why?

Antonio: The first day I had to stay with my little sister because my cousin got sick and my mom took him to the doctor. You know, I can't drive yet. I would have taken my cousin faster. They took the bus. My cousin will stay in the hospital for a few days. I don't know what's the problem; it's something with his heart. He is a lot older than me.

While Antonio's grammatical constructions are acceptable, in U.S. settings, this may not be the response expected by a principal or teacher because it provides more information than requested.

Elements of Communicative Competence

Communicative competence does not apply only to oral language. Communicative competence means competence in all four language domains—both the productive and the receptive. When talking of communicative competence, we need to consider four important elements: grammatical or linguistic, sociolinguistic, discourse, and strategic. Each will be defined below. Examples are provided in Figure 2.5.

1. **Grammatical or linguistic competencies:** involve accuracy of language used (e.g., spelling, vocabulary, sentence formation, pronunciation).

FIGURE 2.5 Elements and Examples of Communicative Competence

Elements of Communicative Competence	Examples
Grammatical/linguistic	• How do you spell ____? • I can't remember the word! • Is the correct word order "I the dog see" or "I see the dog"?
Sociolinguistic	• Which words and phrases fit with this setting and topic? • How can I express a specific attitude (courtesy, authority, friendliness, respect) when I need to? • How do I know what attitude another person is expressing?
Discourse	• How are words, phrases, sentences, and paragraphs put together to create cohesive and coherent communication (conversations, speeches, e-mail messages, reports, newspaper articles)?
Strategic	• How do I know when I've misunderstood someone or when someone has misunderstood me? • Can I think of another way to express my ideas if I can't remember the right word? Maybe I could pantomime or draw a picture?

2. **Sociolinguistic competencies:** entail the use of language in an appropriate manner or style in a given context. These competencies take into account a variety of factors such as rules and social conventions, the status of participants, and cultural norms.

3. **Discourse competencies:** involve the ability to connect correctly formed phrases and sentences into a coherent and cohesive message in a particular style. These competencies involve the ability to be a sender and receiver of messages and to appropriately alternate those roles in conversations or written language.

Stop and Think

How can educators model and teach each facet of communicative competence while simultaneously teaching content? Think about specific examples.

4. **Strategic competencies:** involve the development of strategies such as how to get into or out of conversation, break silences, hold the floor in conversations, and deal with strategies to continue communicating when faced with breakdown in communication.

Native Language and Culture *Native language* is the primary or first language spoken by an individual. It is also called the mother tongue. The abbreviation L1 refers to someone's native language. It is generally used in contrast to L2, the language a person is learning. *Native culture* is the term often used to refer to the culture acquired first in life by a person or the culture that this individual identifies with as a group member.

RESOURCES

For a useful article on promoting native language and culture in English mainstream classrooms, see "Promoting Native Language and Culture in English-Only Programs" in *The ELL Outlook,* by Irujo (2005), at http://www.coursecrafters.com/ELL-Outlook/2005/may_jun/ELLOutlookITIArticle3.htm. For ideas about how to find out information about students' cultures, see the section called "Background" in Chapter 3 of this text.

Stop and Think

While waiting in line for a hot lunch, Marc overhears Mrs. Holton telling several native Russian-speaking immigrant students to speak only English. What can he say or do to advocate for the students while at the same time maintaining a good working relationship with Mrs. Holton?

The Role of Native Languages and Cultures

Norton (1997) claims that "[t]he central questions teachers need to ask are not, 'What is the learner's mother tongue?' and 'Is the learner a native speaker of Punjabi?' Rather the teacher should ask, 'What is the learner's linguistic repertoire? Is the learner's relationship to these languages based on expertise, inheritance, affiliation, or a combination?'" (p. 418). There is an intimate relationship among language, culture, identity, and cognition. Educating ELLs includes not only focusing on language learning but building on students' native languages, cultures, and experiences. Most English language learners are very familiar with at least one other language and have an intuitive understanding of how language and texts work. This knowledge of their first language (L1) will greatly enhance their opportunities to learn English. Research in this area indicates that full proficiency in the native language facilitates the development of the second language (L2) (August & Hakuta, 1997). Native language proficiency can also impact how students learn complex material, such as what is typically encountered in content-area classrooms (Ernst-Slavit & Slavit, 2007).

The key is to consider students' first languages and cultures as resources to be tapped into and built upon. Thinking of our ELLs as "having to start from scratch" is the equivalent of denying the many experiences that children have accumulated before coming to the United States and the vast amount of family and cultural knowledge and traditions that have been passed on to students from the moment they were born. The consequences of denying students' first language can be far reaching because language, culture, and identity are inextricably linked.

Approaches for Using the Native Language in the Classroom   Given the wide variety of languages spoken by immigrant students in the United States today, teachers will not know all of the native languages of their students. Yet teachers can still promote the use of native languages in their classrooms. Below are selected approaches for supporting native language development in K–12 classrooms.

1. **Organize primary language clusters.** Create opportunities for students to work in groups using their primary language. This can be helpful as they discuss new topics, clarify ideas, or review complex concepts.

2. **Label classroom objects in different languages.** Labeling classroom items allows ELLs to understand and begin to learn the names of objects around the classroom. Labels also assist educators and other students to learn words in different languages.

3. **Assign a bilingual buddy to your newcomer.** Having a buddy who speaks the child's first language can be very helpful as the new ELL student learns how to function in the new school and culture. This buddy provides comfort while at the same time guiding the newcomer through different activities (e.g., calendar, circle time, journal writing) and settings (e.g., bus stop, science lab, cafeteria).

4. **Support the use of the native language by using classroom aides or volunteers.** By using the preview-review approach (that is, the translation of key concepts before the lesson starts, followed by review of the new content), aides or volunteers can enhance the learning opportunities of ELLs.

5. **Encourage primary language development at home.** In today's diverse world, bilingualism is highly valued. If students can continue to develop their first language as they learn English, their opportunities as bilingual adults will be enhanced. In addition, when students continue to develop their native language, they can continue to communicate meaningfully in the first language with their parents and relatives.

6. **Use bilingual books.** An abundance of bilingual books in a variety of languages has been published in the United States since the 1980s. These books provide an effective tool for raising students' awareness about diversity and also for fostering literacy and biliteracy development. Figure 2.6 provides a list of strategies for using bilingual books in the classroom; the list was developed by Ernst-Slavit and Mulhern (2003).

RESOURCES

Using Bilingual Books • For additional information about types of bilingual books and an expanded discussion about ways of using bilingual books in the classroom, see Ernst-Slavit and Mulhern (2003) at *Reading Online*. Go to http://www.readingonline.org/articles/ernst-slavit/.

FIGURE 2.6 Strategies for Using Bilingual Books in the Classroom

Introducing a new topic	Literature that relates thematically to a new unit or lesson can acquaint a beginning English language learner with the topic at hand.
Supporting transfer of reading in L1 to L2	Children who can read in their L1 and have learned some oral English benefit from taking turns with an English speaker in reading aloud a bilingual book.
Supporting independent reading	A book in the native language can soothe feelings of frustration and exhaustion common among L2 learners.
Using L1 version as preview	Students can read or have someone read to them the L1 version of a book in order to understand its content.
Using L1 version as review	After a book has been read and discussed in the L2, students can use the L1 version to write about the topic, review issues discussed, or further their understanding.
Reading two versions for self-assessment	Young ESL students enjoy finding out how much English they are learning by counting the words they understand before and after the book is read in the L1 and discussed in the L2.
Comparing and contrasting cognates	Comparing and contrasting words in L1 with English words can contribute to increases in word recognition, vocabulary development, phonic analysis, and structural analysis.
Improving home–school connections	Family members can be actively involved in the education of L2 students, even if their English skills are limited, when books in L1 are available.
Supporting family literacy programs	A great way to start a family literacy program for parents of ESL students is by assisting them in locating books in the L1.
Raising all children's awareness of multiculturalism	Bilingual books and materials in languages other than English can raise all children's awareness through exposure to different languages and scripts.
Helping teachers learn another language	Bilingual books can help teachers and others learn some words in students' native languages.
Encouraging reading for pleasure	One way for students to obtain sufficient amounts of written input is through pleasure reading, whether in L1 or L2.

Source: Adapted from "Bilingual books: Promoting literacy and biliteracy in the second-language and mainstream classroom" by G. Ernst-Slavit and M. Mulhern. *Reading Online, 7*(2). Copyright 2003 by the International Reading Association. Reproduced with permission.

Conclusion

Learning a second language is a complex and lengthy process. While learners follow a similar route in learning a second language, the rate at which they acquire the target language varies depending on a variety of linguistic, sociocultural, and cognitive factors. As students navigate through the process of becoming competent users of English, educators' awareness of their location in the language learning continuum can help them better address the students' needs and build on their strengths.

• Extensions •

For Reflection

1. *Speaking a second or third language.* Do you speak a second or third language? If you do not, do you have a friend who does? Do you or your friend have equal levels of competence across language domains? Think about why some language domains developed more than others.

2. *Types of writing systems.* Look at some of the different alphabets and writing systems for different languages at Omniglot (http://www.omniglot.com/) or at any other website or text. Based on those writing systems, what language do you think would be easier for you to learn? Which one would be more difficult? Why?

For Action

1. *Linguistic diversity.* What native languages other than English are spoken by students in your classroom? In your school, district, and state? Jot down a list of what you believe are the top languages in your area and compare it with information you can find about your school, district, and state. (For information about the different languages spoken in your state and across the United States, visit the website for the Office of English Language Acquisition at http://www.ncela.gwu.edu/stats/3_bystate.htm.

2. *English language proficiency standards.* Find the English language proficiency standards for your state. Then compare those with the 2006 TESOL *PreK–12 English Language Proficiency Standards* (http://www.tesol.org/s_tesol/sec_document.asp?CID=1186). What are some similarities? What are some differences?

RESOURCES

The World-Class Instructional Design and Assessment (WIDA) Consortium consists of 20 partner states, all using the same English language proficiency standards. You may find the list of WIDA states at **http://www.wida.us/index.aspx**.

part two

Components of Effective Lesson Design

Where do I come from?

I come from an unknown place,
a place where nobody wishes to be.
I come from a place where everybody
has nightmares, where mercy does not
exist.

Where suffering is well-known.
I come from a place where obstacles are
always present, and hardness is never, ever
absent. I come from hell disguised as
happiness, a place where many are
unhappy.

I come from a place of defeat.
A place where everyone has fallen and
just a few have triumphantly returned.
A place where I don't want to return,
because it's terrible. I swear.

De donde vengo?

Vengo de un lugar desconocido.
Un lugar donde nadie desearia haber
nacido.
Un lugar donde todos tienen pesadillas,
donde no existe piedad, donde solo existen
penas.
Un lugar donde las trabas son
demasiadas.
Un lugar donde todos son infelices; ***vengo***
de la derrota.
Un lugar donde todos an caido y pocos
han salido.
Un lugar adonde no quiero regresar por
que es terrible en verdad.

Student A. Tomás Flores, used with permission.

● ***How can reading and reflecting on Tomás's poem help his teacher plan her instruction***
to be more effective? Think about this question as you read the chapters in Part Two.

Assessing Student Strengths and Needs

1. Students bring with them different backgrounds, which express themselves as skills, abilities, knowledge, family and community characteristics, and experiences.

2. Students' strengths and needs, including linguistic, content, educational, and cultural, have their roots in these backgrounds.

3. Addressing students' strengths and needs can affect learning of language and content.

4. Teachers can uncover their students' strengths and needs so that they can build on them to help students achieve.

As you read the scenarios below, think about how your classroom context might be like the teacher's classroom depicted in each. Reflect on how you might address the situations that these teachers face.

Nathan Hamma teaches at an elementary school in a district with a 60% ELL population. His sixth-grade class is a mix of native speakers and non-native speakers at different levels. A conscientious teacher, Mr. Hamma tries to meet the needs of all his students by breaking them into groups by language ability and trying to work with the less fluent groups as much as possible. He is a bit frustrated that not all of the students work well in their groups and that some seem uninterested in the lessons. He has noticed that some of his ELLs have a better mastery of different aspects of the class content than others do, but he feels that their language needs are the most important issue to address and that homogeneous language grouping will help with this issue. He is concerned that his ELLs' lack of content and language knowledge will keep them from passing the high-stakes test that all students must pass to go on to junior high.

• • •

Andrew Chen teaches sixth grade at another school in the same district as Nathan Hamma's. His students are also a mix of native and non-native English-speaking students. At the beginning of the year, he spent two weeks gathering information about his students from their files (if they existed), parents, former teachers, and the students themselves. He collected reading and writing samples in both the first language (L1) and the second (L2); background information on students' beliefs, interests, and experiences; and information about what students had studied previously and succeeded in mastering. He discovered that many of his non-native speakers have above-grade-level knowledge in math and science, and that some of the ELLs who seem to have mastered English need extra help working on academic and content-based language. Likewise, he found a range of language and content knowledge among his native English-speaking students. He prepares his instruction while keeping in mind what he has learned about his students. He changes groupings according to content and language knowledge and uses both heterogeneous and more homogeneous groups depending on the lesson topic, language, and tasks. Mr. Chen continues to use strategies such as KWLS and personal journals for each lesson because he knows that the more he knows about his students, the better his lessons will fit their needs.

Stop and Think

Before reading the chapter, what advice would you give the teachers in the scenarios above?

Background

Many authors cite the need for teachers to understand not only the educational backgrounds of students but also the lives of students outside school, including the cultural and linguistic backgrounds of all students (see, for example, Echevarria, Vogt, & Short, 2008; Peregoy & Boyle, 2008), and to plan instruction around this information. As Saville-Troike (1978) notes in her classic but still very relevant monograph, home cultures can play a distinct role in student school success:

> *Students may differ in their willingness to ask questions or volunteer information because of cultural differences in the appropriateness of these behaviors. Teachers should both use and*

allow a variety of procedures, and be sensitive to which procedures are appropriate for which students, and to which differences in behaviors are due to cultural differences between groups and which to individual personality factors. Many students have been incorrectly stereotyped as "shy" because the teacher was requiring inappropriate behavior [from the perspective of the student's native culture]. (p. 44)

Roseberry, McIntyre, and Gonzalez (2001) reinforce this notion, observing that "children may find that they do not know how to show the teacher what they know in ways she can recognize. They may be asked to engage in activities they do not fully understand. And they may find that the teacher talks in ways that are unfamiliar and confusing" (p. 3). For example, students from an oral **culture** may learn content and language better in a storytelling format than from a textbook. Students who are taught at home that it is inappropriate to compete against others might have a hard time participating in competitive tasks in class.

Effective, inclusive teaching includes understanding students' cultures; it is also based on what learners bring with them to the classroom in terms of academic knowledge and knowledge about the world. These *funds of knowledge* (Moll, Amanti, Neff, & Gonzalez, 2001) are cultural and cognitive resources that can be used in planning instruction in order to provide culturally responsive and meaningful lessons that work from a base of student strengths.

These issues mandate the acknowledgment of and connections to students' home cultures and knowledge bases in instruction. That is not to say that every assignment should be tailor-made for individual students, but as described in other chapters in this text, a variety of effective tasks can be used in order to give students access to content and language.

Culture Culture is often defined as a student's country of origin. While researching a student's home country is often a good place to start to understand a student, countries can have more than one culture and often have several. A more accurate definition of culture is the experiences, beliefs, and values that the learner's *community* shares, regardless of its size or location. Understanding the student's community is essential to understanding how a student's culture might affect that student's learning.

RESOURCES

Funds of Knowledge • For more information, see *Funds of Knowledge* by J. Lopez. Go to **http://www .learnnc.org/lp/pages/939**.

Stop and Think

What kinds of knowledge might students bring from home?

Teachers can provide this access only if they understand their students' strengths, needs, interests, and abilities.

Although it is clear that teachers need to understand their students' backgrounds, it is harder to find descriptions of how this information is to be collected and used. While some student information may be gathered immediately from students—such as their names, whether they have attended school previously, and their favorite pastimes—other data must be learned more gradually. Some questions can be asked directly, while some facts can be observed only over time, including specific academic knowledge, preferred interaction patterns, and use of learning strategies. The important issue is that the teacher makes it an explicit aim to collect and integrate as much knowledge about each student as possible.

A teacher can collect information about students in a variety of ways. For example, many teachers use **formal assessments** at the end of a lesson or unit to gather information about student outcomes in content and language. However, the information gained through these assessments does not typically indicate where the students need help and why they succeed in certain areas. If teachers perform ongoing **informal assessments** (checking student process and performance before, during, and after the lesson *and* between lessons), these assessments can reveal information about students and where and why they are succeeding or need help accessing content and language.

One issue in collecting and sorting such data is that of time—with packed curricula, teachers might feel like there isn't enough of it. With student information at hand, however, instruction can be more effective and time will ultimately be saved by having more students succeed. Other concerns in understanding student needs are possible language barriers and privacy issues. However, many districts have interpreters or interpretation services, and there are other resources, some mentioned in this text, to help.

> ***Formal and Informal Assessment*** Formal assessments are standardized across a set of students and typically result in evaluation of some type (e.g., a grade or other mark). They are also known as *summative assessments* and often include end-of-chapter tests, quizzes, and presentations. Informal assessments are used to gather information to inform instructional planning. Also called *formative assessments,* they include teacher observation, checklists, and discussion and interview. These and other strategies are discussed in Chapter 7 in this text.

> **RESOURCES**
>
> See texts such as *School Letters in English and Spanish* from Ammie Enterprises (http://www.ammieenterprises.com/) to assist with home–school communication.

> **Stop and Think**
>
> What are some ways that you can gather information from and about students?

Understanding Strengths and Needs

The first two chapters in this text focused on social and academic language and the relationships between language and content. This chapter focuses on discovering students' language and content strengths and needs by understanding their backgrounds. The sections briefly highlight ways to gather (1) general, (2) linguistic, (3) academic, (4) content, and (5) cultural information about students. The other chapters in Part Two include ways to integrate this information into instruction.

Collecting General Information

As we have already noted, there are numerous techniques for collecting student data. One of the quickest ways to obtain general information about students, particularly about their general backgrounds and perceptions, is to give them a survey at the beginning of the school year. This can be done in the student's first language (L1) if necessary, or pictures and/or photos can be used. Questions, as appropriate, can include the following:

- How many people live in your home? Who are they? Do any of them read and write in English? If so, who?
- Have any of your close friends or relatives gone to school in the United States?
- Did you go to school in your home country? For how long?
- Have you studied English before? For how long?
- Do you come from a big city or from the country?
- What was a typical day at school like for you in your home country or in your previous residence? Did you have homework?
- Who helps you with your homework? Where do you usually do homework?
- What do you like about school?
- What do you do when you are not in school?

The students' responses will assist in understanding some of the home context that may affect students' school performance. Follow-up surveys can be given throughout the year. Note that if the survey asks questions that require yes or no responses, not as much information will be gained as from more open-ended questions. Analysis of the data can be as simple as forming an overall impression of the class or using it to draw a more complete picture of the backgrounds and needs of individual students.

Another way to gather general information about students is through casual conversations with each student. During those times when the teacher is not at the front of the class, she can take notes on short conversations with each student about relevant issues. A para-educator with the same first language as the student can also help with this technique. Brief student-to-student interviews, in which students write or explain what their partners are interested in or how the topic under study relates to their lives, can also be effective. This is especially helpful if you have fluent speakers of both the L1 and L2 who are willing to participate.

A wall-write is another method for gathering general information. In this technique, the teacher hangs sheets of paper on the walls of the classroom. Each sheet has one question or statement ranging from the simple (e.g., "I like to travel" or "Do you have a pet?") to the more complex (e.g., "I think that voting is an important responsibility" or "Where do the majority of your relatives live?"). Students answer the question or sign their names under the statements with which they agree. (No sensitive information should be requested or discussed in such a public forum, of course.) However, this technique can depend on the students' ability to read the questions and answer in writing, something that many ELLs may not yet be prepared to do.

One more technique to collect group data quickly is to use moving questions. As in a wall-write, teachers can use questions or statements. Students who agree or disagree with the statement that the teacher says out loud and/or writes on the board move to different sides of the room, or they move to the corner of the room that provides their response to the question. For example, if the teacher says, "I was born in a big city," students who were born in a big city move to one side of the classroom and students who weren't move to another. This provides the teacher with an easily observable classroom overview and also helps the students to understand some of their general similarities and differences. The teacher can support this activity with photos so that all students can participate.

A slower but possibly richer technique to collect general information about students is to use dialogue journals. In a notebook, students communicate back and forth with the teacher or another student. Students can draw pictures, use both their L1 and L2, and include photos or questions. Teachers write back, modeling the L2 and asking relevant questions. Dialogue journals can also be created on the computer through e-mail exchanges, private blogs, and other technologies. An advantage of using dialogue journals is that students can express themselves and reply in many ways, making it more likely that some information will be gathered in spite of language barriers. For more information about dialogue journals, see Kreeft-Peyton (2000) and Young (1990).

Whatever strategies teachers decide to use, they need to be sure to provide an example of each strategy and to share information about themselves, too. This gives students a better chance of completing the activity successfully and also allows them to know their teachers. A useful resource for thinking about home/school planning is NCREL's (2004) *Putting the Pieces Together: Comprehensive School-Linked Strategies for Children and Families,* available from http://www.ncrel.org/sdrs/areas/issues/envrnmnt/css/ppt/putting.htm.

The strategies described above are summarized in Figure 3.1. There are many more techniques that follow these patterns. In addition to general information, they can also be used to collect more specific student information, as noted later in this chapter.

> ## RESOURCES
>
> **Dialogue Journals** • For additional information on dialogue journals, see J. Peyton (1993), *Dialogue journals: Interactive writing to develop language and literacy,* available from the Center for Applied Linguistics (**http://www.cal.org/resources/Digest/peyton01.html**), or J. Staton (1987), *Dialog journals,* available from the ERIC database (ED284276).

Gathering Information on Learners' Language Backgrounds

Most school districts have one or more standardized language tests such as the Language Assessment Scales (LAS; McGraw Hill) to measure and place students into English as a second language (ESL) programs. Typically, however, such tests are used only to ascertain which students should receive special services at what level. Standardized tests typically do not show, for example, whether students understand commonly used language such as

FIGURE 3.1 Techniques for Collecting General Student Information

Technique	Explanation
Survey	General questions are asked in a questionnaire format.
Conversations	Teachers or other communicants have casual conversations as time allows.
Wall-write	Students answer questions or reply to statements by signing their name or responding on a piece of paper taped to the wall.
Moving questions	Students answer a question by moving to one side or corner of the room.
Dialogue journals	Students communicate with the teacher or another student on a regular basis, using a variety of modes for writing journal entries and responses in the form of journal entries.

indirect instructions and commands (e.g., "I like the way Mary is sitting" that really means "Billy, get off the table!" or "Would you like to do your arithmetic now?" that really means "Do your arithmetic now!" [Saville-Troike, 1978]). While students are in the ESL program, classroom teachers can work with the ESL teacher to discover students' language abilities and needs. Once students exit the ESL program (or if they did not receive services but still need language help), classroom teachers need to find out more about the language students know and can use. During this process, teachers need to keep in mind that social language ability (basic interpersonal communication skills [BICS]) and academic language ability (cognitive academic language proficiency [CALP]) develop at different rates, as we noted in Chapter 1. In other words, simply observing students talking with their friends on the playground using social language may not be a good indicator of their true ability to use and understand academic language.

Teachers can start the discovery process by asking basic questions about students' language backgrounds. These questions can be developed from frameworks like the CAN DO Descriptors mentioned in Chapter 2 and can include the following:

- What is your first language? Do you speak another language? If so, which?
- What can you do in your first language that you can't yet do in English?
- What language do you usually speak with your friends?
- What language do you usually speak with your family?
- What language do you dream in?

FIGURE 3.2   Activities for Assessing Language Needs

Activity	Purpose
Story retelling: After reading, students describe what they understood.	Get a general idea of what the student focused on (main ideas? details? isolated vocabulary?) and what the student understood from the story.
Role playing: Students act out what they know or what they understood about a topic or reading.	Provides students with an alternative way to show what they have comprehended (and thus what they still need to understand).
Oral reporting: Students produce a short extemporaneous or formal oral report about a topic.	Pronunciation, vocabulary use, productive grammar, and presentation skills can be evaluated while the teacher listens.
Brainstorming: Students generate ideas informally either in groups or alone.	Vocabulary and other language use can be assessed as students participate in brainstorming both orally and in writing.
Playing games: Students participate in games involving language reception and production.	While students are relaxed and engaged, their language use and understanding can be observed.

Language process and progress can be evaluated in any number of ways, from casual observation to observation checklists to formal testing. Because language can be understood and produced in many ways, teachers can provide different modes of input and allow students to show what they know in different ways. Activities to help assess student language include those listed in Figure 3.2 and many others.

RESOURCES

Informal Assessments • Examples of informal language assessments can be found at the website for Informal Language Assessment: http://jeffcoweb.jeffco .k12.co.us/is/web/docs/MAST/Informal_Language_ Sample_for_use_with_Interpreter_1-31-05.doc.; and from Colorin Colorado (2007), Using Informal Assessments for English Language Learners (http://www .colorincolorado.org/article/14318).

Understanding Educational/Academic Background

In addition to language background, each student's educational background is important for teachers to investigate. One of the first places to look for academic information about students is in their school files. If a student has been in the district for a while, this file may contain test scores, previous grades, teacher comments, data on previous educational experiences, an individualized education plan (IEP), notes on academic strengths and weaknesses, and information about family context. Questions that might help teachers understand students' educational backgrounds include the following:

- How many years has the student been in school? How many of those years were spent in the United States?
- What is the last grade level the student attended?
- Can the student read and write in the native language? How well?
- What help does the student have to study?
- Where does the student need the most help?

Although some of this information may be available from school records, sometimes such records do not exist, and knowing how many years and where students attended school is not always enough to know what they have experienced or continue to experience. Other questions about their educational background that can be important are whether they are accustomed to collaboration or independence and/or rote or creative learning, types of testing they are familiar with, their and their parents' expectations for student and teacher behavior, and what grades mean to them and their families (Peregoy & Boyle, 2008). Surveys and discussion can be useful techniques for gathering this information. Answers to these questions can help teachers understand which school-based strategies they might need to teach, not in order to replace students' home traditions and expectations but rather as another tool to help them succeed. For example, Saville-Troike (1978) notes that "students should be taught, at least by the secondary level, that asking questions and volunteering information is not considered inappropriate or overly aggressive in school, but rather is valued, and often rewarded with a higher grade. Teaching this, and guiding students to behave accordingly, is part of teaching the second culture" (p. 44). Some ELLs may even need to be shown that it is okay to raise their hand to ask to go to the bathroom or get a drink.

RESOURCES

School Strategies • For ideas about collecting academic information, check these resources: School Strategies Scale (http://dennislearningcenter.osu.edu/sss/sss.htm) and School Climate Survey (http://goal.learningpt.org/winss/scs/sampques.asp?survey=E).

Discovering Content Background and Knowledge

Understanding students' languages and academic backgrounds is important, but equally essential is discovering students' levels of content knowledge. Sometimes teachers can use student files, the curriculum for the previous year, previous teachers' input, and academic testing to discover some of the content that students should or do know and what they need to learn. Using surveys, discussion, and other techniques mentioned in this chapter, teachers can collect additional data. Most important is to separate content knowledge and language knowledge. Just because a student cannot express something in writing in English doesn't mean that the student doesn't know it. Allowing students to express their content knowledge and their needs through drawing, acting, singing, playing, and other modes can provide the teacher with a well-rounded picture of students' understandings (and misunderstandings).

One useful technique for understanding and activating student content knowledge is the use of a KWL or KWLS chart or one of its many modifications. At the top of the chart, column headings are (1) Know, (2) Want to Know, (3) Learned, (4) Still Want to Learn. The first column along the left side of the chart is filled in with upcoming content. For example, if the students will be studying weather, this column might contain

"the water cycle," "tornado," "hurricane," "sleet," or other ideas and concepts from the upcoming lesson. Before the lesson or unit, students fill in the "Know" column (in a group or individually) with information that they already know about the topic. Teachers can encourage students to write, draw, or use other modes. They can then complete the "Want to Know" column, asking questions or describing what they hope to understand from their study. After the unit or lesson, students finish the last two columns. Using this technique, teachers can discover student knowledge, interests, and progress and build on this information in an ongoing way.

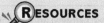

RESOURCES

KWLS • Find a KWLS template at ReadWriteThink (http://www.readwritethink.org/lesson_images/lesson398/kwls2.pdf).

RESOURCES

Interest Inventory WebQuest • To get started developing an inventory, go to http://faculty.citadel.edu/hewett/web_files/interestweb.html.

KWLS can assist teachers in understanding some things about students' interests, but in order to choose content that will engage learners, a more in-depth exploration of their interests might be warranted. Interest inventories, or surveys of student interests, are useful tools for finding out this kind of information. Teachers can create their own interest inventories or they can find ready-made inventories on the World Wide Web or through other teachers. These can be addressed to students or parents, and they can focus on general information, provide pictures that students respond to, or ask topical interest questions with specific science, math, or social studies content. Some resources for KWLS and interest inventories are listed in Figure 3.3. Teachers can also discover students' interests through conversation and many of the other techniques outlined in this chapter. Of course, any technique must fit the ages and abilities of the students or it will not be as successful as it could be.

FIGURE 3.3 Techniques for Understanding Content Knowledge and Interests

Technique	Purpose/Examples
KWLS: A chart in which students note what they know, what they want to know, what they have learned, and what they still want to learn.	To discover specific knowledge and interests that students have before and after lessons or units.
	KWL template from Teach-nology: http://www.teach-nology.com/cgi-bin/kwl.cgi
	KWL generator: http://www.teach-nology.com/web_tools/ graphic_org/kwl/
	KWHL chart: http://www.ncsu.edu/midlink/KWL.chart.html
Interest inventories: General and specific surveys that describe students' interests.	To understand the different interests among students in the class.
	General: Student Interest Inventory (elementary) www.sanchezclass.com/docs/student-interest-inventory.pdf
	The Learner—Interests (elementary and secondary): http://www.saskschools.ca/curr_content/ adapthandbook/learner/interest.html
	Questions addressed to parents: Parent Inventory http://www.circleofinclusion.org/english/pim/ eight/parent.html
	How to Implement a Student Interest Survey: http://www.ehow.com/how_2058230_ implement-student-interest-survey.html

Exploring Cultural Background

The most crucial information to gather for some students is cultural background. Peregoy and Boyle (2008) note that understanding some of students' religious beliefs, cultural preferences and prohibitions, and home responsibilities can help bridge the divide between home and school by helping teachers choose how to organize their instruction and understand

FIGURE 3.4 Common Teacher Behaviors

Behavior	Might Be Misunderstood	Cultural Group That Might Misunderstand
Sitting with legs crossed and your shoe pointed or shoe sole turned toward your students.		
Making the "okay" sign with your thumb and first finger.		
Telling your class to take a "bathroom" break.		
Shaking hands with a parent.		
Waving with your whole hand.		
Touching a student on the head, giving a high-five, or patting a student on the back.		
Signaling to a student by using one finger.		
Taking a student's photograph.		

students' reactions to it. Saville-Troike (1978) adds that it is very important to know who in the family is an appropriate person to reach. Teachers can also find out students' and their families' values, beliefs, roles associated with gender and age, expectations of schooling and teachers, and attitudes toward English language and cultures. Saville-Troike (1978) notes that the point of gathering cultural knowledge is to accept and accommodate "the student's native culture to the extent possible; the teacher, indeed the whole educational system, should seek to expand and enrich the existing repertoire of teaching styles, instructional activities, and even administrative procedures to provide for the cultural diversity of students" (p. 43).

Stop and Do

Cultural Knowledge • Examine the list in Figure 3.4 and mark with an X the common behaviors that might be misunderstood by students from different cultures. For the list items you mark, if you can, note the cultural group of the students who might misunderstand. (Answers can be found in the appendix of this text.)

To understand students' cultural backgrounds, Robertson (2007) suggests that teachers "start by researching your students' native countries, cultures, and educational systems. You may even want to study the historical figures, musical and artistic traditions, geography, and biodiversity of these countries so that you can connect your lessons to something that the students already know" (n.p.). The brief overviews of every country in the world provided in Culturegrams (http://online.culturegrams.com/) include text-based and video information that both teachers and students can use. Many school libraries have access to these materials.

As noted previously, however, there can be many cultures within a country, and people are individuals within those cultures, so surface information is not enough. For deeper questions about culture, Saville-Troike's (1978) *A Guide to Culture in the Classroom* provides 20 categories with sample questions and explanations of why the answers might be important to know. Categories include Natural Phenomena, Time and Space, History and Traditions, and Decorum and Discipline; Saville-Troike provide a general framework for understanding their significance. In "Getting the Answers," Saville-Troike describes how teachers might go about obtaining the information they need. This resource is essential reading for all teachers and a great place to start understanding how culture can affect learning in classrooms.

Other techniques for gathering cultural and family data include some already mentioned in this chapter, for example:

- Interviews with parents and community members. These can take place at school, in the home, or in a safe community setting. The home visit guide found on pages 195–196 can help facilitate such events.

- Dialogue journals. For students who prefer to communicate orally, technologies such as Voxopop (http://www.voxopop.com/), an oral discussion board, are excellent tools.

- Personal narratives and stories in the L1 or English. These can be supported by technologies such as PowerPoint so that students can make them as clear and comprehensible as possible.

Still more techniques include having students create graphical representations of important life events or experiences in quilt squares, cartoons, or picture-book formats; encouraging visits from parents who are willing to share parts of their culture, whether native or non-native; and having students create cultural journals in which they note how their lives are or

Stop and Think

What barriers to communication might teachers find when attempting to understand more about students' cultures? Think of ways to overcome these barriers.

are not like those in the books they read, the people they meet, and the school life in which they participate. Saville-Troike (1978) recommends an approach that is relativistic and flexible for all teachers. No matter which strategies are used, it is crucial that teachers do not expect that all students from one country or even one culture share the same traditions and taboos, and they must be sure that students are treated like the individuals they are.

Guidelines for Understanding Student Strengths and Needs

In addition to the techniques offered previously in this chapter, three important guidelines can assist teachers in collecting information and thinking about the diverse learners in their classrooms.

Guideline 1: Model the Techniques

It is quite possible that the techniques and strategies suggested in this chapter might be strange or inexplicable to some students, regardless of their background. In these cases, the teacher can model how, for example, to use a dialogue journal or KWLS chart and suggest why survey data and other information is necessary. Sharing appropriate personal stories and then relating them to learning helps students understand this connection.

Guideline 2: Try Not to Assume

In one fourth-grade classroom, a new student from China wet his pants in class three days in a row. The teacher assumed that he had a medical or psychological problem and contacted both the school administrators and the parents. When the teacher was finally able to speak with a parent, the parent explained that the student was unsure of the rule and was embarrassed to ask whether using the facilities during class was permitted and what the procedure was for leaving the room during class. There are many other stories (for example, teachers believing that students who didn't look them in the eye didn't know the answer, or students being punished for not participating in practices forbidden by their home culture) that show how important it is for teachers to find out rather than assume.

Guideline 3: Embrace Variety

Saville-Troike notes that "[t]eachers are models; what they value and respect is often valued and respected by their students as well" (p. 44). She suggests that these values, and

Stop and Think

After reading Chapter 3, what advice would you give to the teachers in the chapter-opening scenarios?

those of the cultures of all students in the classroom, should be explored and, as necessary, be the subject of explicit instruction. Because there is such diversity in the backgrounds and interests of any group of students, teachers may use a variety of methods, strategies, techniques, and modes to help all students access content and language, and, according to Saville-Troike, should never assume there is one best way to teach anything.

Figure 3.5 summarizes these three basic guidelines for language instruction. Additional guidelines are presented throughout this book.

Conclusion

Students learn more and better when they can use their individual funds of knowledge to support their learning (McIntryre et al., 2001). Understanding student strengths and needs means that teachers are more aware of what helps learners succeed and in what areas. There is a lot more to say about the hows and whys of understanding students' backgrounds and experiences, and additional activities and techniques can be discovered through Web searches, in conversations with teacher peers, and in books about teaching. The most important aspect is teacher awareness about the need to keep eyes and ears open to understand students. The importance of teacher awareness will be reviewed in Chapters 4, 5, and 6. These chapters discuss planning instruction based on an understanding of student strengths and needs.

FIGURE 3.5 **Guidelines for Understanding Student Needs**

Guideline	Process
Model the techniques and strategies that you want learners to use.	Explain the purpose of data collection and how the technique works. Share personal information on culture, interests, and other topics to pique student interest and create community.
Never assume there is one best way to teach anything.	Ask students about their behavior before judging it.
Embrace variety in planning and instruction to accommodate the diverse needs and backgrounds of all learners.	Use a variety of methods, strategies, and modes to help students access content.

• Extensions •

For Reflection

1. *Assessing student needs.* What other ways can you think of for assessing student strengths and needs? Think about the ways you and your students do or will communicate. How can you use such communication to find out more about your students?

2. *Reflecting on barriers.* In what ways might students' home cultures conflict with the culture of schooling in the United States? Think of some examples of student behavior that you have seen in classrooms and that provoked a specific reaction in you. Might there have been an explanation for that behavior other than the one that occurred to you?

For Action

1. *Learn about culture.* Review the free CultureGram at http://www.culturegrams.com/products/Bulgaria .pdf. List facts and ideas that might cause conflict or misunderstanding for students from this country and culture in U.S. classrooms. List ways in which you might build on knowledge of this culture.

2. *Create a culture survey.* Read Saville-Troike's (1978) work (see the References at the end of this text). Use some of her questions to create a culture survey for your current or future class. Explain why you chose those questions.

chapter 4

Writing and Teaching
to Language Objectives

• Key Issues •

1. All teachers are language teachers.
2. Students' language and content strengths and needs provide a foundation for creating learning objectives.
3. Content objectives support facts, ideas, and processes.
4. Language objectives support the development of language related to content and process.
5. Objectives must be directly addressed by lesson activities.

As you read the scenarios below, think about how your classroom context might be like those of the teachers depicted. Reflect on how you might address the situations these teachers face.

Mary Alvarez was concerned. Her fourth-graders, a mix of native English speakers and English language learners (ELLs) with a variety of different skills and knowledge, seemed to understand the math content she was teaching, but they could not express it in ways that would help them to pass the written math exit test for fourth grade. Their lack of appropriate math vocabulary and process writing skills made their explanations difficult to evaluate. Ms. Alvarez's understanding was that, if students were exposed to language and grammatical structures, they would be able to pick them up. However, her students did not seem to be doing so with any consistency during her math lessons.

• • •

Peter Morello conducted ongoing, formative assessment in his high school biology class. He closely monitored the students' progress toward mastering the content objectives and incorporated scaffolding at every opportunity. He felt that his students were not really grasping the concepts he was teaching, and when it came time to present their understandings, the students had many spelling and grammar errors and could not adequately express what they had found during their lab investigations. When he mentioned this problem in the faculty lounge, other teachers agreed that it was an issue. It was not only the ELLs, however; many of the other students were not picking up what they read in their texts and they could not express themselves in academic English. Like some of the other content teachers, Mr. Morello felt that the English and English as a second language (ESL) teachers should be addressing these issues with students while he focused on science content.

Stop and Do

Before reading the chapter, discuss with your classmates why the students and the teachers in the scenarios may be having problems. What information or understandings can provide solutions for the teachers?

Background

Both teachers in the chapter-opening scenarios recognize that their students need language help. Like many teachers, however, they have misunderstandings about how language learning occurs and a lack of knowledge about how and why to integrate content and language. Teachers can help students access the academic content of the class; however, if language is a barrier to access, then they must also consider ways to help learners access the language they need. Contrary to Ms. Alvarez's belief in the scenario, students do not "absorb" language without scaffolding and focused attention, just like they need for learning content (Crawford & Krashen, 2007). A specific focus on central skills and concepts is critical to learning both language and content (Long, 2001).

This specific focus on language is important in all classrooms, whether content is presented in an elementary classroom in a thematic unit or in a secondary classroom as a discrete subject. This focus is important because, as we outlined in Chapter 1, each content area has jargon, technical vocabulary, and a genre that is specific to that content area. Because ESL and other language teachers may not be well versed in the vocabulary and discourses of all the content areas, regular classroom teachers are probably best suited to teach these types of language with the support of language educators. In essence, all teachers are language teachers to some extent, even if they teach the language of only one content area, as they often do at the secondary level.

Chapter 3 focused on understanding students' needs, backgrounds, and interests. Although content standards and goals for specific grade levels are often prescribed in statewide curricula, the objectives and activities that help learners reach those goals can and should be based on what teachers discover about their students. This chapter focuses on integrating social and academic language needs into content lessons so that all students can access the academic content. An important aspect of teaching language across content areas and themes is understanding how to develop appropriate and relevant language objectives as part of lessons with a content focus. The development of language objectives and activities that support the objectives will be the main emphasis of this chapter.

Understanding Objectives

Different texts call learning objectives by different terms, but it is the idea behind them that is important rather than the exact label. In this text, **objectives** are statements of attainable, quantifiable lesson outcomes that guide the activities and assessment of the lesson. Objectives differ from **goals** and **standards,** which can also be called learning targets and are very general statements of learning outcomes. Objectives are also different from **activities** or **tasks,** which explain what the students will do to reach the objectives and goals. Objectives typically follow a general format, as outlined in the formula below.

"Students will be able to" + <u>concrete, measurable outcome</u> + **content to be learned**

Learning Objectives • Note that starting an objective with the words "Students will" is not the same as SWBAT because "Students will" indicates what activities the students will *do* rather than the *outcomes* that they are expected to achieve from participating in the activity.

RESOURCES

Learning Objectives • For a variety of examples and more action verbs, see "Learning Objectives: Stems and Samples" from Education Oasis (**http://www.educationoasis.com/instruction/bt/learning_objectives.htm**).

The three parts of this formula are equally important. First, "students will be able to"—often abbreviated SWBAT—indicates that what follows in the objective are criteria against which a student's performance can be evaluated after the lesson. Second, the concrete, measurable outcome presents the criterion that the evaluation will focus on. The chart in Figure 4.1 presents a list of possible action verbs that can be used to state the measurable outcome. Finally, the third part of the objective states the exact content to be learned and sometimes also includes to what degree it should be mastered (100% accuracy, 9 out of 10 times, etc.).

Content Objectives

Most mainstream teachers are accustomed to writing content objectives. **Content objectives** support the development of facts, ideas, and processes. For example, in a unit about the Civil War, one of the content objectives might be:

SWBAT <u>name</u> **three of five central causes of the Civil War in writing.**

FIGURE 4.1 Measurable Verbs

abstract	contrast	dramatize	introduce	recall	skim
activate	conduct	employ	investigate	recognize	solve
adjust	construct	establish	list	record	state
analyze	criticize	estimate	locate	relate	summarize
arrange	critique	evaluate	modify	reorganize	survey
assemble	define	examine	name	repeat	test
assess	demonstrate	explain	observe	replace	theorize
associate	describe	explore	organize	report	track
calculate	design	express	perform	research	translate
carry out	develop	formulate	plan	restate	use
categorize	differentiate	generalize	predict	revise	verbalize
change	direct	identify	prepare	select	visualize
classify	discover	illustrate	produce	sequence	write
compare	distinguish	infer	propose	simplify	
compose	draw	interpret	rate	sketch	

Source: Adapted from *Action Verbs for Learning Objectives* © 2004 Education Oasis™ http://www
.educationoasis.com

Others might include

> SWBAT <u>list</u> **the major battles of the Civil War.**

> or

> SWBAT <u>recite</u> **the first section of the Gettysburg Address.**

Which objectives the teacher chooses may depend on the dictates of standards, grade-level requirements, and curricula. Whatever criteria are used for choosing them, those objectives should be developed based on what students already know and need to know and provide a strong guide for the development of the rest of the lesson.

Stop and Do

Look at the standards and other content requirements for teaching in your current or future area(s). Write one or more content objectives that might be appropriate for the students that you plan to or do teach. Refer to Figure 4.1 for action verbs. Then review others' objectives and see what questions you still have about content objectives.

⬗ **R**ESOURCES

Standards • Find state and national standards by content area on the Education World website at **http://www.educationworld.com/standards/index.shtml.**

Language Objectives

While content objectives emphasize facts, ideas, and content processes, **language objectives** support the development of language related to the content and process. This relationship

FIGURE 4.2

The Relationship Between Content and Language Objectives

Content Objectives
The *ideas/facts/processes* student will learn as a result of the lesson

Format
Students will be able to +
<u>measurable/observable outcome</u> (verb)
+ **specific content**

Example
SWBAT <u>identify</u> **three central causes of the Civil War**.

influence

Language Objectives
The *language* that students need to meet the content objectives and participate in task processes

Format
SWBAT + <u>measurable outcome</u> (verb)
+ **language skills, functions, grammar, strategies, or vocabulary required for the task**

Example
SWBAT <u>use</u> **past tense verbs correctly**.

---

is shown in Figure 4.2. Although some content standards and curricula do address general language and communication goals, language objectives are specifically based on helping students access the content of a particular lesson. Because there may be many language objectives that could help learners access the content of each lesson (too many to address in one lesson), they are also created based on the teacher's knowledge of students' current language skills and abilities.

Constructing Language Objectives   The first step in creating language objectives is to determine social and academic language needs based on content objectives. Language needs can fall into these five general categories (adapted from Echevarria, Vogt, & Short, 2008):

1. **Vocabulary:** Including concept words and other words specific to the content, for example, words that end in *-ine,* insect body parts, parts of a map, precipitation, condensation, and evaporation.

2. **Language functions:** What students can do with language, for example, define, describe, compare, explain, summarize, ask for information, interrupt, invite, read for main idea, listen and give an opinion, edit, elicit elements of a genre.

3. **Grammar:** How the language is put together (its structure), for example, verb tenses, sentence structure, punctuation, question formation, prepositional phrases.

4. **Discourse:** Ways students use language, for example, in autobiographies, plays, persuasive writing, newspaper articles, proofs, research reports, speeches, folktales from around the world.

5. **Language learning strategies:** A systematic plan to learn language, for example, determining patterns, previewing texts, taking notes.

Stop and Think

Can you think of more examples of the five kinds of language listed previously? Can you think of other types of language that students might need in order to meet the content objective in Figure 4.3?

For example, the chart in Figure 4.3 shows some of the language in these categories that students might need in order to meet the stated content objective in a lesson on the Civil War. Depending on the teacher's understandings of her students' language needs and on what she sees as the most important language elements to emphasize, she might choose one or more of the following language objectives for this lesson:

- SWBAT spell **the following vocabulary correctly: economy, secession, federal, abolition.**
- SWBAT listen carefully for **main ideas from a reading on the Civil War.**
- SWBAT use past tense verbs to write **complete sentences.**

There are many variations on language objectives, and the basic formula presented above can be used for all of them. There are also variations on this basic formula that add

FIGURE 4.3 Determining Language Needs

Content Objective: SWBAT state **three of five central causes of the Civil War in writing.**

Vocabulary	Grammar	Discourse	Functions	Strategies
slavery	Past tense	Narrative and report genres	Identify main ideas	Take notes
North	Complete sentences		Make a statement	Listen strategically
South			Summarize	
economy			Define words	
secession			Use cause and effect	
federal			Spelling	
abolition			Arguing	

FIGURE 4.4 Sample Language Objectives

- SWBAT use **comparatives** (e.g.,*bigger, wider, higher*) to **compare geographic**
              structure   function
  features.

- SWBAT use the words ***north, south, east,*** and ***west*** to **direct** peers to a specific
                                  vocabulary   function
  map location.

- SWBAT **ask** for information **from native speakers.**
            function   context

- SWBAT use **interrupting techniques** correctly **during discussion.**
                         function   context

context, grammatical structure, and other elements to the objectives. Examples are presented in Figure 4.4.

Stop and Do

First, review the objective(s) you wrote for the Stop and Do about content objectives on page 57. List all of the potential language that students might need in order to access the information and achieve the objective. Then choose the most important language, without which students could not possibly access the content, and write one or more language objectives that address this language need.

Figure 4.5 demonstrates an abbreviated process for determining language objectives for a variety of content areas. The topic of the lesson is first established (column 1) and the content objective(s) are created (column 2). From the content objective(s), a list of words (language) needed to access the content is developed (column 3). Student backgrounds are considered (column 4), and then language objectives that address student needs are produced. Notice that the objective presents the language to be learned or used first, and then the context or conditions in which it will be learned or produced.

Every content objective does not necessarily require a language objective, and some lessons do not have language objectives at all because all students can access the content with skills and vocabulary that they already possess. However, it is important to examine possible language barriers to content in every lesson and to address them if needed.

In summary, the important features of language objectives include the following:

- They derive from the content to be taught.
- They consider the strengths and needs of students.
- They present measurable, achievable outcomes.

FIGURE 4.5 **The Objective Development Process**

Topic	Content Objective	Sample Language Needed	What Students Already Know	Possible Language Objective
Arctic animals	SWBAT identify the habitats of Arctic animals by writing the name and the place.	Vocabulary such as the names of the animals and habitats, spelling, defining.	They know the names, but not the definitions, of the habitats.	SWBAT write the definitions of Arctic animal habitats.
Our community	SWBAT describe five important community landmarks.	Adjectives, present tense, prepositions of location.	They can use many adjectives but need more. They know simple present tense.	SWBAT use prepositions of location accurately.
Ancient Greece	SWBAT explain three contributions to current life made by the ancient Greeks.	Past tense, present tense, sentence format, connectors (*in addition, another*, etc.).	They know how to make past and present tense sentences.	SWBAT use connectors correctly in oral and written texts.
Sports	SWBAT demonstrate the rules of American football.	Sequencing (*first, second, third, next*); modal verbs (*can, can't, should, have to, must*); football vocabulary.	They have already learned the vocabulary.	SWBAT use sequencing words to explain a series of events or items using correct sequence of words.
Argument	SWBAT compose a five-paragraph argumentative essay.	Essay format, paragraph format, sentence format, topic sentences, conclusions, logic, argument support.	They understand paragraphs and sentences, but they do not know about persuasion/argument.	SWBAT construct an argument with three reasons to support their position.
Graphs	SWBAT compare the effectiveness of pie charts, line charts, and bar graphs given specific data.	Comparatives; vocabulary such as *graph, chart, data*; present tense.	They know the vocabulary.	SWBAT write present tense sentence using comparatives.

Teaching to the Language Objectives

Creating language objectives is a good start for addressing the social and academic language needs of students, particularly ELLs, but equally important is that lesson tasks address the objectives. This chapter presents some guidelines for making sure that students meet the language objectives. Chapters 7–11 present specific ideas for teaching to a variety of language objectives.

Guideline 1: Integrate Language and Content

Just as tasks that address content objectives are integrated into the whole lesson rather than being addressed one by one, language objectives should also be integrated into the lesson and not taught in isolation from it. For example, these objectives were chosen for the Civil War lesson:

Content: SWBAT <u>state</u> **three of five central causes of the Civil War in writing.**

Language: SWBAT <u>use reading strategies</u> to uncover **main ideas from a reading on the Civil War.**

The teacher *could* teach about the central causes of the Civil War, separately teach how to identify main ideas, and then hope that the students will apply their knowledge to their Civil War task. This process, however, is problematic in several ways. First, it indicates to students that language is separate from content when it is actually derived directly from the content. In other words, teaching the language objective without content removes much of the context for the language. Second, it breaks up the lesson into chunks, each of which constitutes a separate preparation for the teacher. This is neither an efficient use of the teacher's and students' time, nor is it an effective way to teach language.

A better choice is for the teacher to integrate the content and language. So, for example, while the students are looking for the causes of the Civil War in their textbooks, the teacher can ask them how they figure out what the causes are, and the students can make a list of strategies to find main ideas. They can practice together by finding the first cause of the Civil War and explaining to each other how they found it. This choice makes the lesson more efficient (by teaching two objectives at the same time) and

Decontextualize To decontextualize means to consider something alone or take something away from its context. As noted in Chapter 1, some authors believe that all language is contextualized to some extent, but treating language separately from content takes away the specific context that gives the language meaning, making the language more difficult to understand and use.

Stop and Do

Look at Figure 4.5. For each objective, underline the concrete, measurable outcome and circle the content to be learned. Check your answers with a partner.

effective (helping students see how language and content are related and moving them toward reaching both objectives).

Guideline 2: Use Pedagogically Sound Techniques

In the past, language was typically taught through drill and practice, exercises with few context clues, and mechanical worksheets. Research has found that these techniques are effective for very few students in very limited contexts. Effective language instruction, in addition to being integrated into content instruction, should meet the following basic criteria:

1. **It is authentic.** This means that it comes from contexts that students actually work in and that it is not stilted or discrete just for grammar study. It is language that students need for a real purpose.

2. **Language is taught both explicitly and implicitly.** Students are both directly exposed and indirectly exposed so they can use strategies to figure out some meaning on their own.

3. **It is multimodal.** Students are exposed to language through different modes such as graphics, reading, and listening and they can respond in text, drawing, and voice.

4. **It is relevant.** Not all students in a class need all of the language instruction. The teacher can choose to whom the lesson is aimed (small groups, individual students, the whole class) to make it relevant.

5. **It is based on social interaction.** Collaboration and cooperation help learners test their assumptions about language.

> **RESOURCES**
>
> **Instructional Strategies** • In addition to the techniques and strategies described in this text, others can be found in many excellent guides. See, for example, Herrell and Jordan's (2007) *Fifty Strategies for Teaching English Language Learners* (third edition) and *Making Content Comprehensible for English Learners: The SIOP Model* (third edition) by Echevarria, Vogt, and Short (2007).

Guideline 3: Break Down the Language

Each language objective can actually imply a variety of aspects. For example, for students to learn past tense, they have to understand what it means in a time sense and also that there are regular and irregular past tense verbs (e.g., those with *-ed* added, those with alternative changes), different spellings (e.g., go/went), and different pronunciations (e.g., sometimes the *-ed* ending is pronounced "ed" and sometimes it is pronounced "t"). As with any content, the instructional approach can go whole to part or part to whole or both ways, depending on how students learn best. For example, the teacher might have students read a passage and ask how we know when the events happened (whole) and then review

FIGURE 4.6 Basic Guidelines for Helping Students Meet Language Objectives

Guideline	Example
Integrate language and content	Contextualize the language instruction by using content as the language source.
Use pedagogically sound techniques	Language instruction should be authentic, multi-modal, both explicit and implicit, relevant, and based in interaction.
Break down the language	Teach wholes and parts to address the different learning needs of students.

the various aspects of past tense (parts). Or the teacher and students can point out the different aspects of past tense verbs in a required reading first and then work toward a more general understanding of how it helps us know when events occurred. Either way, the parts of past tense should be examined in light of their use in class content.

Figure 4.6 summarizes these three basic guidelines for language instruction. Additional guidelines are presented throughout this book.

Stop and Think

After reading the chapter, what would you tell the teachers in the chapter-opening scenarios to help them with their concerns?

Conclusion

Every teacher is a language teacher, at least in part, because the language of the content areas requires students to learn social and academic language in order to access the content. Teachers can use their content objectives, which support facts, ideas, and processes, to determine language objectives, which support the development of language related to content and process. Then, by following principles of good pedagogy, teachers can integrate the language and content in lesson activities. Following this process helps make learning more efficient and effective and ensures that all students have a chance to succeed. As crucial as this is, the next chapter shows that there are additional important components of lesson design that teachers can master in order to help all students achieve.

• Extensions •

For Reflection

1. *You as a language teacher.* How are you, or will you be, a language teacher? Think about the ways you and your students use or will be required to use language in your classroom. What do these uses mean for your teaching?

2. *Choosing modes.* Think about a lesson you have observed or taught. How can you include more modes so that students are exposed to language in a variety of ways?

For Action

1. *Meeting the standards.* Choose one of the content standards from your current or future grade level or content area. Develop one or more content objectives and then create language objectives for the same standard.

2. *Break down language.* Choose a grammar point, language function, or discourse. Using any resources that you need to, list all the aspects of your choice and describe how you might use steps to teach your choice to your current or future students.

chapter 5

Connecting
to Students' Lives

• Key Issues •

1. All students bring experiences and knowledge to school.

2. Connections between students' lives and the task demonstrate to students reasons for listening and participating in tasks.

3. Connecting tasks and topics to students' lives increases engagement.

4. Connections can be made by teachers or students.

As you read the scenarios below, think about which students might be more engaged in the lesson.

At Ben Franklin Elementary, sixth-grade teacher Anita Johnson is introducing a new math unit on fractions. "This week we're going to finish pages 73–84 in our math books. The unit is about multiplying and dividing fractions. The test will be next Monday. I'll show you the basics before we get started."

A general groan arose from the class.

"Why do we have to know this?" one student asked aloud.

"Because it's in the curriculum," replied Ms. Johnson. "Now, let's get to work."

• • •

In the other sixth-grade class at Ben Franklin Elementary, Kristin DeLuca is also introducing the unit on fractions. She tells the class, "I want to tell you a story before we start our new math unit. The other day I was making cookies. I thought I was measuring one-half cup of flour, but after I had dumped the flour in the bowl along with some other ingredients, I realized that I had accidentally used the one-third cup measure instead of the one-half cup measure. I didn't have enough ingredients to start over, and I had to bring the cookies to a dinner I was attending that night. How do you think I fixed this problem?" As the students offer possible solutions, Ms. DeLuca has an opportunity to emphasize the importance of knowing about fractions in daily life. She proceeds to ask the students: "Has anyone in this class ever had an experience like this?" and "Why is it important to understand fractions?" Then she says, "Remember when we talked about how math is important in real life? Fractions have a lot of uses. Let me read you this short story about how knowing fractions saved someone's life. But before I do that, let's talk about a couple of important vocabulary words. . . ."

Stop and Think

Before reading the chapter, think about how you might introduce an important concept so that all students have access to the ideas.

In the chapter-opening scenarios, the approaches of the two teachers are completely different. This does not mean that students cannot or will not learn in both situations. However, Ms. DeLuca is giving her students more opportunities and reasons to access the content and language of fractions by connecting the content to her students' lives and funds of knowledge. By also providing scaffolding in the form of vocabulary support, she helps more students to participate.

Chapter 3 focused on understanding students' strengths, needs, backgrounds, and interests, and Chapter 4 introduced the topic of creating language objectives based on those needs. Although providing language objectives and teaching to those objectives based on students' language needs are excellent steps for helping students access lesson content, these steps may not be enough for students from diverse backgrounds. This chapter focuses on making initial connections to student backgrounds to help students link to their previous learning and to their lives outside school.

Teachers can often introduce their lessons with connections to students who have lived in their area or been in their school for a while or who are familiar with mainstream culture and lifestyles. However, newcomers and students with different experiences might find it more difficult to connect to lessons, and teachers need to think deeply to find a common connection to reach all students. The development of connections and finding ways to involve students in lessons through these connections are the focus of this chapter.

Background

Educators in a variety of academic areas have written recently about the need to connect content and pedagogy to students' lives. These connections are important, as Perez (2004) notes, because:

> *When students make the connections between learning and living, they see the authenticity of reading, writing, thinking, listening, speaking, and problem solving in everyday tasks.* (p. 368)

In other words, making connections can make learning meaningful for students (Echevarria, Vogt, & Short, 2008). In turn, learners may be more motivated to learn the content and language that they need in order to work toward their life goals. In addition, teachers who connect new learning to students' backgrounds increase student comprehension (Christen & Murphy, 1991; North Central Regional Education Laboratory, 1995; Taboada & Guthrie, 2006; Ziori & Dienes, 2008). Another important result of making connections is what Clifford (2008) calls "far transfer," or the ability of students to use their learning in new, unfamiliar situations. In other words, making connections can provide students with greater opportunities for achievement both inside and outside school.

It is important to note that, if teachers do not understand their students' needs, interests, and backgrounds, they will not be able to make clear connections or help their students make these connections. The strategies for collecting information about students outlined in Chapter 3, are the first step toward making connections with students. The next step is to use the information to make clear and effective connections among content, language, and the students' lives.

Understanding Connections

There are three main types of connections that are important for students. As Echevarria, Vogt, and Short (2008) note in their Sheltered Instruction Observation Protocol (SIOP), two of these are (1) explicitly linking to students' background experiences and (2) explicitly linking past learning and new concepts. The first is what can be called a **personal connection,** or a clear connection to students' lives outside school. These connections answer the "So what?" or "Why is this important?" types of questions for students. The second is an **academic** or **content connection,** which is a connection to previous school learning—often an earlier lesson—so that transitions are clear and learning builds on previously addressed academic language and experiences. These two connections, personal and academic, fall under the category of "activating prior knowledge" (Lewis, 2008). In addition to these two connections is (3) a **pedagogical** or **instructional connection,** which includes strategies and choices that the teacher makes to address student needs, interests,

FIGURE 5.1　Summary of Connection Types

Type	Explanation
Personal	Links students' lives and lesson ideas.
Academic/content	Links students' past learning and new concepts.

and background directly. Making a pedagogical connection includes preteaching vocabulary, providing students with choices of ways to express themselves, and many other strategies. Pedagogical connections will be discussed in Chapter 6. Personal and academic connections, summarized in Figure 5.1, will be described in more detail in this chapter.

Making Personal Connections

Where the curriculum is less restricted and teachers and students can choose topics and questions to explore together, it is easier to make connections to students' lives. Where the curriculum is more prescribed and readings preselected, there are many ways to make connections, but it might be harder to

Stop and Do

Look at the worksheet in Figure 5.2. Before reading further, try to fill in the blanks with a personal connection that all students might be able to make for the lesson topic that is printed in the first column.

FIGURE 5.2　Creating Personal Connections

Lesson Topic	Personal Connection
Example: Thanksgiving	Celebrations
Maps	
Battle of Bull Run	
The Parthenon	
Penguins	
Sacagawea	
Geometric proofs	
Simple addition	
Washington, D.C./capital	

think about how to make them applicable to all students. For example, some students may have never celebrated Thanksgiving or may not have, in their home culture, a similar feast. Others may have no idea about American wars or have never seen snow. How can personal connections to these topics be made?

To help students make a personal connection to the lesson content, the teacher can start by thinking about what the main topic or idea of the lesson is. The next step is to think of ways, based on knowledge of students' backgrounds, that students might have experience with this main topic. If there is no real link, the next step is to go from the very specific content of a lesson to a more general exploration of the experiences included within the topic, and then choose the one that most of your students have likely had some experience with. For example, for a lesson that includes the content objective "Students will be able to explain the purpose of Thanksgiving," the teacher might think:

- **Specific focus:** *Thanksgiving*. Other countries don't celebrate this U.S. holiday, so my ELLs may not know about it.
- **More general idea:** *Feasts*. Many other countries and cultures do have holidays, some of which include feasts. It's not certain that all of my students have had a feast.
- **Most common idea:** *Celebrations*. All countries and cultures have some kind of celebration. This would be a good place to start to make connections with students' lives.

In another instance, the teacher might go through this thought process for the objective "Acquire the knowledge and skills necessary to perform scientific inquiry":

- **Specific focus:** *The Western idea of inquiry*. This notion is based in culture and is not necessarily the way inquiry is conducted in other parts of the world. My students probably need some background information to understand the purpose.
- **More general idea:** *Detectives*. Not every place has detectives, and even most native English-speaking students have probably not thought carefully about the process of detective work. In fact, what they have seen on television dramas about police work might have given them inaccurate notions about what really occurs during an inquiry process. This might be a useful way to think about or develop a future task.
- **Most common idea:** *Asking questions*. All languages have questions, even though they are asked of different people and take different forms. Therefore, all students can connect to this idea. This is also a great opportunity to introduce this grammar point!

After a connection has been made to the students using this general idea that they already understand, the teacher can involve the students in discussing their personal connections and then narrow the topic back down to the specific focus of the lesson.

When students are familiar with the process, they should be encouraged to find their own connections between their lives and the material to be studied. Students can participate in quick-writes, pair discussions, brainstorming exercises, and a variety of other tasks to help them see how the material relates to their lives. Teachers can ensure that students make the connection and can show them that their background knowledge is valued.

Making Academic Connections

Most teachers *can* make connections to students' previous learning easily, noting how the present lesson relates to past or other content or language learning. The issue is whether they *do* or not. Making this connection can be as simple as asking students, "Who remembers what we studied last week? Tell me something about it. . . . This week, we're going to build on those ideas in order to . . ." Although seemingly a simple idea, making this link can help students see the flow of their learning and associate past personal connections with content. For example, a lesson may have these two objectives: (1) Students

> ### Stop and Do
>
> Choose a partner and review your choices for personal connections in Figure 5.2. Can you think of anyone who might not be able to make the personal connection you chose? Would children in poverty, ELLs, and students of different ages be able to relate? When you are finished reviewing, look at the possible answers in Figure 5.6 at the end of this chapter.

will be able to use past tense verbs in discussion; (2) students will be able to describe central events from the history of their state that shape its current form. In seeking a connection to all students, including those who are not from the state, the teacher may think:

- **Specific focus:** *History of the state*. Not all students are from the state and those that are may not have a connection to its history.
- **More general idea:** *History of their community*. Some students probably know something about community events, but they may not know much about its history if they were not here when that topic was studied.
- **Most common idea:** *Personal histories*. All students have pasts that they have talked and written about in class. This is a good way to connect the content objective to students' lives and to give them a meaningful reason to use past tense (the language objective).

Which connections the teacher chooses depends on the content, language, and students, but those connections should provide a strong motivation for students to learn and use the language and content of the lesson and the background to access both. Students should also be encouraged to make connections themselves as their background and the connection to it helps them access 1) language and 2) content through the same kind of process. Being able to think critically and make connections is an important skill in itself, in addition to the benefits it provides for learning specific material.

Building Background Knowledge

It is important to make academic and personal connections to the lesson objectives, but teachers cannot make connections to background that does not exist. If students do not have any background in the language, concepts, theme, or content that comprises the lesson, teachers can use a number of techniques during their lesson or unit introduction to help students build the background that they need to access the content and language. Direct instruction can be effective in building background knowledge (Strangman & Hall, 2004). Several possible techniques are outlined below and summarized in Figure 5.3.

RESOURCES

Building Background Knowledge • See the list at the end of Strangman and Hall (2004) (http://www .cast.org/publications/ncac/ncac_backknowledge. html#links) for a variety of other resources for building background knowledge.

1. *Preteach and reinforce vocabulary.* Vocabulary should be pretaught (or at least reviewed) if it is essential to understanding the next component of the lesson. Simply giving a list of words with the definitions and having students use them in a sentence does not teach them vocabulary. There is not room here to mention all the ways that teachers can help their students learn vocabulary, but one important idea is that the vocabulary should be used many times in many contexts (before, during, and after the task) to help students comprehend and use it.

RESOURCES

Vocabulary Teaching • For more tips and ideas about vocabulary teaching, go to everythingesl.net. See also books by Fisher and Frey (2008) and Spencer and Guillaume (2009).

FIGURE 5.3 Summary of Background-Building Techniques

Technique	Purpose
Preteach and reinforce vocabulary	Provide students with ways to understand and talk about important concepts.
Cue-do-review	Help students link new and old content by comparing and contrasting.
Field trips and hands-on experiences	Provide students with real-time experience with the lesson topic.
Visitors	Provide background through questioning, discussion, and display.
Visuals	Provide examples of the concept or language and ways to explore links among ideas.

2. *Cue-Do-Review and other techniques.* Explore http://www.onlineacademy.org/modules/a304/lesson/lesson_2/xpages/a304c2_40700.html. In Cue-Do-Review, students compare the new concept with something they already know well, linking past learning and new ideas. Bulgren, Lenz, Deshler, and Schumaker (1995) explain:

> In the first phase, "Cue," the teacher cues students that the routine will be used to present critical information and prompts them to attend to and participate in it. In the "Do" phase, the Linking Steps are used to present the Concept Diagram. Finally, in the "Review" phase, students' understanding of both the concept information and the analytical process is checked and reinforced. (n.p.)

3. *Field trips or hands-on experiences.* If students have never really looked at the leaves on the trees around them, or if they come from somewhere where there are not many trees, teachers can take students on an exploration walk outside at the beginning of the lesson on leaves. Likewise, if students studying angles need background knowledge, they can visit homes under construction to look at angles (this can be linked to a personal connection by having them look for angles in their own residences). For a lesson that includes a language objective for students to use appropriate vocabulary in public speaking, students can watch videos of famous speeches and note important elements. Video field trips can also be used for experiences students cannot or should not have in person, for example, an erupting volcano, the growth of a plant from seed to full fruition, or an experiment for which the school does not possess the appropriate equipment. Teachers can use discussion or response logs to make sure that students are making connections.

4. *Visitors.* For a lesson on community helpers, for example, students who aren't familiar with the responsibilities of people in specific occupations can benefit from a visit from workers in those areas. Students can ask questions and explore aspects of the occupation with these guest speakers. For a unit on China, visits from Chinese community members can help dispel incorrect assumptions and build new knowledge.

5. *Visuals.* Pictures, videos, and other realia can help students get a clear idea of a concept or

RESOURCES

Instructional Videos • If there is something students need to see, there is probably a video about it on the Web. Great resources include YouTube, Teacher Tube, and About.com's "Free Educational Videos on the Web."

RESOURCES

Free Graphic Organizers • Search the Web for free organizers, or go directly to these websites for free organizers: teachervision.com, about.com, educationworld.com, teach-nology.com.

RESOURCES

Background Knowledge • A useful example that supports building student background knowledge is available from McGraw-Hill at http://teachingtoday.glencoe.com/userfiles/file/background_info_visual.pdf. Technology can also help build student background knowledge. For example, see Linda Joseph's lesson plan at http://www.infotoday.com/MMSchools/may02/cybe0502.htm and read how she helped her students build background knowledge using a variety of technologies.

language item. Graphical organizers such as concept maps, webs, and flowcharts help students organize new information and make links between it and other ideas.

Developing connections is the first step in helping students access the content and language outlined by the lesson objectives. The next step is to help students make these connections by integrating them into the lesson introduction. This is the subject of the next section.

Integrating Connections

In general, once lesson objectives are set, the next step in planning instruction is to create a lesson introduction or "anticipatory set." Lewis (2008b) notes that the purpose of the anticipatory set is, in large part, to make connections. It should:

- Provide continuity from previous lessons, if applicable.
- Allude to familiar concepts and vocabulary as a reminder and refresher.
- Tell the students briefly what the lesson will be about, being sure to point out and discuss the language and content objectives for the lesson.
- Gauge the students' level of collective background knowledge of the subject to help inform instruction.
- Activate the students' existing knowledge base.
- Whet students' appetite for the subject at hand.
- Briefly expose the students to the lesson objectives and how you will lead the students to the end result (p. 1).

To build background for students, teachers can think about their answers to the following questions, based on information that they have collected about their students:

1. What about this topic might interest the most students? (personal connection)
2. What have they already learned that relates to this topic? (academic connection)
3. What additional information do they need before the lesson starts? (building background knowledge)

Figure 5.4 provides examples of how connections can be integrated into the anticipatory set of a variety of teacher-created lessons. (In the lessons in this figure, the teachers

FIGURE 5.4   Examples of Anticipatory Sets that Make Connections

Content Area/Topic/ Grade Level	Anticipatory Set (Lesson Introduction)
Science: conservation (Grade 2)	Hold up common examples of paper, plastic, glass, and aluminum/tin products and ask students questions such as "Does your family buy or use any of these products?" "Where do these come from?" "What are they made from?" Write what students know about these products on the Know portion of a KWL chart. Display the learning targets and read them to students. Introduce the new science vocabulary and ask students to listen for it in a short reading. With partners, students discuss what they think the words mean and then share their ideas with the class.
Math/geometry: polygons and nonpolygons (Grades 3–4)	Point out the student-friendly learning targets written on the board. Invite students to take out the "Polygon Treasure Hunt" worksheets that they completed at home. Briefly discuss the previous lesson's discoveries about polygons. Have students, in pairs, share their polygon treasure hunt discoveries from home. As needed, ask questions about their process and outcomes. Link to the current lesson by reading with students a story about the pyramids.
Communications: media literacy (Grade 7)	Ask students, "Does anyone know what advertising is?" "How and where have you experienced advertising?" "How did it make you feel?" Link to the previous lesson by noting, "Remember when we talked about conveying a theme and knowing your audience? Today we are going to talk about how media can influence your thinking and decisions." Preteach new vocabulary by defining new words with students and adding them to a word wall.
Language arts: inferences (Grade 3)	Begin the lesson by talking about guessing. Ask students some issues or topics that they guess about and ask them to make guesses about certain common ideas. Connect to "educated guesses" and what makes a guess good or bad. Explain the link between guesses and inferences. As the discussion progresses, students write definitions for *guess*, *inference*, and *prediction* in their vocabulary journals.

refer to standards, goals, and objectives collectively as learning targets.) Teachers can encourage students to make connections in a variety of ways, from asking guiding questions to letting students brainstorm, to having students listen to a story and point out the main ideas. The anticipatory set is the starting point for the rest of the lesson and can help or hinder its success.

Stop and Think

Evaluate the ideas in Figure 5.4. Try to point out the personal and academic connections and any background building. Is anything missing from these anticipatory sets? Can you think of any ways to introduce the concepts that might work better for your current or future students?

Guidelines for Making Connections

Making connections is a good start for helping students access the social and academic language and content of lessons, but equally important is what students do with the connections that are made. The guidelines below explain further.

Guideline 1: Be Deliberate

Teachers can carefully plan to make academic and personal connections and help students build any background necessary for each lesson. Equally important is to check that students have actually made the connection and that it has served its purpose of piquing students' interest and preparing students to engage in the lesson's language and content. To find out, teachers can ask, review, observe, and reiterate as necessary.

Guideline 2: Help Students Transfer Connections Back to Their Lives

Connections should be obvious and ongoing throughout the unit. Techniques mentioned in this text, such as having students keep a journal in which they link their learning to their lives, can be effective tools for avoiding student questions such as "Why are we doing this again?" during the lesson or unit.

Guideline 3: Consider Culture

Connections may need to be made in different ways and for different reasons depending on the cultures of your students. For example, if students do not understand how leaving the classroom for a field trip is part of the classroom learning process, background may have to be built for this connection strategy. Similarly, if students are asked to brainstorm to make connections but are not familiar with the procedure for brainstorming, explicit instruction in brainstorming might be warranted. If the teacher sees that some students cannot or will not participate, this means rethinking how and which connections are made.

Figure 5.5 summarizes these basic guidelines. Additional guidelines are presented throughout this book.

Stop and Think

After reading Chapter 5, what, if anything, would you have the teachers in the chapter-opening scenarios change in their instruction?

Conclusion

There is no doubt that making personal and academic connections from instruction to students' backgrounds and interests (and vice versa) is central to their ability to access the language and content of a lesson. It also encourages students to take a personal interest in

FIGURE 5.5 Summary of Guidelines for Making Connections Between Students' Backgrounds and Lesson Content

Guideline	Example
Be deliberate.	Check that students have made connections and that students are interested and prepared to engage in the lesson. If they are not, use additional connections and background building as necessary.
Help students transfer connections back to their lives.	Use techniques that encourage students to see the links throughout the lesson and/or unit.
Consider culture.	Use explicit instruction as needed to help students understand the process and content of the connections.

FIGURE 5.6 Possible Connections, from Specific to Common, for Figure 5.2

Lesson Topic	Personal Connection
Maps	Globes Traveling Locations of places we know
Battle of Bull Run	U.S. Civil War Civil wars Conflict
The Parthenon	Greece Religious architecture Important buildings
Penguins	*Happy Feet* Arctic animals Birds
Sacagawea	Indians Explorers Helpers
Geometric proofs	Theorems Deductive reasoning Winning an argument with logic

(continued)

FIGURE 5.6 continued

Lesson Topic	Personal Connection
Thanksgiving	Holidays Feasts Celebrations
Simple addition	Math Playing games (scoring, counting spaces, etc.)
Washington, D.C./capital	The United States capital State capitals Important places

and be engaged with the content and language. However, this is only the beginning of planning effective lessons for diverse classrooms; making instructional connections in lesson tasks is also essential, as we will describe in Chapter 6.

• Extensions •

For Reflection

1. *Personal connections*. Think of ways in which your background connects with the content in one of the areas you teach or will teach. How might the connections you make differ from the connections that might be made by students from Mexico, from a poor area of town, or from a different age group?

2. *Think back*. Reflect on a lesson or class that you found inspiring, exciting, or engaging. What connections did the teacher make for you, or did you make for yourself, that piqued your interest and encouraged you to engage?

For Action

1. *Reviewing strategies*. Choose an activity for activating prior knowledge from the West Virginia Department of Education Strategy Bank (http://wvde.state.wv.us/strategybank/activating.html) or another Website. Integrate this strategy into a lesson. Focus on activating both content and language knowledge.

2. *Adapt a lesson*. Find a lesson that you have created or have downloaded from the World Wide Web. Check the lesson for language and content objectives and effective personal and academic connections, then improve the lesson by adding and/or editing as needed.

RESOURCES

Lesson Plan Sites • There are many websites that provide lesson plans on the Web. Try these: The Lessons Plan Page, The Educator's Reference Desk, Scholastic, Discovery Education.

Designing Engaging Tasks

• Key Issues •

1. Tasks are designed to help students meet objectives.

2. Tasks must be engaging in order for students to learn.

3. Engaging tasks make pedagogical connections between students' backgrounds and needs in relation to lesson objectives.

4. Tasks should incorporate culture and be culturally responsive.

5. Students can help design and carry out tasks.

As you read the scenario below, think about issues that the principal needs to address with Mr. Carhart.

 Dr. Johnson, the principal of Franklin High School, was conducting the mandatory annual review of his teachers. Mr. Carhart, a ninth-grade social studies teacher, had turned in a lesson plan in the district's required format, including language objectives and connections to students' backgrounds. During the required observation of this lesson in Mr. Carhart's social studies class, Dr. Johnson listened to groups of students present very similar speeches about the causes of the Civil War. Dr. Johnson noticed that there seemed to be a lot of down time in the class during which students in the audience were off task and not paying attention. In addition, the English language learners (ELLs) in the class were sitting in a group together and did not seem to be actively listening at all. Dr. Johnson was interested in hearing Mr. Carhart's purpose for this task and what he thought about the behavior of his students during it.

Background

Having students present to the class is a technique that is commonly used in schools. In the chapter-opening scenario, however, the principal, Dr. Johnson, has some justifiable concerns. If students were not spending time on task, and the ELLs were not engaged at all, chances are that they were not learning as much as they could (Bonine, 1999; Brophy, 1988; Meltzer & Hamman, 2004).

Stop and Think

Before reading the rest of Chapter 6, think about how you might change the task that Mr. Carhart's students are involved in so that students are more engaged in the content and language and can meet lesson objectives.

The amount of time that students spend on task is clearly related to the amount of engagement that they feel. Creating language objectives to help students access and understand goals and making connections in the lesson's introduction to help initiate engagement are important steps in helping students engage. However, the design of learning tasks must also emphasize access and engagement.

Understanding Engagement and Tasks

Engagement

An engaging task does not necessarily mean one that is fun but rather one that is worth doing because it is inherently interesting or meaningful to students in some other way. Studies in learning, brain research, psychology, motivation, and second language acquisition clearly show that engaged students achieve more (Bruner, 1961; Dhority & Jensen, 1998; Meltzer & Hamman, 2004; Vygotsky, 1986). This is particularly true for ELLs and other diverse students because engagement in tasks can mitigate the effects of factors outside school that may otherwise interfere with achievement (Csikszentmihalyi, 1990; Guthrie, Shafer, & Huang, 2001). As Egbert (2007) notes:

> *Engagement includes student* involvement *and* ownership. . . . *An engaging task means that students spend more time on task and have deeper focus, leading to greater success. In order to engage students, teachers should understand their needs, wants, and interests as relevant to their [learning]; in other words, to comprehend their learning goals.* (n.p.)

Meltzer and Hamman (2004) refer to engagement as "persistence in and absorption with reading, writing, speaking, listening, and thinking even when there are other choices available" (p. 10). They propose three strategies, supported throughout the literature on engagement, for engaging students in tasks that integrate content and language:

1. *Making connections to students' lives* by creating opportunities for authentic interactions with people, objects, and experiences that initiate student interest. In other words, tasks should be authentic and relevant for learners.

2. *Having students interact* with each other and with language. Tasks should be cooperative and/or collaborative in both focusing on language and using language for authentic purposes.

3. *Creating responsive classrooms,* or considering students' needs, wants, abilities, and interests. In other words, tasks should be differentiated, challenging, and scaffolded. (Egbert, 2007)

Clearly, understanding students' backgrounds and interests, as suggested in Chapter 3, is central to student engagement.

Elements of Tasks

An understanding of tasks is also crucial to creating engaging ones. Tasks can be divided into two overlapping components: process and product. **Task process** is "what happens when the learning takes place" (Smith, 2003, n.p.); in other words, the process is what the students do and how they do it. Process can include whether students work in groups, what kind of language they use, and what tools they employ in doing a task. **Task product** can be seen as the outcome of this process or the end result of the task. Products can include written essays, plays, art pieces, dioramas, and many other (usually concrete and graded) artifacts. In the past, more emphasis was typically placed on task products, but the process is equally important because engagement and learning depend on what happens during it.

> **Stop and Do**
>
> Before reading further, list the elements of task process and product (think about what is involved in designing tasks).

Elements of task process and product that teachers can consider intentionally in their task design are listed in Figure 6.1.

FIGURE 6.1 Elements of Task Process and Product

Elements of Task Process	Elements of Task Product
Instructional groupings	Audience
Modes	Mode
Task structure	
Time and pacing	
Scaffolding	
Resources/texts	
Teacher/student roles	
Procedural tools	

Elements of Task Process   Regardless of the content of the task, the elements of the process that require thought and careful design are the same. Each of these elements will be described next.

Instructional groupings.   Instructional grouping includes how many students work together and also with whom they work. In different tasks or different parts of one task, students can work individually, in dyads or trios, in large groups, or as a whole class. In addition, students can work in either **homogeneous** or **heterogeneous** groups that should be determined by aspects such as ability level, first language, interest, and/or skill. Which of these groupings is part of the design of a specific task depends on what the task is meant to accomplish. It also depends on how students connect to the groupings. For example, students who come from educational backgrounds where group work was prevalent may prefer collaboration and may need help working individually, and students who are used to working individually may prefer that approach and also need to learn skills for working in groups. Students in diverse classrooms benefit from teachers balancing the use of many participation structures (Peregoy & Boyle, 2004): from teacher-directed activities to small cooperative groups, to solo work. Students also profit from frequent opportunities to interact with each other and with the teacher during instructional activities.

Modes • Language modes include listening, speaking, reading, writing, viewing, and representing. Modes should be integrated in all tasks, unless the task is specifically designed to focus on one mode.

Modes.   In addition to the basic **modes** of reading, writing, listening, and speaking, teachers and students can use graphics, video, art, music, storytelling and other modes that incorporate student backgrounds and help students access the content and language of the lesson. Students learn by interacting in all of these modes. Completing written worksheets, while useful for remediation and practice, should not be the main task of a lesson.

Task structure.   Tasks can be open, partially structured, or highly structured. The task structure can determine how students get information and how they express themselves during the task. For example, in a structured task, the teacher may ask students to complete individually a predetermined set of task steps using specific materials, or in a more open task, students may choose which materials they use and how they arrive at the product. Whether the structure is cooperative or competitive, open or structured, or some combination, teachers can make sure that students understand how to participate via explicit modeling or instruction of group processes and language.

Stop and Think

What other specific modes can you think of in which students can receive and/or produce language and content?

Time and pacing.   Because they are such a diverse group, students do not get the same work done in the same amount of time. Some students work faster, some slower; some have language or content barriers; others complete the overall requirements but do not get deep into the topic. In designing a task, teachers need to consider how much time different students need while also considering how to provide enough scaffolding that students can complete their tasks. Having a set of task extensions or additional tasks that students are expected to tackle when they complete the required task sooner than expected can help them spend classroom time to best advantage.

Scaffolding. The Center for Research on Education, Diversity & Excellence (1998) notes that teachers can scaffold student learning by modeling, eliciting, probing, restating, clarifying, questioning, and praising, as appropriate. This can be done in a carefully planned way and when the teacher sees that students need help during a task. Students can be scaffolded in both content and language, particularly in the informal, intercultural, instructional, and academic language to which they have not previously been exposed. These kinds of scaffolds can also be provided by other students and paraprofessionals, class guests, carefully constructed computer programs, and the use of dictionaries and other reference works. If students are given too much scaffolding, however, they may not feel challenged and may become bored; if too little scaffolding is available, the task may seem too difficult and some students may flounder. The idea is to plan scaffolding so that there is just enough challenge to keep students engaged, regardless of their level. Understanding students' backgrounds helps in designing lessons that have the appropriate amount of scaffolding.

Resources/texts. Lesson texts and other content and language resources must be at appropriate levels. Text sets, consisting of texts with similar content but a variety of language levels, can be assembled from different sources. Other resources should be used if they help students meet the objectives and can engage students in doing so.

Teacher/student roles. Who is the expert? Who gives help? Who asks questions? Who talks?

Scaffolding Scaffolding means providing support of the appropriate type and level of difficulty.

Stop and Do

Think about the ways that you scaffold instruction or have had instruction scaffolded for you. Make a list of scaffolds that may work for different groups of students.

RESOURCES

Scaffolding • Tom Snyder Productions offers software packages that contain a variety of scaffolds and modes and thus provide access for diverse students. For more information, go to **www.tomsnyder.com**.

Stop and Do

Search the Internet for a text set centered around a specific content topic. Find at least one reading that can be used with each of the following three student groups: improving, grade level, and above grade level in language ability and knowledge.

RESOURCES

Text Sets • National Geographic Explorer comes in Pioneer and Pathfinder editions, both with the same cover and illustrations so that elementary school students do not know who has the easier text. The focus of both is on content and language. For more information and additional resources, see **http://magma.nationalgeographic.com/ngexplorer/pioneer/teachers/**.

Research shows that when the answer to most of these questions is the student, the more likely it is that students will be engaged and achieve (Meltzer & Hamman, 2004). Tasks should be developed with the intention that students will be active and engaged in learning rather than recipients of it. For example, instead of lecture, teachers can ask essential questions (McKenzie, 1997; Prensky, 2007) that lead students to create, with the teacher, a process for answering them.

Differentiation Differentiation of instruction means designing instruction based on student abilities, interests, and backgrounds. The purpose is to help all students reach the same goal but to do so in a way that works for each student.

RESOURCES

Differentiation • See these useful texts and websites: *Differentiated Instruction* by T. Hall, 2002 (http://www.cast.org/publications/ncac/ncac_diffinstruc.html); *How to Differentiate Instruction in Mixed-Ability Classrooms* (2nd ed.), by C. Tomlinson, 2001, Alexandria, VA: ASCD; and many other useful resources from the Association for Supervision and Curriculum Development (ASCD) (www.ascd.org).

Procedural tools. Tools include everything from books to pencils, to visitors, to blogging software. Teachers need to determine which tool(s) has the best fit for the task. If computers are not really necessary, they probably should not be used. Likewise, if a book cannot give the best idea of the content or language, a different tool should be chosen. This tool–task fit is important because it takes the focus off the tool and keeps it on the content and language of the lesson. In other words, tools should not get in the way of learning.

One, some, or all of the elements of the task process can be designed to be engaging based on a teacher's understanding of her students and the curriculum. In addition, by allowing *students* to make some of the design choices, teachers can differentiate both task process and product. **Differentiation**, in turn, promotes greater access and engagement.

Elements of Task Product The elements of task process are clearly instrumental in engaging students and supporting achievement. Several aspects of the task product are also important and will be discussed next.

Audience. Students are typically more engaged in their products when they will be viewed by an audience other than the teacher. A letter written to a scientist or politician, a book to be read to students in other classes or be placed in the library, or a model to be entered in a competition is more likely to engage students than worksheets or writing assignments that the teacher grades and then students "file" in the nearest trash can.

Modes. How can students complete their products? As in the task process, modes have an important role. Speaking, writing, drawing, acting, singing, constructing, and creating are among the many choices teachers can make. While designing what the students will produce, teachers can review the lesson objective verbs (see Figure 4.1) and create the objectives broadly enough that students have a chance to express themselves in ways that they can be understood. Students can also be given choices about how to represent their learning.

Assessment of both the process and the product should help students see relationships among objectives, connections, and the task, including both the process and the product. Assessment is discussed further in Chapter 7.

Pedagogical Connections

Engagement comes when task elements—of both process and product—are designed to work for students. To design effective tasks, teachers can make pedagogical connections; in other words, they should think about the backgrounds and interests of their students while designing tasks. Such connections can lead to student success. For example, Oh (2005) notes that successful learning tasks in her classroom were those in which her students were encouraged to produce products using their creativity and experiences, including creating short stories, poems, raps, mobiles, video clips, quilts, puppet shows, and PowerPoint presentations. Murray (1999) likewise describes projects in which students chose the topic or procedure for their learning and recorded in some way how the course content connected to their daily lives. These ideas, and the general techniques described below, are based on the teacher's understanding of the diversity of learners within the classroom.

Techniques for Making Pedagogical Connections

The Center for Research on Education, Diversity & Excellence (1998) recommends the pedagogical strategies in Figure 6.2, which teachers can employ to make instructional connections to student backgrounds. Another principle is to use culturally relevant resources such as minority or first language literature, film, and artifacts. Teachers can also promote cultural awareness, engage students, and enrich the presentation of content by integrating facts from a variety of cultures where they naturally fit into the lesson. Figure 6.3 presents examples of tasks into which teachers have integrated cultural facts. Pedagogical connections, or the design of tasks that support achievement for all learners, work with personal and academic connections to provide students with both access and reasons to engage.

> **Stop and Think**
>
> What topics do you know enough about to include cross-cultural facts? Which do you need to learn more about?

Guidelines for Task Design

In addition to the suggestions above, two additional guidelines can help teachers create effective tasks.

FIGURE 6.2 Principles for Connecting Instruction to Students' Lives

1. Listen to students talk about familiar topics, such as home and community.
2. Respond to students' talk and questions, making on-the-spot changes that relate directly to their comments.
3. Interact with students in ways that respect their speaking styles, which may be different from the teacher's, such as paying attention to wait-time, eye contact, turn taking, and spotlighting.
4. Connect student language with literacy and content-area knowledge through speaking, listening, reading, and writing activities.
5. Encourage students to use content vocabulary to express their understanding.
6. Encourage students to use their first and second languages in instructional activities. (p. 2)

FIGURE 6.3 Integrating Cultural Facts

Topic	Example
Rocket inquiry	During construction of a paper rocket and study of gravity and force, teacher integrates facts about space programs in different countries and the international space station.
What's going on in the sky?	In a lesson about weather, with a focus on rain, the teacher notes folk beliefs about rain, including the South African rain-maker queen and other cultures' rain dances.
Rosa Parks	During the lesson, the teacher mentions other nonviolent protesters, including Gandhi and the Dalai Lama, and their contributions to the world.
Persuasion	The teacher integrates different cultural views of persuasion, demonstrating with television commercials and other forms of advertisements.
Plants	The teacher and students discuss contributions from researchers and botanists around the world to the work of modifying and improving plants.

Guideline 1: Give Students a Reason to Listen

In the chapter-opening scenario, students were listening to practically the same presentation over and over. From their reactions, it is clear that they have little incentive to listen, even though the teacher has asked them to. To make this task more engaging for students, Mr. Carhart has many options. For example, he could ask the students to take notes for an upcoming test, or to list differences in the information that the groups found. Even better, he could design a jigsaw activity, asking each student group to present on a different aspect of the war, providing information to their peers that they would need to synthesize in order to complete their final product. Whether students are required to fill out a graphic organizer or ask two questions of the presenters, students always need a reason to listen to ensure that they do.

Guideline 2: Do Not Do What Students Can Do

The more students have invested in a task or lesson, the more engaged they tend to be. Teachers who give students choices and allow them more **autonomy** in making instructional decisions will find the students more involved in their learning. By understanding students' backgrounds, teachers can design specific roles for students in tasks and lessons that they would not have previously considered. Figure 6.4 presents some tasks that students can do and that teachers typically take responsibility for.

> **Autonomy** Learner autonomy refers to the amount of responsibility that learners take or are given for their own learning, including the extent to which they make choices about task process and product.

Stop and Do

With a partner, list other tasks that students can do and that teachers often do not allow them to do.

FIGURE 6.4   Tasks Students Can Do

- Write test questions.
- Help their peers review.
- Lead a brainstorming session.
- Explain tasks.
- Form groups.
- Decorate the classroom.
- Provide feedback.
- Search for resources.
- Find cultural facts.
- Create choices for products.

FIGURE 6.5 Guidelines for Designing Engaging Tasks

Guideline	Example
Give students a reason to listen.	Do not assume that students will listen because they are supposed to. Give students a task that they cannot complete unless they have listened.
Do not do what students can do.	Students are more likely to engage in tasks in which they have an important role. Think about what students can do through each step in the lesson design process.

Stop and Think

After reading the chapter, what advice would you give to the principal and teacher in the chapter-opening scenario?

Providing students with reasons to listen and letting them participate in instructional planning can facilitate student engagement and thereby their success. Figure 6.5 summarizes these guidelines as reinforcement. Additional guidelines are presented throughout this book.

Conclusion

The careful design of task processes and products can result in student engagement, particularly when the backgrounds and needs of all students are considered. Instructional connections, the integration of cultural knowledge, and a focus on student autonomy contribute to achievement for all students. The measurement of lessons and student process and outcomes is the subject of Chapter 7.

──────────── • Extensions • ────────────

For Reflection

1. *Task process.* Think about times that you have given students worksheets or been given worksheets by a teacher. How might students be involved in the information they must learn in a more active way?

2. *Task product.* What's the most interesting product you have created? What made it engaging to you?

For Action

1. *Organizing task design.* Use the elements chart in Figure 6.1 to make a checklist of elements you want to remember to include in your lessons.

2. *Standards and culture.* Look at the standards for your content area and/or grade level. Find cultural facts that you could integrate into lessons on the topics that the standards require.

chapter 7

Assessing Tasks, Lessons, and Students

• Key Issues •

1. Teachers can assess their lessons before, during, and after their implementation.

2. Teachers can assess student progress toward both content and language objectives and demonstrations of knowledge in both areas in student products.

3. Assessments should be integrated into the lesson and focus on students' ways of knowing.

As you read the chapter-opening scenario, think about the issues that it raises about assessment.

 Li Lee had been in Ms. Hamilton's class for 4 months. The second-grader was responding to the language objectives that Ms. Hamilton included in each lesson and appeared to be learning English quickly. Li also really enjoyed the hands-on science lessons in class, particularly when Ms. Hamilton could help Li make connections to her former life in Korea. Ms. Hamilton was perplexed, however, at Li's science test scores: Li consistently scored at the lower end of the class on the short, multiple-choice exams, but her performance in class indicated that she should be doing much better. Ms. Hamilton wondered if Li needed more time with the English as a second language (ESL) teacher or whether she might have some kind of disability.

Stop and Think

Before reading Chapter 7, think about how you might discover why Li's science test scores are so low.

Background

Assessment is an important component in both lesson design and implementation. It can be used to evaluate how the lesson meets guidelines for good pedagogy *and* how students react to the lesson. Many outstanding resources for teachers describe all aspects and types of assessment; see, for example, Burke, 1994; Ioannou-Georgiou and Pavlou, 2003; O'Malley and Pierce, 1996. This chapter focuses on a specific subset of principles that underlie the development and integration of effective assessment for diverse learners.

Understanding Assessment

Some authors (e.g., Wiggins & McTighe, 1998) suggest that assessments be created by first identifying the desired results (learning targets), and then deciding what evidence would be effective in measuring those results. In their view, the design of tasks and other parts of the instruction should then be built with the assessments in mind. Whether teachers use this backward design strategy or a linear, beginning-to-end design, the principles that guide the development of assessments do not change. Overall guidelines for assessing student learning include those in Figure 7.1.

Teachers usually cannot do much to meet the guidelines shown in Figure 7.1 when they are implementing major graduation or other standardized tests because the use of such assessments is usually closely prescribed. However, teachers can certainly consider the guidelines when constructing and using classroom-based assessments or those that are developed by the teacher for her classroom. Whether the assessment is of the lesson or task, the process or product, the more closely the assessment fits these guidelines, the more useful it will be in understanding students.

It is easy to get confused by all the jargon surrounding assessment. The difference between assessment and evaluation is one crucial point that is often misunderstood. **Assessment** refers to the general process of gathering data about something or someone, while **evaluation** refers to a final judgment (i.e., assigning a grade or a rank). In other words, not all assessment is evaluation. Teachers *can* use assessments to make an evaluation, or they can use the data they gather for goals such as changing instruction,

91

FIGURE 7.1 General Guidelines for Assessment

Guideline	Explanation
Directly related to objectives	Measures progress toward and attainment of the lesson objectives.
Authentic and/or meaningful to the students	Provides useful and accurate feedback. Helps guide students and instruction. Avoids evaluating students based only on testwiseness.
Occurs in multiple contexts	Allows students to show what they know in different ways during and after the task or lesson.
Ongoing	Used at various times during the task or lesson.
Integrative	Assesses both language and content.
Balances depth and breadth	Combines alternative assessments and standardized assessments.

Source: Chao, C. (2007). "New Emphases in Assessment" (Chapter 15) in J. Egbert and E. Hanson-Smith (Eds.), *CALL Environments: Research, Practice, and Critical Issues.* Alexandria, VA: TESOL, Inc.

Testwiseness Testwiseness is the understanding of how to take tests well. Students can be weak on understanding content, but if they are testwise, they can figure out ways to use the test structure to pass.

supporting students, and reviewing real achievements with students. Most teachers perform evaluations on a regular basis, but evaluation is certainly not the only purpose for assessment.

Purposes of Assessment

Assessment has many purposes: some are administrative or programmatic; others pertain mainly to the classroom teacher. Types of assessments that serve administrative or programmatic purposes include placement tests, standardized exit tests, program evaluations, and graduation tests. These assessments are useful to a variety of stakeholders; however, they do not provide direct lesson information to teachers but rather are measurements of accountability (evaluations).

Classroom assessments, on the other hand, include reviews of lesson design, student progress, and student products. Some are for evaluation purposes; others serve to monitor student progress and thus help learners move ahead, develop an awareness of their abilities, and figure out what goals they should aim for. **Traditional classroom assessments,** or those that are typically used for evaluation purposes, include quizzes, tests, and structured papers. These assessments are the same for each student and typically require students to choose an answer. Traditional assessments generally provide a score that designates how students have mastered individual (discrete) content or language items. **Alternative assessments** are alternatives to traditional assessments and consist of any open-ended method that uncovers what students know and can do as students create an answer. Alternative assessments include verbal reporting, observation, oral interviews, demonstrations, retellings, role plays, portfolios, journaling, and many other activities. Some of these assessments are described in Figure 7.2. Alternative assessments are used to design or redesign instruction, showing student growth between assessments. Traditional assessments are often a required part of the curriculum, but teachers can also add a variety of alternative assessments in

RESOURCES

Alternative Assessments • For a variety of great information and links, see Kathy Shrock's Guide for Educators—Assessment and Rubric Information at http://school.discoveryeducation.com/schrockguide/assess.html#alternative.

Stop and Do

Before reading further, list the assessments that you have used, experienced, or read about. Note what and who they can be used to assess.

FIGURE 7.2 Alternative Assessments

Type	Explanation
Observation	Teachers can make informal observations of students during tasks or use a more formal checklist to look for specific items.
Oral or written interviews	Teachers can interview students individually or in groups on any aspect of the task or theme.
Demonstrations	The use of props (realia) can help students remember what they want to say and to follow a structured plan for expressing themselves.
Oral or written retellings	After a reading, the students retell what they understood. Teachers can understand how students comprehend, e.g., whether they focus on details or main ideas.
Role plays	For students who do not have a lot of productive language or who feel comfortable with drama, acting out understandings can help them show what they know.
Portfolios	Teachers help students indicate what they know by assembling and explaining a variety of their work.
Journaling	Dialogue journals, double-entry reading journals, math journals, and even group journals can help students express their understandings without fear of being evaluated.

FIGURE 7.3 Traditional and Alternative Assessments

	Traditional Assessments	Alternative Assessments
Overall purpose	Evaluate knowledge of discrete items.	Review process and product; gather a more holistic understanding of student knowledge and abilities.
Audience	Parents, administrators, government stakeholders.	Parents, teachers, students.
Examples of methods	Multiple-choice and true-false tests, structured essays, discrete-item quizzes.	Verbal reporting, observation, oral interviews, demonstrations, retellings, role plays, portfolios and journaling.
General use of results	Document aspects of student learning; screen and/or diagnose, place, and exit students; determine graduates.	Improve instruction, provide student examples and progress reports to parents, help students understand their strengths and weaknesses.

order to capture the varied and complex learning that takes place in classrooms. Figure 7.3 contrasts traditional and alternative assessments.

Assessing Student Process and Product

Adapting Traditional Classroom Assessments

Traditional assessments do have disadvantages; most problematic is the idea that all students should be measured in the same exact way. However, they are often efficient, simple, and useful for getting a general overview of class performance. Because they are so predominant (and often required) in classrooms, teachers can consider adapting traditional assessments where possible to work more like alternative assessments. For example, **hybrid** test or quiz questions include features of both traditional (e.g., multiple-choice and true-false) and alternative (open-ended, student-centered) assessments. This type of assessment may be an effective option for classrooms with diverse learners. Hybrid multiple-choice and true-false questions can include a box in which students can explain their answers, providing teachers with information about both the effectiveness of the question and the students' answering process. This is particularly useful with diverse

FIGURE 7.4   Examples of Hybrid Test Questions

1. The Milky Way galaxy is shaped like a

   a. doughnut.

   b. pretzel.

   c. ball.

   d. spiral.

   Why did you choose this answer?

   ┌───┐
   │   │
   └───┘

2. T F In *Pride and Prejudice*, Jane Austen is making fun of the food of her era.

   If you chose "False," make the statement true.

   ┌───┐
   │   │
   └───┘

learners, who may understand the questions or answers in a variety of ways. Examples of hybrid questions are shown in Figure 7.4.

Alternatively, teachers can ask students to rate the questions and/or the test, indicating what they thought was fair or not fair, clear or unclear, important or unimportant. Even a review with students at the end of a commercially produced, standardized classroom test can help teachers and students understand what their next goals should be.

> ### Stop and Think
>
> What other ways can you construct hybrid assessments from traditional assessments?

Student Roles in Alternative Assessments

The Chapter 6 guideline "Do not do what students can do" also applies to designing assessments. Students can and should be involved in the creation and review of classroom assessments. This involvement helps them to understand the objectives, empowers them by engaging them in their own evaluation, and provides clear direction for the language and content that they need to access during the lesson.

The process of working with the teacher on assessment can also facilitate the building of classroom trust and understanding. Students can participate by writing test questions, providing individual or group assessment choices, developing instructions and **rubrics** for projects that express relevant outcomes, and even scoring and providing feedback

> **Rubric** A rubric is a scoring tool for alternative assessments. It contains criteria, developed by teachers and/or students, that are linked to the content and language learning objectives. Rubrics can be used by students to self-assess or by other members of the classroom community to comment on student process and product.

for other students. Teachers can use the student assessment creation process as an assessment in itself: it can assess how students understand what they are supposed to learn and how they are to learn it.

Lesson Examples

Chapter 11 provides complete lessons with assessments integrated into them. For the purposes of this chapter, Figure 7.5 shows the relationships in three lessons among the essential lesson components described in this text. Note how the lesson objectives are explicitly related to the connections that students are asked to make, and that they also determine the tasks and assessments. Some of the lessons choose less formal (ungraded) assessments, which are quite appropriate for initial lessons in a unit. Other lessons include assignments that will be graded. All of them use a variety of assessments and follow some of the guidelines presented previously in Figure 7.1. Assessments can be preplanned into the lesson, as in Figure 7.5, but there should always be room to add additional assessments if the teacher or students see a need to collect further information.

Stop and Do

Review the assessment plans in Figure 7.5. How do they follow the guidelines presented in this and other chapters? Suggest adaptations for any issues that you see.

Homework

Another commonly used form of practice and assessment is homework. Homework often consists of worksheets or reading assignments. For English language learners (ELLs) and other diverse students, particularly if they do not have help in English at home, these tasks are not very effective. More effective might be activities and assessments that incorporate the characteristics of engaging tasks noted in Chapter 6. Interactive homework (Van Voorhis, 2001; Epstein & Van Voorhis, 2001; Epstein, Simon, & Salinas, 1997) is one type of homework that can be effective for all learners.

Interactive homework assignments are "homework assignments that require students to talk to someone at home about something interesting that they are learning in class" (Epstein et al., 2002, n.p.). Parents (or other guardians) have a small but essential role in interactive homework tasks. One of the bases for interactive homework is the idea that family involvement in a child's schooling can result in higher achievement (Egbert & Salsbury, 2009). Schools can also benefit from the knowledge brought to school by

FIGURE 7.5 The Relationships Among Lesson Components

Context	Objectives SWBAT:	Connections	Tasks	Assessments
Third-grade science: plants	• Identify what plants need to stay alive. • Define and use plant vocabulary. • Recognize good discussion skills. • Write complete sentences.	• What are some things that you need every day to stay alive? • We'll study what living organisms need to stay alive. • What is an organism? What is a plant?	• Vocabulary word wall. • Review how to participate in a classroom discussion. • Brainstorm. • Complete diagrams with vocabulary words. • Journal according to model.	• Observation of discussion. • Class rating of discussion. • Observation of vocabulary use during tasks. • Final product completion and accuracy. • Journaling to check complete sentence use, questions, and interests.
Eighth-grade English: persuasion	• Identify persuasive techniques. • Organize thoughts to be persuasive. • Use adjectives to illustrate an idea.	• How many of you have seen an ad that made you want something? • Review the meaning of *opinion* and other vocabulary words.	• Discuss persuasive techniques and the role that adjectives play. • Add adjectives to word wall. • Analyze ads and complete a worksheet on techniques, pointing out adjectives.	• Observation during discussion. • Worksheet review. • Matching/fill-in-the-blanks test on identifying techniques.
Fourth-grade social studies: wood	• List common products that come from trees. • Explain how this natural resource can be renewed. • Write complete sentences.	• What products do you use that come from trees? • "We studied about tree rings and how trees clean the air. Now we will see . . . ."	• Review and practice how to write complete sentences using tree products information. • Organize a scavenger hunt for wood products. • Discuss the scavenger hunt.	• Observe during brainstorm to see what students know. • Observe/discuss with groups of students during the scavenger hunt. • Short written quiz that students answer with complete sentences.

parents and other family members, particularly those of diverse backgrounds (Egbert & Salsbury, 2009). Interactive homework includes the following features:

- Teachers guide involvement and interaction.
- Parents do not "teach"—students are responsible for learning and sharing.
- Parents interact with children in new ways.
- Teachers show children that they understand the importance of family interaction.
- Tasks are engaging and challenging.
- Interactive homework is assigned two to four times per month. Family interaction is expected to be 10 to 15 minutes per task, and two to three days may be given for completion.
- Tasks are content- and language-based, relevant, interactive, and written in simple language.
- Teachers provide follow-up and student sharing (Egbert & Salsbury, 2009).

Interactive homework assignments that focus on content can be conducted in the language of choice for ELLs, making it more likely that they will understand the content and be able to complete the tasks. If this homework is being used as an assessment of student understanding, this is an important advantage over worksheets.

Examples of interactive homework tasks for the lessons in Figure 7.5 are the following:

1. **Plants:** Students will create interview questions about plants to ask their family member. They can record, write down, or draw the answers they receive. Questions and prompts can include "What is your favorite plant?" or "Tell me about something you've grown."

2. **Persuasion:** The student briefly explains persuasive techniques to the family member. The student then interviews the family member, asking which technique is most persuasive to her or him and why. The student records the information and adds whether he or she feels the same way as their family member. In class, students compare answers and discuss.

3. **Wood:** The student and the family member hunt for wood products in their home and the student records the findings. The student interviews the family member about which wood product is most valuable to her or him and why. The student shares the findings with the class.

ⓇESOURCES

Interactive Homework · For more information, see Battle-Bailey (2003) at http://www.ericdigests.org/2004-4/homework.htm.

Stop and Do

Find an interactive homework activity on the TIPS website at http://www.csos.jhu.edu/P2000/tips/index.htm. Adapt the activity to fit a class that you are teaching, have observed, or have participated in. Describe why you think this activity will work for the students you have in mind.

These tasks allow students to share their knowledge, and they allow teachers to assess whether students understood both the homework assignment and the lesson.

Additional Guidelines for Assessment

In addition to the suggestions above, the following two guidelines can help teachers design effective assessments during lesson development.

Guideline 1: Be Transparent

One important concept that affects assessment and supports student achievement is transparency. For example, teachers need to help students see the relationships among the lesson parts (connections, objectives, tasks, assessment). Students should also be aware of how task elements affect process and outcomes. In the same way that students should not wonder why they are addressing a topic or participating in a task, students should understand essential lesson components; this type of transparency leaves the components open for discussion and possible change, helping to keep students engaged and achieving.

Teachers can start with transparency at the beginning of the lesson by using the following suggestions:

1. Make sure that students know what the language and content objectives are and how they will be assessed. Post them on the board, refer to them, and discuss them as needed.

2. Model and explain the task, linking the task process to objectives.

3. Explain what the product expectations are and how achievement can be demonstrated in relation to the objectives.

Such transparency also allows students to play a bigger role in assessment because they understand the focus and procedures of the lesson.

Guideline 2: Reconsider Grades

Grades do not indicate actual knowledge and performance, which are the goals for many assessments. Grades for content knowledge, particularly for ELLs, can be lower than they should be because of issues with the student's English language proficiency. However, teachers can score content knowledge separately from language proficiency. To score content knowledge, teachers can use the results of multiple assessments to determine how well ELLs understand key concepts, how accurate their responses are, and how well they demonstrate the processes they use to formulate responses. Language can be assessed

FIGURE 7.6 Additional Guidelines for Assessment

Guideline	Example
Be transparent	Help students understand the role of assessment. Clearly list and discuss objectives and other components of the task or lesson.
Reconsider grades	Separate language and content grades to provide a more realistic picture of student achievement.

on a scale of progress or according to a rubric based on the English language standards for the grade level and content area.

Figure 7.6 summarizes these guidelines. Additional guidelines are presented throughout this textbook.

Assessing the Lesson

Once the lesson is complete and incorporates the essential components—including assessments—teachers can evaluate lesson design to make sure that the lesson is appropriate and relevant and meets student needs. Whether the lesson design is effective for diverse learners, particularly ELLs, can be measured in a number of ways before, during, and after the lesson (Chapman & King, 2005). These evaluations can be used to improve the lesson. Suggestions include the following:

1. Before
   - Use a component checklist based on ideas in the chapters. Teachers can create their own checklists with the components (objectives, connections, engaging tasks, assessment) and relevant guidelines, or they can use parts of the "Preparation" and "Building Background" sections of the Sheltered Instruction Observation Protocol (SIOP) (Echevarria, Vogt, & Short, 2008). An example of a component checklist is provided in Figure 7.7.
   - If something is missing or does not meet the guidelines, adjustments can be made to the lesson before it is implemented.
2. During
   - Teachers can use observation and discussion with students to determine whether the lesson is going as planned and whether that plan is appropriate for the students.

FIGURE 7.7 **Example of a Lesson-Component Checklist**

✓ Component

Language objectives

- ❑ Are tied to standards.
- ❑ Are tied to content objectives.
- ❑ Are based on student needs.
- ❑ Are measurable.
- ❑ Are presented to students.

Connections

- ❑ Are based on student interests, needs, backgrounds, abilities.
- ❑ Tie current topic and tasks to past lessons.
- ❑ Tie current topic to students' personal lives.
- ❑ Tie lesson tasks to students' personal lives.
- ❑ Are assessed for relevancy and accuracy with students.

Tasks

- ❑ Address both content and language objectives.
- ❑ Are engaging.
- ❑ Are authentic.
- ❑ Are relevant.
- ❑ Are multimodal.
- ❑ Are explicit.
- ❑ Are implicit.
- ❑ Break language down as necessary.
- ❑ Are culturally responsive.
- ❑ Are learner-centered and/or -produced.
- ❑ Focus on process and product elements.
- ❑ Provide students with reasons to listen.

Assessment

- ❑ Is ongoing.
- ❑ Is authentic.
- ❑ Uses multiple measures.
- ❑ Provides practice and review.
- ❑ Is transparent to all participants.
- ❑ Homework is relevant, engaging, and interactive.

- If there are problems with the lesson, teachers and students can make just-in-time adjustments, keeping the objectives, connections, and relevant process in mind.

3. After
   - Teachers can review the lesson, jotting down observations of individual students or the whole class. They can note when time on tasks and engagement were or were not obvious and where it seemed students needed more help in accessing the language and/or content. Teachers can also observe to what extent the objectives were met and create ideas for revising the lesson.
   - Teachers can also have others review the lesson, including asking students how it went, what the most effective parts of the lesson were, and how the lesson could be improved to better suit their needs.
   - This information can be incorporated into the next iteration of the lesson.

Stop and Think

After reading Chapter 7, what advice would you give to the teacher in the chapter-opening scenario about Li's low science test scores?

Assessment of the lesson is an important part of effective lesson design and provides a firm foundation for ongoing lesson design.

Conclusion

Chapter 7 presented principles and guidelines for the measurement of both lessons and student processes and outcomes. Teachers can use a large array of assessments for assessing student progress toward both content and language objectives. Most important for the assessment of diverse learners is to focus on students' ways of knowing, providing them with opportunities to express their understandings and how they came to those understandings. In turn, teachers can use this information to design effective lessons.

• Extensions •

For Reflection

1. *Reviewing tests.* Find examples of standardized tests that your current or future students may take. Think about how you might help ELLs and other diverse students be successful on these tests.

2. *Use your personal experience.* Think about your teacher education classes. Did you have an opportunity to show what you knew? Did you ever feel that you were evaluated unfairly? Why? What can you apply from this experience to your own teaching?

For Action

1. *Justify your grading.* Write a letter to your principal explaining why you are including a grade report for each student that has separate grades for language and content and what these grades mean.

2. *Meet the guidelines.* Choose an assessment type (for example, oral retelling or a portfolio) from a lesson or book. Describe how this assessment contributes to a lesson meeting the general guidelines for assessment listed in Figure 7.1.

part three

Designing Lessons
for Academic Success

How to Make Your Classroom Fun

How many times do you find more than 50% of your students . . . asleep during your class? How many students say: "That class is really boring"? Don't you wish it could be different? Well, here are some ways to make your classroom fun.

- *The first step you have to take is to give more freedom to your students, at the beginning it could be a little bit hard, but with some time it will be easier. Trust them and trust what they say, if you trust them, they will trust you.*

- *Second, have stuff done at school, give all of your work at class, try to fit everything on your schedule, to get done as quickly as you can, and do not send work to be done at home. No one likes to go home after school and still have stuff to do.*

- *Third, show videos and movies; the majority of students learn better and [more easily] when they see and hear than when they hear the voice of the same person only. There are a lot of educational videos and movies that . . . will help you.*

- *Last, but not least, have some time in class to talk about other stuff, such as things that happen during the day, news, music, movies. Your students will enjoy doing that and everyone else, including you, will learn something new every day.*

If you follow all of [these] steps, you are going to see the change, for good, of your students.

Santiago S., used with permission.

● *How do these arguments from an ELL student fit with what you've read in this and other books and learned in other ways about teaching? What does that say about tapping students as co-facilitators of classroom instruction?*

Unlocking the
Language of Science

• Key Issues •

1. Science texts, materials, and processes may present many challenges to English language learners (ELLs).

2. Hands-on, inquiry-based, and experimental science activities provide an ideal setting for learning language and content simultaneously.

3. The specialized language of science is filled with technical terms and features needed to describe the natural and physical world.

4. Practicing compare-and-contrast and cause-and-effect methods and the language of scientific inquiry can benefit all students, particularly ELLs.

5. A key component in learning to "talk science" is to analyze the Greek and Latin roots as well as the prefixes and suffixes that permeate scientific language.

• Potential Challenges for ELLs •
in the Science Classroom

- Students may be familiar with lectures and rote memorization of concepts but unfamiliar with hands-on, experiential approaches.

- Students may not be familiar with science labs or equipment.

- Content in class is often covered very fast.

- Directions are usually multistep and complex.

- Making guesses and drawing conclusions may not be part of students' prior science experiences.

- The language of science (vocabulary, language functions, and grammar and discourse characteristics) is specific and vast.

- Sentence structure in science texts is complex, and the use of the passive voice is pervasive.

- Many concepts are explained on one page of a science textbook.

- Working with a partner or in groups may be a novel way for ELLs to learn.

- Assessments do not always match classroom or lab activities.

- Students familiar only with the metric system will not know ounces, pounds, tons, pints, quarts, gallons, inches, feet, yards, miles, and the Fahrenheit scale.

- Some ELLs may have strongly held religious beliefs that may be a source of conflict with the science content.

Rita Harrington was accustomed to working with ELL students in her sixth-grade geology classroom. After all, she had been teaching for 12 years in a large, multilingual suburban school district. This school year, however, marked her first time teaching a newcomer from Afghanistan. She admitted to herself that she was a bit nervous at the thought of the crucial role she would play in the development and expansion of Yasir's understanding and capabilities in geology—especially because she didn't speak a word of Dari Persian!

Stop and Think

Before reading Chapter 8, what advice would you give Rita Harrington regarding teaching science to ELLs?

Science Education: A Focus on Inquiry

Knowing science involves making meaning of scientific knowledge and vocabulary. Prior knowledge and personal experience play key roles in acquiring new knowledge.
(Lee & Fradd, 1998, p. 16)

The science classroom is an ideal setting for ELLs to learn both language and content, particularly if the emphasis is on inquiry-based learning and activities are hands-on and experimental. Unlike traditional science teaching, which often consisted of long lectures, rigid, step-by-step experiments, and a focus on rote learning of selected science concepts, the *National Science Education Standards* (National Research Council, 1996) advocate for a broader approach to scientific inquiry where students have more opportunities to interact with the materials, the teacher, and each other.

RESOURCES

For more information about National Science Education Standards, see National Research Council (NRC) at **www.nationalacademies.org/nrc/**.

The science standards, with their key principle of "science for all," emphasize inquiry as the means for students to become scientifically literate. Inquiry is described as a multifaceted activity that involves the following:

- **Making** observations.
- **Posing** questions.

- **Examining** books and other sources of information to see what is already known.
- **Planning** investigations.
- **Reviewing** what is already known in light of experimental evidence.
- **Using** tools to gather, analyze, and interpret data.
- **Proposing** answers, explanations and predictions.
- **Communicating** the results.

Scientific Inquiry Refers to the diverse ways in which scientists study the natural world and propose explanations based on the evidence derived from their work. Inquiry also refers to the activities of students in which they develop knowledge and understanding of scientific ideas, as well as an understanding of how scientists study the natural world" (*National Science Education Standards,* 1996, p. 23).

In this light, inquiry requires identification of assumptions, use of critical and logical thinking, and consideration of alternative explanations. To participate successfully in the science classroom, students need to learn the academic language and ways of thinking necessary to pose questions, read a variety of documents (e.g., textbooks, lab directions, online material), record data, document observations, venture conclusions, discuss findings, and write lab reports. Hence, the role of language and literacy in the science class is critical.

The Specialized Language of Science

> *Science is, in itself, a language and each different science (biology, physics, chemistry) is a separate language. Science involves the acquisition of concepts and processes, specific vocabulary, phrases, and terminology. The ability to manipulate this language and its processes will provide the necessary instruments for the mastery of the science curriculum.* (Carrasquillo & Rodríguez, 2005, p. 438)

"Talking science" (Lemke, 1990) is essential to the process of *doing science*. Students cannot conduct experiments, write reports, or study the human body without using appropriate terminology and language structures that characterize the specialized language of science. This science register is filled with technical terms and features needed to describe the natural and physical universe. It uses academic language features such as describing natural phenomena, formulating hypotheses, proposing alternate solutions, inferring processes, gathering and interpreting data, generalizing, and reporting findings. According to Zwiers (2008), the language used in science tends to:

- **Describe relationships of taxonomy, comparison, cause and effect, hypothesis, and interpretation.** Unlike language arts and history, science texts have few stories or narratives. The text structure is dense and hierarchical (topic, subtopics, details).

- **Describe procedures explicitly via the use of language functions,** such as *observe, measure, calculate, predict, graph, examine, align,* and *connect.* Language functions are used primarily in lab directions and lab reports.

> **Language Functions** "Language functions are an important component of school.... They refer to how language is used in the communication of a message. Much of what is said in the classroom is for a purpose, such as greeting, congratulating, requesting permission to speak, requesting help, responding to a question, giving instruction, or explaining" (Gottlieb, Katz, & Ernst-Slavit, 2009, p. 18).

- **Connect abstract ideas illustrated by various media.** Photos, diagrams, graphs, charts, math and chemistry symbols, lab experiences, and text all overlap to communicate concepts.

- **Use generalized verbs in the present tense to describe phenomena, how something occurs, and why.** These generalized verbs include words like *produce, engender, power, energize, propel.*

- **Appear to be highly objective.** First-person perspective and emotion are removed in order to attempt to imbue statements with more credibility (i.e., "just the facts, not your opinion").

- **Use many new and big words with new meanings, many of which are nominalizations.** Examples of such words are *condensation, refraction, induction, resonance, reaction, radiation, fusion, erosion,* and most other *-ation* words (Zwiers, 2008, pp. 85–86).

> **Nominalization** Nominalization is any process by which a noun is formed from a verb or adjective, for example, *convection, defluoridation, desalination,* and *sedimentation.*

For ELLs to achieve academic success in the science classroom, they need to learn to talk science. Conversely, participation in meaningful science activities enhances the process of learning scientific language.

> *The relationship between science learning and language learning is reciprocal and synergistic. Through the contextualized use of language in science inquiry, students develop and practice complex language forms and functions. Through the use of language functions such as description, explanation, and discussion in inquiry science, students enhance their conceptual understanding. This synergistic perspective is a relatively new view of curricular integration.* (Stoddart, Pinal, Latzke, & Canaday, 2002, p. 667)

While the use of diverse language functions (i.e., what we ask students to do with language) might be beneficial for conceptual knowledge, it may generate difficulties because each language function demands a different way of using language. Language functions used in science include *classify, compare, describe, detect, discover, hypothesize, investigate, infer, measure, observe,* and *record,* among others.

As discussed in Chapter 1, the academic language needed to navigate and succeed in the science classroom includes multiple competencies, including a wide range of specific vocabulary items, grammatical constructions, language functions, and discourse features. Each competency is discussed below.

RESOURCES

Academic Vocabulary Lists. • See, for example, Chatham County Schools Essential K–8 Science Vocabulary at **http://www.chatham.k12.nc.us/central_office/instructional_services/docs/esv/K_essential_sci_vocab.pdf**; Essential Vocabulary for 9–12 students for Illinois school district U-45 at **http://www.u-46.org/roadmap/files/ACVOC%2007-08/HSScience%20ACVOC%20.pdf**; The Tennessee Project, with lists from K–12 organized by content, at **http://www.rcs.k12.tn.us/rc/departments/ITS/Teacher_Resources/State_Department_WordList_Final.pdf**; Grades 6–8 vocabulary lists in English with Spanish, Khmer, Lao, and Hmong translations at **http://www.fresno.k12.ca.us/divdept/sscience/Vocabulary.html**; and biology, physics, and physical science vocabulary word lists at **http://www.eldoradopublicschools.com/uploads/pdfs/Academic%20Vocabulary/academic%20vocabulary%20science%20ehs.pdf**.

Vocabulary

Current studies point to a strong relationship between extensive student vocabulary and academic achievement. During science instruction, ELLs must rely on their second language vocabulary to (1) understand the topic of discussion and (2) produce written explanations about the material read or about the experiment performed. Because a basic core of approximately 2,000 high-frequency words accounts for most words in academic writing (Scarcella, 2003), effective science teachers can provide explicit and deliberate vocabulary instruction. Academic vocabulary in science, as in other content areas, can be grouped in three categories: general (terms used across content areas), specialized (terms associated with science), and technical (terms associated with a specific topic in science). Figure 8.1 presents examples of types

FIGURE 8.1 Examples of Scientific Vocabulary Used in Different Disciplines

Scientific Discipline	General Academic Vocabulary	Specialized Academic Vocabulary	Technical Academic Vocabulary
Astronomy	• star • planet • moon • rotate	• nebula • galaxy • nova • pulsar • telescope	• red giants • white dwarfs • supernovae • neutron star • Olbers's paradox

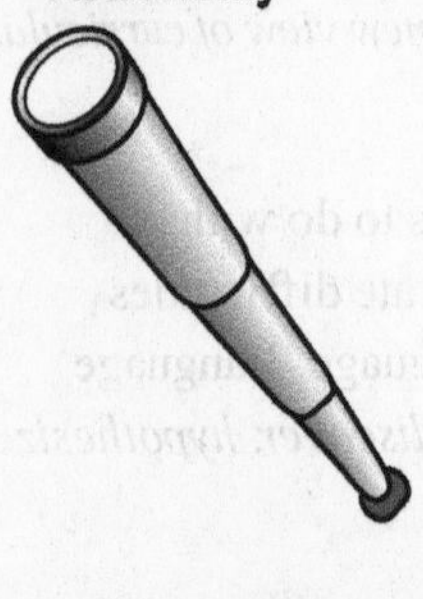

FIGURE 8.1 continued

Scientific Discipline	General Academic Vocabulary	Specialized Academic Vocabulary	Technical Academic Vocabulary
Biology	• nucleus • categories • class • order	• insect • reptile • mammal • amphibian • microscope	• Animalia • Phylum • Echinodermata • Holothuroidea • Dendrochirotida
Chemistry	• nucleus • bond • solution	• atom • isotope • proton • neutron • electron • hydrometer • mass spectrometer	• periodic table of elements • BR=bromine • C=carbon • FE=iron • HG=mercury • Boyle's law
Geology	• mineral • fault • soil	• volcano • lava • magma • eruption • earthquake • seismograph	• igneous • metamorphic • sedimentary
Physics	• force • lift • nucleus • pressure • power • resistance	• barometer • fulcrum • particle • voltage	• supernovae • Bohr model • infrasonic • magnetic flux

Stop and Think

1. In Rita's upcoming geology lesson, which language functions can you reasonably predict that she will ask students to use?

2. Think back to a science lesson you recently taught, prepared, or observed. What language functions were present in the lesson? Were those language functions explicitly taught to the students? Were specific terms needed to "do" the science taught explicitly?

of vocabulary used in different scientific disciplines. There are many well-researched lists of vocabulary terms needed in science, ranging from general to technical, organized by discipline.

An effective way of helping students learn scientific vocabulary is by highlighting the different meanings of words. Thus, a beam is a ray of light in some contexts and a heavy piece of timber in others. This approach is particularly important because ELLs may not know how to select the correct definition in a dictionary.

Looking over the upcoming lesson on the Earth's interior and plate tectonics theory, Rita easily recognized the need to teach vocabulary such as words with multiple meanings:

mantle
(1) the top shelf above a fireplace
(2) a coat or cloak
(3) cerebral cortex (anatomy and physiology)
(4) the part of mollusks and brachiopods that secretes material forming a shell (zoology)
(5) the layer between the Earth's core and crust (geology)

crust
(1) part of a pie
(2) the outer part of bread
(3) the top, hard layer of the Earth

core
(1) the center portion of certain types of fruit (biology)
(2) an item related to computer memory
(3) the layer of the Earth below the mantle

Other terms to review include *tectonic plates, inner* and *outer core, inferences,* and *layers.* Because Rita was planning on using posters, videos, worksheets, and brown hard-boiled eggs as models for students to explore the Earth's interior, she thought about the kinds of language functions and grammatical features that Yasir and all her students would need to participate in all the activities. Next, Rita reviewed her state and the Teachers of English to Speakers of Other Languages (TESOL) English language proficiency standards for ideas of activities suitable for Yasir's beginning level. She also decided to provide some support and guidance to Yasir by pairing him with Thomas, a student with great social skills and good problem-solving talents. With all this planning, Rita felt a bit more relaxed. She was off to good start.

Grammatical Features

The language of science, used to describe the physical and natural world, is characterized by a variety of grammatical features. Some of these features may pose challenges to ELLs who may lack familiarity with those usages. A case in point is the use of the passive voice, that is, instances where the subject who performs the action is ambiguous (e.g., "a two-step analysis was performed"). The use of the passive voice may obscure the meaning of a sentence. For some ELLs, the challenge may increase if they do not have a passive voice structure in their first language (Zwiers, 2008). Additional grammatical features that characterize the language of science include the following:

- Grammatical metaphor
- Syntactic ambiguity
- Complex noun phrases
- Cause and effect
- Time order
- Compare and contrast
- Formulas and symbols (e.g., $f=ma$, $e=mc^2$)

Grammatical Metaphor Substitution of one grammatical class or structure by another, for example, replacing "she emerged" with "her emergence." *Emergence* deviates from the traditional pattern where processes are verbs, participants are nouns, properties are adjectives, and logical relations are conjunctions. ***Syntactic Ambiguity*** A type of linguistic ambiguity that results in sentences being interpreted in more than one way, for example: *Flying planes can be dangerous.* This sentence can mean either that flying planes *is* dangerous, or flying planes *are* dangerous. ***Complex Noun Phrases*** Sentences made by the addition of multiple modifiers, for example, *life, life science, life science industry,* and *life science industry technologies.* ***Time Order*** A word or phrase that helps readers make the step from one sentence to the next or from one paragraph to the next. Some examples are *soon, then, now, while, meanwhile, already, first, second, last.*

Discourse

Science writing is precise and filled with detail. This often makes for long and complex sentences, as the analysis of the following sentence suggests:

> *The osmoregulatory organ, which is located at the base of the third dorsal spine on the outer margin of the terminal papillae and functions by expelling excess sodium ions, activates only under hypertonic conditions.* (The Writing Center, 2007, para. 12)

Several items make this sentence complex. First, the action of the sentence (*activates*) is far removed from the subject (*the osmoregulatory organ*) so that the reader has to wait a long time to get the main idea of the sentence. Second, the verbs *functions, activates,* and *expelling* are somewhat redundant.

RESOURCES

For strategies to teach ELLs how to access science textbooks, see Alex Ragan's article in The *ELL Outlook,* "Teaching the academic language of textbooks: A preliminary framework for performing a textual analysis," at http://www.coursecrafters.com/ELL-Outlook/2005/nov_dec/ELLOutlookITIArticle1.htm.

Another aspect to consider is related to science books. Science textbooks make it difficult for English language learners to discern between main and supporting ideas. For example,

Science texts develop concepts and skills through the use of argumentative, procedural, and descriptive genres and use different fonts, font sizes, colors, pictures, and graphic organizers to signal the organization and the importance of concepts and skills. Because these graphic elements involve so many signals, they can be confusing for those not used to them. (Simich-Dudgeon & Egbert, 2000, p. 30)

Stop and Think

1. Select a discourse feature from the list about diverse genres and visual-graphical representations.

2. Now look at the list of grammatical features presented earlier. Which grammatical features are used most often in that discourse type?

3. Do these features vary within the same discourse type? If so, when do they vary?

In general terms, scientific literacy involves more than just texts. It involves understanding very diverse genres and visual-graphical representations, as exemplified in the following list:

- Lab directions
- Research reports
- Data analysis
- Case studies
- Scientific texts
- Tables
- Posters
- Description of scientific inquiry
- Online documents
- Write-up of experiments
- Charts

Strategies for Learning and Talking Science

As discussed above, science materials and tasks often require the use of diverse grammatical and discourse structures. All students, particularly ELLs, need practice in using these structures. The examples provided in the next section highlight the importance of practicing and learning the language of scientific inquiry, the ubiquitous text structures of compare-and-contrast and cause-and-effect methods of inquiry, and Greek and Latin roots.

Learning the Language of Scientific Inquiry

Teaching science as inquiry provides students with opportunities to develop enriched understandings of the physical and natural sciences. As students investigate phenomena, they develop the ability to ask questions, explore aspects of the world around them, and use their observations and scientific knowledge to construct reasonable explanations for questions posed and phenomena encountered. One way to assist students in talking and writing about the scientific inquiry process is by having examples of sentence starters or stems. For this purpose, students and teacher can jointly create a poster with examples of language needed throughout the different phases of scientific inquiry, as depicted in Figure 8.2.

Compare and Contrast

Compare and contrast is the process of identifying how things are similar and different. This process forces students to evaluate and synthesize how two things are alike (compare)

FIGURE 8.2 Sentence Starters Needed During Scientific Inquiry

Phases of Scientific Inquiry	Sentence Starters for Each Phase
Identify a problem	• I wonder . . . • I have noticed . . . • I observe . . . • I was confused by . . .
Generate a guess or hypothesis	• I think/believe . . . will happen because . . . • If . . . , then . . . • It's possible that . . . • It will most likely . . .
Plan an experiment or inquiry	• Let's try . . . • What would happen if . . . ? • I will gather . . . • We have to be sure to . . .
Conduct an experiment	• Do we have all of the . . . ? • What should we do next? • How did . . . react to . . . ? • How will we measure . . . ?
Collect and organize data	• Did you record/write down the . . . ? • How much . . . ? • Where do we record our findings? • Should we use a table or a graph?
Analyze and interpret data	• . . . means that . . . • The data from . . . show . . . • This doesn't make sense when compared to . . . • My evidence is . . .
Report results	• The research demonstrates that . . . • The data show . . . • Based on the data, it is likely that . . . • Our research supports . . .

and how they are different (contrast). There are many examples of graphic organizers to assist students in comparing and contrasting. Figure 8.3 is a list of commonly used vocabulary words when comparing and contrasting two items. Figure 8.4 is an example of a Venn diagram used to compare and contrast permanent magnets and electromagnets.

FIGURE 8.3 Vocabulary that Signals Compare and Contrast Structures

Compare	Contrast
at the same time	but
in comparison	conversely
in the same manner	however
in the same way(s)	nevertheless
like	nonetheless
likewise	on the other hand
similar	rather
still	yet

FIGURE 8.4 Venn Diagram Comparing and Contrasting Permanent Magnets and Electromagnets

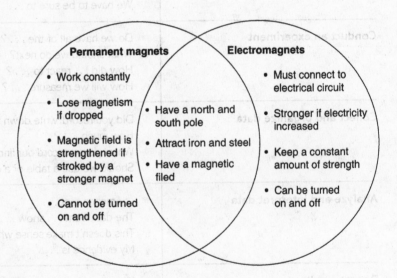

Permanent magnets
- Work constantly
- Lose magnetism if dropped
- Magnetic field is strengthened if stroked by a stronger magnet
- Cannot be turned on and off

- Have a north and south pole
- Attract iron and steel
- Have a magnetic filed

Electromagnets
- Must connect to electrical circuit
- Stronger if electricity increased
- Keep a constant amount of strength
- Can be turned on and off

Cause and Effect

Cause and effect indicates the relationship between two things when one causes the other to happen. For example, if we water our plants too often, they will die. Too much water is the cause; the death of the plants is the effect. Determining a cause-and-effect relationship is essential for explaining how things happen the way they do.

In science, this text structure is used to show order, inform, speculate, and change behavior. One way of helping students learn the cause-and-effect text structure is by teaching

FIGURE 8.5 Words and Phrases that Show Cause–Effect Relationships

accordingly	due to	nevertheless	that is how
as a result of	for	since	therefore
because	for this reason	so	thus
consequently	if . . . then	so that	

signal words (also called secret code or nerd words in elementary classrooms) that show cause-and-effect relationships. See the examples in Figure 8.5.

Teaching Greek and Latin Roots

A key component in learning to talk science for all students involves the analysis of Greek and Latin roots because they generate the overwhelming majority of science terms. Helping students brainstorm the origin and meaning of technical words might unveil potential connections among the meaning of the word, the student's language background, and the science register. For example, for Spanish, Italian, Portuguese, and Catalan speakers, the terms *aquatic, aquarium, aquanaut, aqueduct,* and *aquifer* might not be too difficult to learn because the prefix *aqu-* is very similar to the word they have for water (*agua* in Spanish, *acqua* in Italian, *água* in Portuguese, and *aigua* in Catalan). Remember, some ELLs might know more academic language than they think! See examples of Greek and Latin roots in Figures 8.6 and 8.7.

FIGURE 8.6 Greek Roots

Greek Roots	Definition	Example of Usage
agro, agros	field, earth, soil	agrobiology, agronomy
archaeo, archaios	ancient, old, original	archaeology, archaic
bios	life, living things	biology, biopsy
chroma, chromato	color	chromophil, chromophore
chrono, chronos	time	chronograph, chronometer
demos	people	demographics, pandemic
dendron	tree	dendrochronology, rhododendron
gastro	stomach	gastroenteric, gastropod
gram	something written or drawn	electroencephalogram, telegram

(continued)

FIGURE 8.6   continued

Greek Roots	Definition	Example of Usage
hemo	blood	hemoglobin, hemophilia
hydro	water	hydrocarbon, hydrodynamics
metron	measure	metronome
neuron, neuro	sinew, string, nerve	neurology, neuromuscular
pous, pod	foot	octopus, podiatrist, pseudopodia
scopos, skopein	spy, watcher, to see	microscope, telescope
therme	heat	thermocline, thermometer
zoion	living being, animal	zooid, zoology

FIGURE 8.7   Latin Roots

Latin Roots	Definition of Root	Example of Usage
anima	life, soul, breath, mind	animate, inanimate
aqua	water	aquanaut, aquatic
arbor	tree	arboreal, arborvitae
avis	bird	aviation, avian
cavare, cavus	hollow	cavern, cavity
dens, dentis	tooth	dentate, denticle, dentin
generare, genus	origin, race, species, kind, to beget, produce	gender, generate
herba	grass, herb	herbal, herbarium
laborare	to work	laboratory
mare	sea	marine
mors, mortis, mori	death, to die	mortality, mortuary
mutare, mutatum	to change	molt, mutation
nox, noct	night	equinox, nocturnal
oculus	eye	binocular, oculomotor
sepsis	putrefaction, rotten, poison	septic, septicemia
sol	sun	solar, solstice
toxicare, toxicum	to smear with poison	toxemia, toxin, toxicology
spirare	to breathe	expire, inspiration, respiratory
vivere, vita	to live, life	revive, viviparous

Stop and Think

1. Using the chart in Figure 8.6, how would you define the word *biometric*?

2. How does knowledge of the Greek roots in the word *gastropod* (a class of mollusks containing snails and slugs) change how you think about snails and slugs? What impact do you think such knowledge would have on your students?

RESOURCES

Latin and Greek Roots • For additional information on Latin and Greek roots, see: Jessica's Common Prefixes, Suffixes, and Root Words at **https://www.msu.edu/~defores1/gre/roots/gre_rts_afx2 .htm**; Lit Café at **http://library.thinkquest.org/17500/data/infobar/latin.html**; and Infoplease at **http://www.infoplease.com/ipa/A0907036.html**.

Stop and Think

Many scientific terms are built on Latin and Greek roots. For example, in Earth science, the three basic types of rock are **metamorphic, igneous,** and **sedimentary**. These three terms mean "shape-changing," "fire," and "sit," respectively. Knowing the meaning of these roots helps students not only in the science classroom but also in other content areas. Think about Kafka's *Metamorphosis* and Ovid's *Metamorphoses*; about *igniting* students' imaginations, or about how many people are leading *sedentary* lifestyles. Look at the lists of Latin and Greek roots in Figures 8.6 and 8.7 and identify roots that originate terms used across different content areas.

Rita and Yasir survived the geology lesson. In fact, Yasir learned terms and concepts about the Earth's interior and tectonic plates, and the entire class learned about the ancient Cimmerian plate and about Yasir's experience during the 2002 earthquake in northern Afghanistan. And everyone also learned how to say "egg" in Dari Persian!

Conclusion

Language is at the heart of the process of scientific inquiry. For English language learners, this means that they have to learn the language to describe scientific phenomena; at the same time, they must learn the concepts and processes and how to "do" inquiry. Science teachers need to examine the language of science and determine the kinds of language support all students, but particularly ELLs, need to meet the content objectives successfully. Lessons can be adapted to develop vocabulary, construct background knowledge, modify texts, and build on what students already know.

• Extensions •

For Reflection

1. *Think back.* ELLs are often able to participate in the science class sooner than in other content-area classes when science is experimental, hands-on, and inquiry-based. Reflect on the times when you taught a lesson or when you as a student partici- pated in that kind of lesson. Were learners engaged? Did students learn the concepts and processes? Was it successful?

2. *Examining language from a different perspective.* Look at the sample of Arabic text below. What would help you understand its meaning? How can you apply these ideas to your classroom context?

يولد جميع الناس أحراراً متساوين في الكرامة والحقوق . وقد وهبوا عقلاً وضميراً وعليهم ان يعامل بعضهم بعضاً بروح الإخاء .

Source: From Omniglot at http://www.omniglot.com/writing/arabic.htm

For Action

1. *Student version of scientific inquiry language.* One important strategy for learning to "talk sci- ence" is to help students generate a chart to talk about the scientific process. You can do this with your students by using a chart similar to the one in Figure 8.2. Make sure to explain difficult terms in the left-hand column, such as *hypothesis, validity, generalize,* etc.

2. *Science textbooks.* Page through a science text- book. Look both at the content and the format. What features of this book might be challenging for ELLs? What can you do to help students learn how to read scientific materials?

Unlocking the
Language of Mathematics

Key Issues

1. The mathematics reform movement, with its current emphasis on communicating mathematically, may pose some challenges for English language learners (ELLs).

2. The language of mathematics uses unique symbols, technical language, and diverse representations.

3. Mathematics may not always be a universal language; there are many variations across languages and cultures.

4. Mathematical language used in tasks, tests, texts, and teacher talk can have many confusing usages.

5. Explicit instruction, speech modification, and modeling are necessary for students to learn the language of mathematics.

Potential Challenges for ELLs
in the Mathematics Classroom

- In many countries school mathematics curricula emphasize calculations, not communicating mathematical thinking.

- Many students have never seen or worked with manipulatives and might not take a lesson using manipulatives seriously.

- In some countries, periods are used instead of commas when representing large numbers and

- commas instead of periods when representing decimal numbers.

- Many ELLs are familiar with the metric measurement system and are not familiar with measurements like feet, pints, miles, ounces, etc.

- Students must read mathematics not only from left to right, but also right to left, up and down, and diagonally (in the case of tables, diagrams, and graphs).

- Some students are used to learning mathematics by rote memorization.

- In some countries, word problems are introduced in the upper grades.

- Estimating, rounding, and geometry are first taught in the upper grades in many countries.

- There are many distinct vocabulary terms used only in mathematics.

- Mathematics textbooks are tightly packed with concepts.

Lewis Gandolfi was pleased with his plans for teaching a lesson on estimating with a jar of pennies. He had planned it carefully so all his third-graders would (1) actively participate in the activity, (2) feel comfortable guessing and estimating, and, (3) learn to develop various ways to arrive at the answer. As he thought about his six ELLs, he opted to mix them across groups and jotted a list of much-needed vocabulary, grammar, and discourse features to review before the lesson:

Vocabulary
- guess
- estimate
- round off numbers
- range
- cents
- dollars
- penny

Grammar
- ways to express amounts
- using cents and dollar signs

Discourse
- word problems
- graphs

The next morning, Lewis introduced the lesson by discussing the difference between a guess and an estimate and reviewing terms and phrases from the math wall. Then Lewis showed students his jar with 300 pennies and asked them to make group guesses. He took about half of the pennies out of the jar (the students decided when it was "about half") and asked for volunteers to count aloud in piles of ten. When a brief pause occurred after the third pile was counted, Lewis promptly counted in Italian (his grandfather's native language) and asked if someone wanted to count to ten in another language. Before he knew it, his ELLs had counted in Korean, Spanish, Russian, Vietnamese, and Urdu, followed by two native English speakers who knew French and German. Lewis was ecstatic and grateful that his improvisation had jazzed up the activity, and he continued with the lesson.

Stop and Think

With the information provided, how do you think Lewis's lesson proceeded? Why? What would you do to plan a lesson like this one?

Mathematics Reform: "The New Math"

In 1989, the National Council of Teachers of Mathematics (NCTM) identified a clear set of standards for teaching and assessing mathematics, which were reinforced and elaborated upon in their more recent document (NCTM, 2000). These five standards apply to all grade levels and provide mathematics educators with a solid base upon which to build instruction and curriculum:

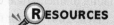

RESOURCES

For more information, see National Council of Teachers of Mathematics (NCTM) at http://www.nctm.org/standards/default.aspx?id=58.

1. To understand and value mathematics.
2. To reason mathematically.
3. To communicate mathematics.
4. To solve problems.
5. To make connections to contexts and other academic subject areas. (Ernst-Slavit & Slavit, 2007)

In 1991, NCTM produced an accompanying document that makes recommendations for teacher professional standards. The document encourages teachers to:

- Select mathematical tasks to engage students' intellect and interest.
- Provide opportunities to deepen students' understanding of mathematics and its applications.
- Orchestrate classroom discourse in ways that promote the investigation and growth of mathematical ideas.
- Help students use technology and other tools to pursue mathematical investigations.
- Help students seek connections to previous and developing knowledge.
- Guide individual, small group, and whole class work. (NCTM 1991, p. 1)

According to the NCTM documents, teachers need to select activities that grow out of real-world problems relevant to the learner. This focus on real-world connections

Applying Mathematical Skills to Solve Real-World Problems • The following example illustrates how problem solving in authentic contexts can be used to improve learning for students from diverse cultural and linguistic backgrounds. In a seventh-grade classroom in Salinas, California, Latino students are huddled over a model of a bridge that they have constructed. They are trying to determine the proportions needed to build a slightly different bridge—one that is three and a half times larger. By focusing instruction on themes such as architecture (bridges), astronomy (space), and statistics (baseball), mathematics is taught in highly contextualized situations where the focus is on the acquisition of conceptual knowledge, problem solving, and application of mathematical skills to concrete problems. (McLaughlin & McLeod, 1996).

may be very different from what many of our ELLs have experienced in their mathematics classes in their countries of origin, where lessons may have involved working on algorithms, manipulating mathematical expressions, and solving "recipe-type" problems (Ernst-Slavit & Slavit, 2007). Prior to the 1989 NCTM standards, mathematics education in the United States also tended to focus on calculations, algorithms, and teaching what Skemp (1987) called "rules without reasons."

As part of their reform recommendations, the standards and the ensuing NCTM documents placed equity, communication, and "mathematics for all" at the heart of mathematics reform. While these are indeed important goals, placing communication at the center poses some serious challenges for students who are learning English as an additional language. For these students, it is no longer enough to come up with the correct answer to a problem; now students have to explain—using phrases and sentences—how they arrived at that solution. Hence, for ELLs to achieve in mathematics, they need to acquire conceptual and procedural mathematical knowledge in addition to learning to "talk math," that is, to use the specialized language of mathematics.

The Specialized Language of Mathematics

A key question that must be asked is whether or not an assessment measures students' mathematical skills or their proficiency in English. . . . ELLs must process and interpret information in a language in which they are not fully proficient to be able to perform the mathematical tasks. (Gottlieb, 2007, p. iv)

Many say that mathematics is a language by itself. This is because mathematics uses a set of meaningful symbols to express ideas using conventional English syntax. For example,

$$2(4 - 3) + (4 + 3x) = 33$$

can be read as "two times four minus three plus four plus three times x equals thirty-three." Unlike the English language, however, where you read from left to right, in mathematics, as in the example above, you have to first complete the computations within the parentheses or brackets before you can multiply by the first number on the left.

ELLs with prior school experiences in their countries of origin may find that familiar symbols, expressions, and methods differ from those they encounter in U.S. classrooms. These barriers become increasingly challenging as students engage in story problems that can be worded in many different ways. Although there are many similarities among number systems across the world, mathematics (particularly as taught in schools) may not be a universal language for all! See Figure 9.1 for selected examples.

FIGURE 9.1 Selected Examples of Different Representations and Computing Methods

	In the United States	In Other Countries
Numbers and letters might be written differently	For example: l 7	In some countries (e.g., Germany and Latin America) 1 has serif and 7 has a stem. l 7
Multiples of thousands are separated by different symbols	Commas are used to separate multiples of thousands, for example: 285,215	In some countries (e.g., France and Spain) periods are used to separate multiples of thousands. 285.215
Different methods are used for solving division	For example: $$\begin{array}{r} 16 \\ 4\overline{)64} \end{array}$$	In some Spanish-speaking countries, (e.g.,Peru, Colombia, Chile). division problems look as follows: $$\begin{array}{r} 64\lfloor\underline{4} \\ 16 \end{array}$$

ELLs also encounter difficulties when attempting to translate literally a mathematical concept expressed in words into a concept expressed in symbols. For example, the algebraic phrase

the number *a* is five less than the number *b*

is often translated into

$a = 5 - b$

when it should be

$a = b - 5$

> **Mathematics Register** The particular use of language associated with mathematics. In linguistics, a register refers to a variety of a language used in a particular context and for a particular purpose.

The development of the **mathematics register** is a critical component of developing mathematical understanding in all students, including ELLs. In this chapter, we discuss different types of vocabulary, unique grammar features, and forms of discourse used in the teaching and learning of mathematics.

Vocabulary

Amoebas multiply by dividing.

The mathematics register includes a variety of words, phrases, and expressions. As discussed in Chapter 8, these words and expressions can be classified according to three

FIGURE 9.2 Types of Vocabulary in Mathematics

Vocabulary Type	Definition	Examples
General academic vocabulary	Terms used in the mathematics classroom and in other subjects	• combine • describe • consequently
Specialized academic vocabulary	Terms associated with mathematics	• quotient • hypotenuse • angle
Technical academic vocabulary	Terms associated with a specific mathematics topic	• perfect numbers • quadratic equations • least common denominator

Source: The authors gratefully acknowledge National Middle School Association for pemission to use information from the following previously published article: Slavit, D., & Ernst-Slavit, G. (2007). *Teaching mathematics and English to English language learners simultaneously.* Middle School Journal, 39(2), 4–11.

categories: general academic vocabulary, specialized academic vocabulary, and technical academic vocabulary. Figure 9.2 presents definitions and examples for each category.

In addition, Wong-Fillmore and Snow (2000) list a series of words that pose many challenges for ELLs, such as terms that express various kinds of quantitative relationships as well as everyday words that provide logical links in sentences typical to mathematical word problems (see Figure 9.3). Another challenging aspect for ELLs is the use of many different words to refer to the same mathematical operation (see Figure 9.4 for examples). Teaching students to identify key words in word problems and displaying them prominently will assist students in identifying the kind of operation they need to pursue.

Representing information in nonlinguistic ways is also an important consideration when "talking math" (Lemke, 1990). For example, the idea of slope can be expressed using graphs of lines, algebraic symbols and formulas, tables of values, or contextual information (e.g., *the fixed cost of an item is the slope of a cost function for that specific item*). In addition, a variety of linguistic expressions are commonly used to refer to the general concept of slope, including *rate of increase/ decrease/change, linear change, degree of inclination,* and *rise over run*. Students must draw from all four of the vocabulary types (general academic vocabulary, specialized academic vocabulary, technical academic vocabulary, and social language) when participating in mathematical conversations of this kind.

Stop and Do

Unique Meanings in Mathematics •
Many common English words and terms have unique meanings in mathematics. Examples include *plane, face, bring down, net,* and *negative.* Can you add other terms to this list? How would you help students learn the differences among their meanings?

FIGURE 9.3 **Problematic Words for ELLs Commonly Used in Mathematics Textbooks and Classrooms**

Words That Express Quantitative Relationships		Words That Link Phrases and Sentences and Express a Logical Relationship	
• hardly	• less	• since	• if
• scarcely	• longer	• unless	• because
• roughly	• older	• almost	• unless
• rarely	• younger	• probably	• alike
• next	• least	• exactly	• same
• last	• higher	• not quite	• different from
• most	• many	• always	• opposite of
		• never	• whether

As all teachers of mathematics know, specific language considerations are also needed because of the precise meaning of mathematical terms; for example, *slope* is a "rate of change," but not all rates of change have a slope. Hence, ELL students need to be made especially aware when their language can be imprecise and when it must be precise.

FIGURE 9.4 **Different Terms That Signal the Same Operation**

Mathematical Operation	Examples of Different Terms with Similar Meanings
Addition	add, plus, combine, sum, total of, more than, increased by, greater than, altogether, in all
Subtraction	subtract, minus, less, less than, fewer than, decreased by, difference, lower, take away from, shorter, diminished by, are left, remain
Multiplication	multiply, time, product, as a factor, twice, double, triple, groups of
Division	divide, divided by, quotient, separated in equal groups, shared equally, over, into, how many groups
Equal	is, are, result, make, become same as, equivalent

Grammatical Features

At the sentence level, there are language patterns and grammatical structures specific to mathematics. These include the use of logical connectors (e.g., *consequently, however*) that in regular usage signal a logical relationship between parts of a text, but in mathematics signal similarity or contradiction. The use of comparative structures (e.g., *greater than* and *less than, n times as much as*) and prepositions (e.g., *the temperature fell . . . to 15 degrees, by 15 degrees, or from 15 degrees; divided by, divided into*) pose serious difficulties for students who are trying to learn language and content simultaneously.

Mathematical Discourse

This section discusses three areas of language difficulties: density of mathematics textbooks, word problems, and teacher talk. First, mathematics texts have a denser concentration of abstract concepts when compared to other texts. Students cannot read a mathematics textbook like a newspaper or novel. The conceptual density is too great—even when compared to textbooks in other content areas. Mathematics texts are highly connected, and each word and phrase is important to the process (Zwiers, 2008). In other words, when it comes to language, mathematics textbooks are both wonderful and dreadful: wonderful because they are concise and to the point; dreadful because every single word, no matter how big or small, is packed with information. Skimming through mathematics books is not an option!

Another characteristic of textbooks is that they often expand a basic problem into more sophisticated versions illustrating new concepts. For example, in one section of a mathematics book, students were asked to calculate the perimeter of a park enclosing three skateboard rinks. Then, in the next section, they were asked to calculate the perimeter for the same park, this time with a different polygon shape. Then they were asked to repeat the calculations using a fence with curves, etc. This kind of threading, while helping students build on what they already know, may pose challenges to students who did not understand earlier steps of the problem.

Second, word problems can pose difficulties, such as in the following example by Dale and Cuevas (1992):

Three times a number is 2 more than 2 times the number. Find the number.

Solving this problem requires recognition of how many numbers are involved, the relationships between them, and which ones need to be identified. Figure 9.5 illustrates some of the confusing aspects of the language used in mathematics problems.

Pointing out some of this problematic usage in books and texts and giving explicit instruction in reading and writing word problems are ways of teaching ELLs how to grapple

FIGURE 9.5 Examples of Issues with Word Problems

Confusing Aspects	Examples
Same pronoun is used to refer to different subjects	Suppose <u>you</u> and three friends buy a large pizza. <u>You each</u> pay with a $5 bill. The pizza costs $12.75. <u>You</u> will also pay $.83 tax on the pizza. How much change will <u>you and your</u> friends get? (Houghton Mifflin's *Math Central*, 2001, p. 287)
Unclear directions Will the friend start on pane 1 of window 1 or on pane 3 of window 1? Will he or she then move to window 2 or continue on window 1? Is the comparison among the three friends or between the "one friend" and the "two of you"? What is a "pane"?	There are four windows in the attic and each window has eight panes of glass. One friend cleans every third pane. Two of you clean the rest. Who cleans the least number of panes? (Houghton Mifflin's *Math Central*, 2001, p. 241)
Use of several small words These commonly known words (underlined) take a specialized meaning that is particular to mathematics.	A rock is dropped from a height of 200 feet. During its fall, the rock's height h (in feet) <u>is given by</u> $$h = -16t^2 + 200$$ <u>where</u> t is the time <u>in</u> seconds. Find the height <u>when</u> t = 0, 1, 2, 3, and 3.5 seconds. When does the rock hit the ground? (McDougal Littell's *Math Concepts and Skills*, 2007, p. 623)
Shifting subject referents	Your grandmother started <u>a college fund</u> for her grandchildren 15 years ago with an investment of $15,000 at an annual interest rate of 6½. Find the balance of <u>the account</u> if the account earns simple interest. (McDougal Littell's *Math Concepts and Skills*, 2007, p. 378)

with the unique grammatical features of the language of mathematics. In addition, the use of warm-up activities using mathematical language can give students practice in sentence construction.

Last, a word on teacher talk. Ernst-Slavit and Mason (2009) point to the difficulties teachers may have in clarifying problematic terms and expressions in an ongoing and systematic manner. In their research, they found that even teachers who were aware of the linguistic challenges faced by ELLs and who explicitly discussed trouble usages, such as synonyms (*change, convert*) and homophones (*two, to, too*), missed other potential sources of confusion for their students.

When teachers oversimplify their language to accommodate students' lack of proficiency in English, students may not encounter enough opportunities to develop and practice mathematical language (Irujo, 2007). The line between too much oversimplification and not enough is a fine one, and the need for it varies from student to student. However, with preplanning, intentional teaching, and cumulative experience, educators can become skilled at distinguishing and applying the nuances of simplifying language.

Teaching Strategies for Learning and Talking Mathematics

The discussion above was intended to assist educators better understand the language abilities and needs of their English language learners. But we still must ask, "How do mathematics teachers teach their students mathematical thinking if their students communicate minimally in English?" or "How do I reach my ELLs?" Although there are no simple answers for these questions, the truth is that, in many mathematics classrooms, teachers are using a variety of instructional strategies that have proven useful to reaching all students, but in particular those who are learning English as a second language.

Below we provide selected strategies that support ELLs as they learn how to think mathematically, how to do math, and how to talk math using the mathematics register.

Use a Variety of Instructional Formats and Supports

Students learn in many different ways. Classroom activities can be structured to support many learning styles and strengths. For all students, particularly for ELLs, the use of instructional supports (e.g., discussing a graphic organizer, working with a partner, using manipulatives) increases their understanding of the topic at hand. Below is a list of suggestions:

RESOURCES

Creating a Graph • You can create a graph online with the help of the National Center for Education Statistics at **http://nces.ed.gov/nceskids/createagraph/**.

- Design multisensory lessons (visual, auditory, tactile, kinesthetic).
- Use visuals (graphs, charts, diagrams, models) when possible.
- Use graphic organizers to visually represent mathematical concepts.
- Point to or explicitly connect terms with a visual representation.

- Design hands-on activities.
- Use different technologies.
- Vary groupings throughout the lesson (independent work, pairs, groups, whole class).
- Use real-life problem-solving situations to teach new concepts.
- Make connections across content areas whenever possible.

Introduce New Vocabulary in a Thoughtful and Integrated Manner

Vocabulary is best taught not as a separate activity but as part of the lesson. For example, students who memorize the definition of *cube* without solving a problem or participating in a discussion involving cubes often have a superficial understanding of this term. Manipulatives and visual aides, such as pictures, graphic organizers, charts, and bulletin boards, are good support for these conversations. It has been recommended that the introduction of new vocabulary be limited to less than 12 words per lesson (Fathman, Quinn, & Kessler, 1992). In addition, teachers can better communicate with their ELLs if they limit the use of idioms, speak slowly, and use visuals and gestures. Breaking the lesson into smaller units and pausing or stressing key terms is also helpful.

Identify and Highlight Key Words with Multiple Meanings

In addition to the problematic words and phrases discussed earlier, ELLs can have difficulty with words that have multiple meanings in social and academic language or in other content areas. For example, the word *table* can refer to a times table for multiplication facts or a table of values for graphing functions. *Table* may also have very different meanings and usages in nonmathematical contexts, such as timetable in social studies, table of contents in language arts, water table in physical science, and periodic table in chemistry.

Identifying and carefully planning the use of any such words that you anticipate using in a lesson can support students' efforts to follow the subsequent line of discourse.

Modify Your Speech

One important aspect of teaching ELLs includes providing comprehensible input (Krashen, 1981), that is, when teachers modify their speech to facilitate communication and enhance students' understanding. Often, however, modification is understood as meaning "simplification," and while that strategy might be helpful in the short term, it is not the only adjustment teachers can make to promote understanding. Below is a list of additional suggestions:

- Enunciate clearly and slowly without speaking louder (ELLs are not hard of hearing; they are second language learners).
- Pause between sentences or concepts.
- Use gestures and visuals to enhance meaning.
- Avoid using idioms and slang.
- Use key words frequently.
- Repeat, rephrase, restate.
- Simplify the language used rather than the mathematical concepts taught.
- Particularly for difficult mathematical content, allow non-English-language group discussion or the help of teaching assistants.
- Focus on the content, *not* on the form, of students' responses. Respond to inappropriately phrased language by modeling the appropriate grammatical form instead of correcting.
- Be aware that additional wait-time may be needed when teaching ELL students.

Wait-Time Wait-time refers to the time that students are given to respond to a question posed by the teacher.

The concept of **wait-time**, a phrase coined by Mary Budd Rowe (1972), refers to the time students are given to respond to a question posed by the teacher. Studies by Rowe and others showed that, in most classrooms, students were given no more than 1.5 seconds before teachers continued talking or students provided an answer. In classrooms where teachers paused between 3 and 7 seconds after asking high-level questions, students responded more thoughtfully and their achievement increased.

Use Preview and Review

This technique provides a lesson introduction (which can be given to all students or only to ELLs) via a handout, an outline of the entire lesson on the board or overhead, and a list of key words. This preview provides context for the lesson, and small-group discussion can support any of these steps. After the lesson, a review of its main aspects, including both key content and language features, can be provided to further clarify or reinforce learning goals as well as key terms.

Kristie, a middle school teacher, uses the preview and review technique in all of her classes, including those with ELLs. Her use of preview is extended through the use of a "hula skirt," a piece of paper folded down the middle and cut horizontally into four or five strips on each side. The students are asked to write key terms and definitions on the left and provide a visual on the right. These terms are then used during the lesson, and the students make regular use of the "hula skirt" throughout. Kristie states: "For my ELLs, I always try to use different modalities to get them to understand the vocabulary. The hula skirt is kind of fun, and it gets them to write a definition and connect it to a visual. I tell them I am bad at Pictionary, you know, like stick figures and stuff, so the drawing doesn't have to be perfect. But it really connects them to the meaning of the word." Kristie also uses the "hula skirt" for a game modeled on *Jeopardy* by having one student of a pair of fold and cover the strip with the illustration and asking the other to provide either the word or definition (Slavit & Ernst-Slavit, 2007).

Search for Cognates: Validating Students' Languages and Cultures

Cognates are related in origin and occur most often in English, Greek, Latin, and German, although Farsi and Turkish have English cognates: some examples are, *temperature– temperatura* (Spanish); *citizen–citoyen* (French); *mother–Mutter* (German); *inflation– enflasyon* (Turkish). False cognates, on the other hand, are terms that appear to be similar in two languages and may have similar roots but their meaning is different. Examples of false cognates in English and Spanish are *library–librería* (bookstore); *embarrassed–embarazada* (pregnant); *exit–éxito* (success); *pan–pan* (bread).

> **Cognates** A cognate is a word in one language that is similar in meaning and form to a word in that same language (e.g., *shirt* and *skirt*) or in another language.

Research indicates that students' home languages can play a significant role in learning complex material, including content encountered in mathematics classrooms. This is especially true when students are afforded opportunities to incorporate their home language into classroom discourse. Even teachers who do not speak ELLs' home languages can use this strategy by giving students options for accessing books, handouts, or websites in their native languages, or working with peers or teaching assistants versed in the native languages.

Arthur, a middle school teacher in a building with a large number of Mexican and Central American students, builds on students' knowledge of Spanish by using cognates. Arthur states, "My Spanish-speaking students understand more English than they realize. For example, they know *círculo* [circle], *lateral* [lateral; related to the side], *cuadrado* [a square or special quadrilateral], and even words like *edificio* [edifice], and *casi* [quasi; resembling something]." The use of cognates helps Arthur validate students' first languages, and, at the same time enables students to learn language and content through vocabulary that can be easily identified in its written form.

All students come with varied experiences and knowledge, which can often lead to creative ways of solving mathematical problems. Sharing such samples of student thinking and problem solving is currently at the heart of mathematics education reform. Additional suggestions for tapping students' knowledge include the following:

- Connect students' prior knowledge and experiences to new learning. Find out what students already know about a topic by making a semantic web on the board. Write the topic in the center and record students' knowledge around it.

- Integrate ELLs' culture into lessons whenever possible. Give students opportunities to share examples from schools in their country and different ways of learning mathematics.

- Begin a unit of study by building on students' own questions about the topic.

Use Cooperative Learning and Promote Opportunities for Interaction

It is possible for students of diverse linguistic and educational backgrounds to work together on a common task in pursuit of a common goal. Collaborative groups provide opportunities for students to hear and use the math register, while at the same time developing mathematical understandings. Depending on the students' language proficiencies, this works very well in groups with diverse language backgrounds because students can use English to communicate with all the members of the group. Teachers can provide visuals with key words to support students with emerging language proficiency, even in groups with a variety of home languages.

RESOURCES

Cooperative Learning • For additional information on cooperative learning, see ¡Colorín Colorado! at **http://www.colorincolorado.org/educators/content/cooperative**.

Teach Organizational and Study Skills

Students need to have organization, study skills, and learning strategies to succeed in today's classrooms. Explicitly teaching organizational and study skills is necessary at the elementary and secondary levels. The following list of suggestions for teachers will be helpful for all students, but particularly for ELLs:

- Demonstrate how to read a mathematics textbook.
- Point out key sections and resources in the textbook.

Maddie, a seventh-grade mathematics teacher with students from Mexico, Eastern Europe, and Africa, asked her class to count on their fingers. Maddie noticed that Chimwala began counting with her thumb, others began counting with their pinkies, and most began with their index fingers. After this realization, Maddie asked all her students to share in groups how they use their fingers, or any other body parts, in the counting process. Though she did not choose to do so, Maddie could have extended this discussion into exploring the various algorithms for performing arithmetic on whole numbers that students bring from their various home and school cultures.

- Teach students how to organize notebooks and binders and record homework assignments.
- Teach study and test-taking skills.
- Teach note-taking skills. For beginner English language learners, copying notes is an effective way to begin learning writing conventions.

Create an Atmosphere for Risk Taking and Making Mistakes

Finally, learning a second language, including the mathematics register, has an affective base; that is, when students are motivated, feel at ease, and view their goals as reachable, their learning is enhanced. Students need to be encouraged to ask questions and take risks; making mistakes is part of learning. If students' answers are not correct or if students are not able to follow the emerging lines of discourse, patience may be needed to ensure that student risk taking and participation will continue.

Lewis's lesson was a success! After the spontaneous demonstration of multilingualism in his class, Lewis asked groups to estimate the total number of pennies and recorded the information on a chart under his document camera. Students continued to work in groups to produce their own charts by ordering the numbers. Other activities for this and the following day included (1) finding the differences between the guesses and estimates, (2) rounding the numbers to the nearest ten or hundred, (3) finding the difference between the ranges in each column, (4) expressing the guesses in different forms using cents and dollar signs, (5) generating word problems using data, and (6) discussing what you could buy with that amount.

Conclusion

Mathematics is not limited to computation; it is very much dependent on the language in which it is taught. Current mathematics standards require students to apply computational skills in a variety of real-life problem-solving situations, read and solve word problems, communicate their mathematical thinking, and collaborate with others to complete a task. These requirements demand that students learn to "talk math." Just as archaeologists search for bones and stone materials to understand past civilizations, educators must search texts for challenging words, grammatical structures, and processes that may hinder understanding of mathematics. Explicit and deliberate instruction of terms, concepts, and processes—in addition to the utilization of a variety of instructional supports and classroom arrangements—can enhance mathematics instruction for all students.

• Extensions •

For Reflection

1. *In your ELLs' shoes.* Recall a time when you were learning a second language. Now imagine you had to learn mathematics in that language.

2. *Think back.* Recall your school or college days and reflect on your best and worst math teachers. What did some teachers do to foster or hinder learning? Was there an emphasis on communicating problem-solving strategies? Was there explicit language instruction?

For Action

1. *Adapt a lesson.* Find a lesson or unit on the Internet that is appropriate to your grade level or area of interest. Check if this lesson or unit grows out of real-world problems, is relevant to your students, and focuses on teaching explicit language components needed to understand the lesson. If it does not have any of these features, what adaptations would you need to make?

2. *Interview a student or an adult whose first language is not English.* Find out how the student or adult learned mathematics in his or her schools. Was the emphasis on computational activities or communicating knowledge? Also, find out if, in this person's home country, he or she uses different symbols to represent various concepts.

chapter 10

Unlocking the Language of English Language Arts

• Key Issues •

1. English texts and tasks, with their abundance of idioms, figurative language, imagery, and symbolism, present challenges for English language learners (ELLs).

2. The language arts include reading, writing, listening, speaking, viewing, and visually representing.

3. Educators need to affirm and draw on the different literacy practices that students develop in and out of school.

4. Early elementary grades focus on learning to read; later the focus is on reading to learn.

5. Students benefit from receiving extensive and varied vocabulary instruction.

• Potential Challenges for ELLs • in the English Language Arts Classroom

- English texts have an abundance of idioms, figurative language, imagery, and symbolism.

- Students may not have practice in forming, expressing, and supporting their opinions about a literary work.

- Students may not be familiar with drawing conclusions, analyzing characters, and predicting outcomes.

- Texts use a variety of regional U.S. dialects as well as Middle and Old English.

- Students may lack familiarity with text structures and features.

- English texts have large quantities of unfamiliar vocabulary, homonyms, homophones, and synonyms.

- Students need to become familiar with grammar usage and with many of the exceptions to the rules found in any language.

- ELLs may not be familiar with terminology and routines associated with the writing process: drafting, revising, editing, workshop, conference, audience, purpose, or genre.

It is 9:45 p.m. and Jeff Rosenfeld, a second-grade teacher, has only three more interactive journals to respond to; he takes a sip of his coffee. Last weekend had been a busy time for his students, as evidenced by their journal entries. Opening up the journal of Pierre, an ELL student from Togo, Jeff read the latest entry. Pierre, a native French speaker, talked about attending church with his parents last weekend and then playing with friends he had made in his neighborhood. After writing a reply in which he modeled appropriate word order, Jeff jotted the following on a separate piece of paper:

Language Objectives for Pierre:

- **Word order:** (1) sentences: subject before verb; (2) questions: use of "do" or "did" with verb and placement of subject

- **Tense:** work on simple past tense (regular forms first: play → played; irregular forms later: go → went). Journal showed all present tense. This will be useful in social studies, too.

- **Social studies:** Allow Pierre to use simple past in social studies for now. As he demonstrates mastery, begin teaching present perfect and past perfect in stages.

Tomorrow, Jeff will use this information to plan the coming week's whole-group and targeted small-group language lessons.

Stop and Think

Before reading the chapter, imagine three siblings who just arrived from Ukraine. During their first month in school, each student participated in the reading and discussion of one of the following books:

Ekaterina (kindergarten): *The Very Hungry Caterpillar* (Carle)

Misha (sixth grade): *Hatchet* (Paulsen)

Pavel (eleventh grade): *Beloved* (Morrison)

What language and literacy skills will Ekaterina, Misha, and Pavel need in order to access, understand, and participate in classroom activities? How can teachers prepare students in the early stages of language proficiency so that they can benefit from the discussion of these and other books?

English Language Arts: Preparing Students for the Literacy Demands of Today and Tomorrow

Language and literacy development can be seen as a continuous process that starts at birth with a child's earliest experiences with language. Observations of young children show that the development of oral language and literacy are interrelated processes. As children manipulate books, pencils, and papers, they begin to assume the roles of readers and writers in their everyday play. These early experiences in constructing meaning from text are part of what is called emergent literacy. Later, instruction in the early grades focuses on teaching students how to decode and produce written texts. As students leave the primary grades, the emphasis shifts to comprehension of increasingly complex texts in language arts and other content areas. This change of emphasis, from learning to read to reading to learn, may present many challenges for ELLs because they are learning language and content simultaneously.

Language arts have traditionally focused on the four language domains of *listening, speaking, reading,* and *writing,* including language conventions such as punctuation, spelling, and grammar usage. Recently, however, newer skills such as word processing, Web searching, and designing websites are now also considered part of the language arts.

Visual literacy, that is, the ability to interpret, negotiate, produce, and make meaning from information presented in the form of an image, is now an important aspect of the language arts. For example, it is not uncommon for third- and fourth-grade students to produce PowerPoint presentations containing print and other special features such as pictures, graphics, sound, and video.

In 1996, the National Standards for the English Language Arts, published jointly by the International Reading Association (IRA) and the National Council of Teachers of English (NCTE), recognized the need to consider *viewing* and *visually representing* as part of language arts (see Figure 10.1).

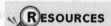 **R**ESOURCES

NCTE/IRA Standards • For a link to the NCTE/IRA Standards for the English Language Arts, see http://www.ncte.org/standards.

Clarification: Six Language Arts or Four Language Domains?

During the discussion of language proficiency in Chapter 2, we addressed four interrelated language domains of listening, speaking, reading and writing. When discussing language acquisition and language learning, these are the four domains that need to be considered. However, for the K–12 language arts curriculum in the United States (as well as in Canada), the inclusion of "viewing" and "representing," in addition to the four language domains, is a response to technological changes in the way we communicate. The intent is to highlight the need for students to learn the techniques and conventions of visual language to become

FIGURE 10.1
NCTE/IRA Six Language Arts

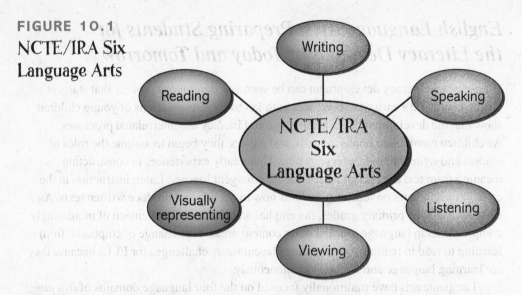

more conscious, critical, and appreciative readers of visual media and more effective creators of visual artifacts.

Multiple Literacies

> *There is an emerging view that literacy is inherently multiple and that literacies are an integral part of the social-cognitive and cultural lives of individuals and communities.* (Bloome & Paul, 2006, p. 293)

The concept of multiple literacies expands our notion beyond that of reading and writing to consider literacy practices across a variety of contexts, using diverse language domains and texts, in different languages, for an array of purposes, to meet the challenges of new and unknown technologies. The concept of multiple literacies emerged as a result of (1) diversification of school systems due to demographic changes and (2) changes in technology that, in turn, have resulted in new forms of literacy (e.g., text messaging, blogs).

If ELLs are to achieve and succeed in the English language arts classroom, educators need to affirm and draw on the different literacy practices that students develop in and out of school. As we prepare students to achieve academically, we must not lose sight of the need to prepare students to succeed beyond the school walls. Students today are not only exposed to printed materials and TV, they are also part of an increasingly multisensory world incessantly vying for their attention via movies, multimedia graphics, radio, music, the Internet, text messaging, cell phones, and computers. As we prepare students for a world that is experiencing an unprecedented technological revolution, we must not lose sight of the existence of multiple and evolving forms of literacy.

Effective Literacy Practices for ELLs in the Elementary Grades

Determining what is best for all students, including ELLs, depends on many factors, such as teachers' own perspectives and experiences; the school, district, and state curricula; the kinds of programs and supports available to the students; and the needs and strengths of the students, among other factors. In this section, we first discuss key elements to consider when developing a literacy program for elementary classrooms with ELLs. This discussion is followed by effective prereading and reading strategies for ELLs. Reading strategies are grouped around two broad categories: beginning readers and intermediate readers.

Key Elements for Improving Literacy for Elementary English Language Learners

When planning literacy instruction for ELLs, educators need to consider their unique strengths and needs, including their distinctive backgrounds and experiences. In addition, teachers might want to consider the following elements when developing a successful literacy program.

Theoretical Orientation   Deciding on the kind of theoretical orientation to reading instruction (e.g., phonics approach, skills approach, whole-language approach, biliteracy) to guide the program is a very important first step. This does not necessarily mean that only one perspective needs to be adopted. Successful teachers of ELLs are often very creative and integrate different approaches in addition to district or state-mandated programs.

Language-Rich Environment   Surrounding ELLs with ample opportunities to hear and use language for meaningful purposes fosters the acquisition of English. Continuous modeling, ongoing feedback, a stress-free environment, and reasons to use the target and the native language all help students become better language users.

Meaningful Literacy   Learning how to read and write should not be equated with disconnected skill-and-drill practices. On the contrary, literacy learning should happen when students are engaged in actual, meaningful literacy acts within real-life environments.

Culturally Relevant Literacy Practices   Cultural practices are central to literacy learning. These practices play a tremendous role not only in how people learn to communicate orally or in written form, but also in shaping the thinking processes of individuals. A classroom environment that acknowledges, responds to and celebrates different literacy practices offers students opportunities to benefit, in a just and equitable manner, from the schooling experience.

Additive Bilingualism Learning a second language should not be equivalent to losing the first language. On the contrary, additive bilingualism is promoted when students' first languages and cultures are celebrated and developed. Additive bilingualism is linked to self-esteem, increased cognitive flexibility, and higher levels of proficiency in the second language.

Additive Perspective on Language As mentioned throughout this book, this key is to consider students' languages as resources. Even when instruction can be delivered only in English, the goal should be to add English to students' linguistic repertoire rather than to replace it.

Emphasis on Academic Language The development of academic English needs to be an instructional goal for ELLs, starting in the earliest grades. Students benefit from having deliberate academic language instruction consistently and simultaneously during language arts and content-area instruction.

Prereading Strategies

Engaging students in prereading activities is one of the most successful strategies for motivating them to read and to activate and build their background knowledge on topics or concepts contained in the reading selection. Activation of relevant knowledge is extremely important for ELLs, who might not feel confident about their ability to read in English. In addition, prereading activities can serve as a vehicle to elicit students' reactions and feelings about ideas and issues contained in the material to be read before confronting those issues in the text. See Figure 10.2 for selected strategies that have proven helpful for many teachers of ELLs.

FIGURE 10.2 **Examples of Prereading Strategies for Developing Motivation, Purpose, and Background Knowledge**

Anticipation guides	Can be designed as a list of three to five statements, related to concepts or issues, with which students are asked to agree or disagree.
Discuss critical terms and concepts	Locate important vocabulary and explain it beforehand by using visuals or brainstorming meanings.
Establish a purpose for reading	Explaining the purpose of the reading selection often helps students focus by having a purpose for the reading.

FIGURE 10.2 continued

Field trips and films	Field trips are ideal activities to build background knowledge and vocabulary on a topic. Films provide a visual context and help build schema.
Graphic organizers	Can be used to record prior knowledge about a concept, topic, or book.
KWL chart (Know, Want to Know, Learned)	Often used as a whole-group activity; helps students activate prior knowledge, identify areas of interest, and reflect on their learning. You can use the following headings: What I Know, What I Want to Know, What I Learned.
Making predictions	Give students the title of the book or text and show some pertinent pictures. Based on this information, have students make two or three predictions as to what they think the book is about.
Preview/simplified text summary	A preview presents the gist of the longer text and is written using relatively simple sentence constructions. Visuals or graphics are also helpful.

Reading Strategies for Beginning Readers

Beginning English readers, whether ELLs or not, are just starting to make meaning from text. While some ELLs might need to be reminded to read from left to right and top to bottom, others might be starting to comprehend the text beyond the sentence level. Beginning readers, regardless of their age, need more familiarity and interaction with the written text. See Figure 10.3 for a list of successful practices to support beginning readers.

Reading Strategies for Intermediate Readers

Intermediate readers are more familiar with reading a variety of texts for a variety of purposes. They can read with greater fluency because they have a larger sight vocabulary. However, they still have difficulty reading texts, particularly if the texts are about unfamiliar topics and have many new vocabulary words. Like their beginning reader counterparts, intermediate readers can benefit from supporting reading strategies like the ones listed in Figure 10.4.

FIGURE 10.3 Strategies for Beginning Readers

Choral reading	During choral reading, all students read aloud from the same selection under the direction of the teacher or leader. It helps students improve sight vocabulary and develop effective read-aloud skills.
Guided reading	Students grouped at similar reading levels read under the guidance of their teacher. When students encounter difficulty reading aloud, the teacher offers explicit instruction to help them better decode or comprehend the text.
Language experience approach	This approach allows children to dictate their stories to an adult or older student based on their personal experiences. Through this approach, students provide the text and the topics that will be the basis for reading instruction.
Literature circles	This student-centered collaborative strategy affords students opportunities to participate actively in the selection, reading, and discussion of a book. Because student members of the circle have a role, with corresponding responsibility, students take ownership of their learning.
Predictable and pattern books	These books offer students opportunities to anticipate or predict what is next because of the patterned structure in the book. Books have repeated segments that are easily learned and allow children to read along with their teacher.
Reader's theater	Students perform a dramatic presentation of a written work in script form. Readers read from a script, and reading parts are divided among the readers. It helps students perfect their fluency and speaking skills.
Shared reading with big books	Children join in the reading of a big book or other enlarged text as guided by a teacher. The teacher points at each word as children read together. This offers children opportunities to participate and behave like readers.
Story mapping	A story map is a visual representation of the settings or the sequence of major events and action of the characters in the story. This strategy helps students visualize story characters, events, and settings and also helps them develop a sense of story.

FIGURE 10.4   Strategies for Intermediate Readers

Cognitive mapping	This graphic drawing summarizes a text and helps readers with comprehending and remembering what they have read.
Directed reading-thinking activity (DR-TA)	This strategy asks students to make predictions about a text and then reread to confirm or refute their predictions. Encourages students to be active and thoughtful readers, thus enhancing their comprehension.
Individual student conference	This strategy involves one-on-one conferences with students and is designed to gather information about each student as a reader and to provide direct, explicit, and targeted support.
Learning logs	Via this personalized learning strategy, students record their responses to reading challenges. Each log is a unique record of the child's thinking and learning over time.
Literature response journals	Encourage children to draw, write, and talk about the books, poems, plays, or any other text they read. Through journaling, students experiment with a variety of writing skills and genres.
Think-alouds	Readers are asked to stop at various points during their reading and think aloud about the processes and strategies they are using as they read. This strategy allows teachers to observe students' thinking aloud during reading to assess comprehension and inform instruction.

Key Elements for Improving Adolescent Literacy

There are important differences between teaching literacy to young children and adolescents. These differences are more pronounced when teachers are working with ELLs.
In the early grades, both ELLs and native English speakers are learning to read and write in English; in middle school and beyond, the focus shifts from literacy skills to the learning of academic content knowledge, skills, and ways of thinking. At the secondary level, there are fewer curricula and materials for ELLs and fewer content-area teachers prepared to address the needs of high school ELLs. Finally, the complexity of the texts, tasks, tests, and teachers' explanations can be overwhelming for students who are learning a new language, adapting to a new culture, and at the same time trying to achieve in the content areas.

Effective Reading Instruction for ELLs

Figure 10.5 provides a useful chart prepared by Fisher, Rothenberg, and Frey based on the findings from *Reading Next: A Vision for Action and Research for Middle and High School Literacy* by Biancarosa and Snow (2006) completed for the Carnegie Foundation.

RESOURCES

Reading Next Report • For a copy of *Reading Next: A Vision for Action and Research for Middle and High School Literacy* by Biancarosa and Snow (2006), see http://www.all4ed.org/files/ReadingNext.pdf.

This report, written by a panel of experts, identified 15 recommendations for addressing the needs of struggling adolescent readers and writers. One main point highlighted by Reading Next is to expand the efforts placed on literacy in the early grades (e.g., Reading First) to include acquiring literacy skills that can serve youth for a lifetime. Figure 10.5 presents nine important strategies from this report and their implications for effective reading instruction with adolescent ELLs.

FIGURE 10.5 Key Elements of Effective Reading Instruction for ELLs

Instructional Practice	Explanation	Focus on ELL
1. **Direct, explicit comprehension instruction**	Teach the strategies and processes that proficient readers use to understand what they read.	• Model, model, model! • Elaborate instruction rather than simplify.
2. **Diverse texts**	Use texts at a variety of difficulty levels and on a variety of topics.	• Ensure access for ELLs through differentiated texts that address the same topic.
3. **Effective instructional principles embedded in content**	Use content-area texts in language arts classes and teach content-area-specific reading and writing skills in content-area classes.	• Use content as a vehicle to teach language—students do not learn language in a vacuum. • Incorporate language teaching throughout the day, throughout different content areas.
4. **Intensive writing instruction**	Form bridges to the kinds of writing tasks ELLs will have to perform in high school and beyond.	• Assign tasks that require high levels of critical thinking and teach the language and strategies need to analyze, critique, justify, etc. • Scaffold writing instruction through talk, visuals, graphic organizers, writing frames, and the gradual release of responsibility.

FIGURE 10.5 **continued**

Instructional Practice	Explanation	Focus on ELL
5. **Motivation and self-directed learning**	Build motivation to read and learn and provide students with the instruction and supports needed for independent learning tasks that they will face after graduation.	• Teach students to take responsibility for learning and engaging as active, not passive, learners.
6. **Ongoing formative assessment**	Learn how ELLs are progressing under current instructional practices.	• Assess all four language domains: reading, writing, speaking, and listening. • Provide focused, selective feedback that differentiates between language and content.
7. **Strategic tutoring**	Provide students with intense individualized reading, writing, and content instruction as needed.	• Group students homogeneously to address similar needs and develop language proficiency when the teacher or aide is present.
8. **Technology**	Use technology both as a tool and a topic for language and literacy instruction.	• Use technology to scaffold understanding through visuals and access to a diversity of sources in multiple formats and languages.
9. **Text-based collaborative learning**	Encourage interaction among students around a variety of texts.	• Group students heterogeneously to provide language models and scaffolds for learners.

Source: Adapted from *Language learners in the English classroom*, revised versions of Tables 2.3 and 2.5. Doug Fisher with Carol Rothenberg and Nancy Frey. Copyright © 2007 by the National Council of Teachers of English. Reprinted with permission.

Effective Writing Instruction for ELLs

Writing well in English is one of the most difficult skills for ELLs to master. Many English language learners are still acquiring vocabulary and syntactic competence in their writing. Students may show varying degrees of English language acquisition, and not all second language writers have the same difficulties or challenges. Teachers should be aware that English language learners may not be familiar with terminology and routines often associated with writing instruction in the United States, including the writing process, drafting, revision, editing, workshop, conference, audience, purpose, or genre. Certain elements of discourse, particularly in terms of audience and persuasion, may differ across cultural contexts. The same is true for textual borrowing and plagiarism. Figure 10.6 depicts 11 key elements

FIGURE 10.6 Key Elements of Effective Writing Instruction for ELLs

Instructional Practice	Explanation	Focus on ELL
1. **Collaborative writing**	Use instructional arrangements in which students work together to plan, draft, revise, and edit their writings.	• Provide opportunities for students to practice oral language to hear and rehearse models of language they can transfer to writing.
2. **Inquiry activities**	Engage students in analyzing data to help them develop ideas and content for a particular writing task.	• Ensure that ELLs are engaged in tasks that require high-level critical thinking.
3. **Prewriting**	Engage students in activities designed to help them generate and organize their ideas for compositions.	• Provide opportunities that encourage students to practice oral language.
4. **Process writing approach**	Integrate a variety of writing activities in a workshop that focuses on extended writing opportunities, writing for authentic audiences and purposes, personalized instruction, and cycles of writing.	• Provide daily opportunities to practice writing. • Link assignments to personal experiences to activate background knowledge.
5. **Sentence combining**	Teach students to construct increasingly complex, sophisticated sentences.	• Use this as a way to teach grammar in context.
6. **Specific product goals**	Assign students specific, reachable goals for the writing they will complete.	• Break down goals as needed to make writing less overwhelming for students who are learning language at the same time as they are learning writing strategies.
7. **Study of models**	Provide students with opportunities to read, analyze, and emulate models of good writing.	• Provide a variety of models before students are required to create a product independently.
8. **Summarization**	Explicitly and systematically teach students to summarize texts.	• Use graphic organizers to help ELLs chunk text for summarizing.

FIGURE 10.6 continued

Instructional Practice	Explanation	Focus on ELL
9. Word-processing skills and tools	Use computers as instructional supports for writing assignments.	• Teach students to use spellcheckers and online thesauruses and dictionaries (including in their native languages). • Provide prescreened websites for research.
10. Writing for content learning	Use writing as a tool for learning content material.	• Build background knowledge before asking students to write. • Provide students with opportunities to talk with peers before asking them to write.
11. Writing strategies	Teach students strategies to plan, revise, and edit their compositions.	• Teach the organization of various genres—the organization of writing can vary from culture to culture.

Source: Adapted from *Language learners in the English classroom*, revised versions of Tables 2.3 and 2.5. Doug Fisher with Carol Rothenberg and Nancy Frey. Copyright © 2007 by the National Council of Teachers of English. Reprinted with permission.

that have proven effective for helping students learn to write well and to see writing as a tool for learning. These instruction practices are based on the work done by Graham and Perin (2007) and Fisher, Rothenberg, and Frey (2007).

The Language of English Language Arts

English language learners face a daunting task. They must acquire a multifaceted knowledge of the English language as they learn demanding grade-level content-area knowledge. They must do all this while native-English-speaking peers continue to increase their knowledge of the English language and its use and application in the content areas. ELLs have a steep path ahead in playing catch-up with their peers in a relatively short time. As they learn with their peers new vocabulary and language features, they also have to learn the social and academic language that their peers have learned since they entered school—and even earlier. ELLs need explicit and systematic practice to develop a competent command of the language of school, including the many features of academic language. Following is a discussion of academic language in the English language arts classroom.

Vocabulary

The difference between the right word and almost the right word is the difference between lightning and a lightning bug.

—Mark Twain

One of the most important challenges facing second language learners is the acquisition of the vocabulary needed to actively and successfully participate in all facets of school. ELLs encounter thousands of different words in texts, group work, classroom discussions, and tests, just to mention a few. And they need to learn many of them in a short time!

Harvard professor Catherine Snow (2005) concludes that, by the time middle-class students with well-educated parents are in third grade, they probably know 12,000 English words and that ideally students should know 80,000 words by the time they graduate from high school. If some students are learning only 75% as fast as their peers, then huge deficits can be accrued.

Like other content areas, the English language arts classroom has its own set of general, specialized, and technical academic vocabulary. Figure 10.7 presents selected examples.

Vocabulary Teaching Strategies   Students can learn and use new words if they have daily opportunities to practice their newly acquired vocabulary. Students gain a deeper understanding of the meaning of words and their relationship to other words when explicit vocabulary instruction is presented daily via diverse strategies that target group of words. Selected teaching vocabulary strategies for all students are presented below.

Root Words   Students learn high-frequency roots from Latin or Greek (see Chapter 8 for examples). Students collect words with the roots and learn their meanings.

Personal Vocabulary Journal   Students select new words and concepts and record them.

FIGURE 10.7 Examples of Vocabulary Types in English Language Arts

Vocabulary Type	Definition	Examples	
General academic vocabulary	Terms used in content areas in addition to English language arts	• convey • theme • symbol	• background • opposite • reference
Specialized academic vocabulary	Terms associated with English language arts	• adjective • adverb • clause	• preposition • tense • diction
Technical academic vocabulary	Terms associated with a specific English language arts topic (e.g., Greek drama)	• catastrophe • catharsis • chorus	• hubris • thespian • parados

Word Games and Word Play　Games are fun ways to have students practice new words.

Word or Concept Maps　A graphic organizer is created for each new word. It helps students engage with and think about new terms in several ways (see Figure 10.8).

Acting Out　Give each student one card with different instructions (e.g., "Open the window slowly"; "Carefully open your book").

Word Sort　Students sort a series of words into various categories; later, they discuss their answers and the categories.

Focus on Cognates　This is an excellent way to build on and make connections to the pre-existing knowledge that ELL students bring if their first language shares cognates with English. See the examples in Figure 10.9.

Vocabulary Guides　This strategy is effective when using grade-level materials that are inaccessible to readers because they contain too many unfamiliar words. Guides can have definitions or synonyms of the difficult terms.

Key Word Method　This mnemonic strategy uses a key word that can be associated with the target word based on meaning and sound and helps students recall the term.

Target word: *carline*   **Meaning:** witch

- Teacher identifies the word *car* (easy to represent visually and it sounds like the first part of the target word).

- Teacher shows a picture of a witch sitting in a car.

- When asked to recall the definition of *carline*, students follow a four-step process:

  1. Think back to the keyword: *car*
  2. Think of the picture: a car
  3. Remember what else was in the picture: a witch was in the car
  4. Produce the definition: witch. (Mastropieri & Scruggs, 1998)

Grammatical Features

Some grammatical features are especially troublesome for ELLs. Some are learned through usage, practice, and feedback, but others take longer and require a deliberate and explicit instructional approach. Although all teachers need to provide opportunities for ELLs to work on grammar, the English language arts classroom is a prime setting for understanding and using correct grammar structures.

Students learning English as a second, third, or fourth language may encounter a variety of challenges as they try to apply the linguistic knowledge from their first language to English. This process is called language transfer. For example, students who speak a Slavic language (e.g., Russian, Croatian, Polish) have difficulty understanding the term *article* in English (where it is used to refer to *the* and *a/an*) because it does not have a direct translation in Slavic languages. For a useful guide on language transfer issues for students speaking Spanish, Vietnamese, Russian, Korean, Arabic, Tagalog, Khmer, Cantonese, Hmong, and Haitian Creole, see *Teacher's Resource Guide of Language Transfer Issues for English Language Learners* (2004), published by Rigby.

In 2003, Robin Scarcella identified 10 major areas of focus for grammar instruction for ELLs: sentences, subject–verb agreement, verb tense, verb phrases, plurals, auxiliaries,

---

Stop and Do

Practicing Idiomatic Expressions • Select several local or online newspaper headlines. Paste them on a poster board and assign each a number. Have students identify the figure of speech in each line by number and explain in concrete terms what the line is saying. Here are some examples:

"Updike's way with words extended to baseball."

"Injured Duran ready to climb right back on that beam."

"AT&T's earnings take a hit in fourth quarter."

"Celebrity parties going head-to-head at Super Bowl."

Next time your students read the newspaper they might enjoy figuring out some witty headlines.

FIGURE 10.8 Vocabulary Teaching Strategies

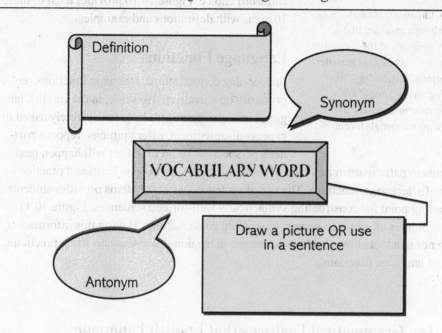

FIGURE 10.9 Cognates for the Word *Star*

	Words for *star*	Languages
	str	Sanskrit
	star	Sinhala
	aster	Greek
	Stern	German
	ster	Dutch and Afrikaans
	stea	Romanian
	stjerne	Norwegian
	setare	Persian
	estrella	Spanish
	estrela	Portuguese
	estêre	Kurdish

articles, word forms, fixed expressions and idioms, and word choice. Figure 10.10 provides a list of these 10 areas with definitions and examples.

Language Functions

In everyday conversations, language functions rely primarily on narratives. However, in the English language arts classroom, students are routinely asked to express disagreement, offer opinions, report a partner's perspective, or predict what will happen next. For students to participate in this kind of academic talk, they need to learn and practice these specific language functions. The use of sentence starters or stems provides students with a starting point for constructing syntactically well-formed sentences. Figure 10.11 includes examples of sentence starters to scaffold conversations. Having this information on a poster or handout allows students to engage in meaningful discussion while practicing a variety of language functions.

FIGURE 10.10 Ten Grammatical Features that English Language Learners Need to Know

Grammatical Features	Example	Incorrect Use
1. Sentence structure All sentences have one subject and one main verb.	My tutor was the only one who helped me.	My tutor only one to help me.
2. Subject–verb agreement Subjects must agree with verbs in number (the s rule).	They come from China. He comes from Kenya.	He come from Kenya.
3. Verb tense The present tense is used to refer to events that happen now and to indicate general truth. The past tense is used to refer to events that happened before now.	My teacher explained how important recycling is for our planet.	My teacher explains how important recycling was for our planet.
4. Verb phrases Some verbs are followed by *to* + base verb. Other verbs are followed by a verb ending in *-ing*.	My teachers convinced me to read many books.	My teacher convinced me read many books.

FIGURE 10.10 continued

Grammatical Features	Example	Incorrect Use
5. Plurals A plural count noun (e.g., dog, plant) ends in an *s*.	She has two dogs.	She has two dog.
6. Auxiliaries Negative sentences are formed by placing *do/did* + *not* in front of a base verb.	Do not cut the trees.	Not cuts the trees.
7. Articles Definite articles generally precede specific nouns that are modified by adjectives.	I speak the Japanese language.	I speak Japanese language.
8. Word forms The correct part of speech should be used—nouns for nouns, verbs for verbs.	We have confidence in our new president.	We have confident in our new president.
9. Fixed expressions and idioms Idioms and fixed expressions cannot be changed in any way. They are treated as a whole.	You need to get your ducks in a row.	You need to get your chickens in a row.
10. Word choice Formal and informal words should be used in formal and informal settings or contexts, respectively.	Dear Dr. Thorne	Hi Dr. Thorne

FIGURE 10.11 Sentence Starters for Scaffolding Conversations

Selected Language Functions	Sentence Starters
Asking for clarification	● I am confused about . . . ● What do you think this . . . means? ● This part . . . does not make sense to me.
Asking questions	● What caused . . . ? ● I wonder how did . . . ? ● What would happen if . . . ?

(continued)

FIGURE 10.11 continued

Selected Language Functions	Sentence Starters
Commenting	• My favorite part so far is . . . • This is confusing because . . . • This is hard because . . .
Connecting	• This is similar to . . . • This reminds me of . . . • The problem here is like . . . because . . .
Disagreeing	• I see your point, but I . . . • My idea/position/answer is a little different because . . . • I got a different result than you.
Expressing an opinion	• I think . . . because . . . • In my opinion . . . • It seems that . . .
Predicting	• I guess that . . . • I anticipate . . . • I'm expecting . . . to happen because it says . . .
Offering assistance	• May I help you . . . ? • It looks like you might need some help. • Maybe we could . . . .
Paraphrasing	• Another way to say it is . . . • In other words, . . . • I hear you say . . .
Suggesting	• Perhaps if you . . . • Have you considered . . . ? • Another idea would be to . . . instead.

Discourse

The English language arts classroom uses a variety of genres, as depicted in Figure 10.12. ELLs may not be familiar with some of these discourse forms or may not feel comfortable preparing a poetic response or a critique because these language forms might not be seen as academic in their countries and cultures. This suggests the need to clearly define and review expectations for each genre.

FIGURE 10.12 Types of Discourse in the English Language Arts Classroom

autobiography	editorial	poetic response
ballad	expository essay	poem
biography	monologue	script
blog	narrative	sonnet
caption	newspaper article	response logs
critique	persuasive essay	webpage

Conclusion

The English language arts classroom is an ideal place for ELLs to learn many of the much needed features of academic language. However, a heavy emphasis on form might not render the best results. ELLs (indeed all students) need to be able to connect what they are learning with what they already know and to build on their linguistic and cultural resources. In that sense, thinking about multiple literacies and not just one provides students the much needed comfort and strength to add additional literacies. Finally, language and literacy instruction is enhanced if it is meaningful to the students, it is done explicitly and systematically, and it takes into account increasingly diverse oral and written practices.

— • Extensions • —

For Reflection

1. *Multiliteracies*. Think about the diverse types of texts and writings you or your students are exposed to in one day. How is written language used within the school setting? Outside the school? For example, if a student takes the school bus in the morning, then walks to her piano lesson, and later attends her brother's basketball game, what kinds of literacy practices does she encounter throughout the day?

2. *Language functions in one hour*. Reflect on one recent lesson you taught or in which you participated as a student. Think about the number of language functions used (that is, what students were asked to do with language) during that one lesson. How might you teach an ELL how to use language functions appropriately?

For Action

1. *Teaching vocabulary.* Select a book that you like from Vocabulary.com (http://www.vocabulary .com//index.php?dir=general&file=books) or another website and locate the list of vocabulary words for that book. Plan how to teach these vocabulary words using two or more of the strategies for teaching vocabulary discussed in this chapter.

2. *Writing and grammatical features.* Analyze selected ELL student writing samples. What evidence do you find of a lack of familiarity with grammatical structures (see Figure 10.10) that might be different from errors made by native English speakers? How could you, as a teacher, help ELLs learn these usages and features?

chapter 11

Unlocking the
Language of Social Studies

• Key Issues •

1. The field of social studies includes many disciplines (e.g., archaeology, history, philosophy, psychology), each with its own set of language demands.

2. Social studies may be the most difficult content area for English language learners because they may be unfamiliar with many of the topics, particularly in relation to history.

3. Many terms in social studies are abstract, hard to translate, and culturally based.

4. Social studies textbooks and curricula assume that students have a great deal of background knowledge—knowledge that U.S. students accumulate over time from one grade level to the next.

5. Many strategies and approaches are available for enhancing the learning experiences of English language learners (ELLs) in social studies classrooms of all types.

As a point of clarification, the National Council for the Social Studies (NCSS) uses the phrase *the social studies* to refer to the overarching group containing diverse disciplines such as anthropology, geography, and political science. When we refer to social studies or social studies classrooms, we mean subjects and locations in the context of K–12 public schools.

• Potential Challenges for ELLs • in Social Studies Classrooms

- Most high school ELLs have not had seven or eight years of instruction in U.S. elementary and middle schools, and their prior knowledge may be significantly different from that of their U.S. peers.

- Social studies vocabulary can be highly technical and abstract.

- ELLs may not be familiar with historical concepts, terms, or U.S. governmental processes.

- Social studies requires very high literacy skills because much of the instruction comes through teacher lecture and textbook reading.

- Textbooks often lack clear and complete explanations of the topics they present.

- Textbooks often use passive voice, intricate sentences, and pronouns that can make it difficult for ELLs to understand passages.

- The worldview(s), perspectives, and values presented in textbooks and public school curricula may be very different from those of ELLs' families and countries.

- ELLs may not be accustomed to offering their personal opinions and challenging texts and others.

The sound of excited, high-pitched voices reached the ears of fourth-grade teacher Sheila Covington scant seconds before Catherine, Angélica, and Kamelya demanded her opinion.

"Miss Covington! Miss Covington!" chimed the girls. "We have a question."

Knowing that a question from these three students could range from the merits of the latest video game to the political situation in the Middle East, Sheila mentally braced herself.

"We don't understand something," began Angélica. "I was born in Mérida, México, which makes me Mexican."

"Yes, and I was born here in the United States, so I'm an American!" asserted Catherine.

"But Kamelya's parents . . ."

"I was born in Russia," stated Kamelya calmly and clearly, "but I am Turkish. Everyone speaks Turkish in my family and that's the only language we speak at home. It was only when I entered school that I learned Russian, but I am not Russian."

"But, Miss Covington, that just doesn't make sense to us," explained Catherine and Angélica.

"Ah, the complexities of a multinational, multicultural identity are tough concepts to explain," thought Sheila. "I have noticed that an increasing number of our immigrant ELL students have complex identities. Now, how can I explore and clarify the ideas of nationality, citizenship, and culture with 9- and 10-year-olds?"

What would you do in Sheila's place?

About the Field of Social Studies

According to the National Council for the Social Studies (NCSS, 2009), social studies is the integrated study of the social sciences and humanities to promote civic competence (NCSS, 2009). The field of social studies within the U.S. context has three important distinctions: (1) it is designed to promote civic competence as determined by U.S. norms; (2) it is cumulative, building on content learned over many years; and (3) it is integrative, incorporating many disciplines such as anthropology, archaeology, economics, geography, history, law, philosophy, political science, psychology, religion, and sociology. All these characteristics contribute to making the diverse disciplines of social studies difficult subject areas for ELLs. The integrative nature of social studies assumes that students have certain knowledge and skills in many other disciplines. In addition, the emphasis on democracy might be completely new for students and in direct contradiction to some of their traditions or political perspectives.

> ## RESOURCES
>
> For more information, see the National Council for the Social Studies (NCSS) website at http://www.socialstudies.org/.

The NCSS further states:

> *The primary purpose of social studies is to help young people develop the ability to make informed and reasoned decisions for the public good as citizens of a **culturally diverse**, democratic society in an **interdependent world**."* (emphasis added; NCSS, n.d., para. 3)

As the chapter-opening vignette illustrates, cultural diversity and the results of worldwide population migration are readily encountered in U.S. classrooms. Today's educators must be prepared to interpret such encounters with sensitivity because the outcomes affect not just academic achievement but the well-being and personal identity of ELL students. As Salinas, Franquiz, and Reidel (2008) point out: "Because late-arrival students have binational, if not transnational, experiences, there is the possibility for potentially divergent understandings of citizenship" (p. 74). In an increasingly diverse society, the plurality of identities challenge traditional views of citizenship and nationality, amplify the notion of global identity, and give credence to Gloria Anzaldúa's poem "To Live in the Borderlands Means You" (1987).

Besides the difficulties inherent in multinational identities, and as the challenges listed in this chapter suggest, some educators believe that social studies may be the most difficult content area for ELLs because of the invisible features of many of the topics in the field. The following list explains some of these features:

1. **Content may be new.** For example, concepts such as *liberty, democracy, taxation, civil rights,* and *free will* might be completely unknown to students coming from countries with long-term dictatorships or dictatorial regimes.

2. **Topics are not only abstract but language-dependent, too.** For example, students will encounter abstract concepts such as *justice, responsibility,* and *First Constitutional Congress,* which require students to depend more on reading and listening.

3. **The field of social studies incorporates many disciplines.** The field of social studies incorporates many disciplines, as listed above, and utilizes numerous skills and processes from math, science, and language arts.

4. **The field relies on extensive background knowledge.** For ELLs who received part of their elementary education outside the United States, the lack of prior exposure to the elementary social studies curriculum may pose enormous challenges because they will need to learn not only the grade-level content but several years of social studies curricula.

5. **History is presented in a linear manner, like a timeline.** This presentation may cause some confusion for students coming from educational systems where history is learned around selected dynasties or periods.

In addition to lack of familiarity with the language and content of social studies, ELLs will encounter additional challenges with a number of classroom activities. For example (and as reviewed in previous chapters), many ELLs may be unfamiliar with group work, debates, timelines, and oral reports. They may never have questioned authors' or teachers' ideas, and they may have never ventured their own opinions before.

Another area that presents challenges for ELLs is the perspective from which U.S. texts are written, that is, from local and national viewpoints. Students coming from other nations may have significantly divergent worldviews. For example, when studying the diverse peoples of the West, Chinese students may feel that textual descriptions of Chinese laborers are incomplete, inaccurate, or biased. Similarly, when studying the continents ELLs may find that their knowledge about the continents is considered erroneous, because in many countries children are taught that there are five continents, not the seven taught in U.S. schools (seven is reduced to five continents by grouping North, Central, and South America as one continent, America). Because social studies is inherently culture-specific, the perspective presented in the textbook and in the school curriculum may be different from what ELLs learned in their native countries.

Disciplines within social studies, however, can provide ideal settings for teaching ELLs. A case in point is world geography. As suggested by Salinas, Fránquiz, and Reidel (2008), an emphasis on cultural geography can be ideal for connecting the content of the curriculum with students' lives. In the area of physical geography, the study of physical features such as plains, mountains, rivers, valleys, and lakes, among others, can be taught using many types of educational supports such as visual aids, hands-on activities, illustrations in textbooks, or searching the Internet.

In sum, academic success in social studies classrooms requires that students acquire much of the background knowledge that children raised in the United States have learned over many years. In the following sections, we discuss some of the particular characteristics of the language of social studies that may pose challenges for ELLs as they try to learn both language and content.

Later that day, after school, Sheila sat down to consider how she could approach the identity issues brought up by Catherine, Angélica, and Kamelya. To generate some ideas, she turned to her copy of *Expectations of Excellence: Curriculum Standards for Social Studies* prepared by the National Council for the Social Studies (NCSS). As she encountered pertinent phrases, she jotted them down. After a few minutes of scanning, she had generated the following list:

- Multidisciplinary
- Perspectives: personal, academic, pluralist, global
- Of the 10 themes and/or organizing strands stated in the standards, these seem to apply the best:
    - IV. Individual Development and Identity
    - V. Individuals, Groups, and Institutions
    - VI. Power, Authority, and Governance
    - IX. Global Connections

Thinking back to exactly what the girls had said, Sheila suddenly realized the implicit meaning buried in the phrase *I am* _____. While common usage of English permits one to say, "I **am** American," as Catherine had done, the actual message conveyed can be multifaceted unless specified by the speaker. For instance, Catherine's statement could be interpreted as:

I am an American **citizen**.

I am an American **national** (meaning "I was born in America")

My **culture** is American.

America is the **continent of my birth**. (Remember: Canadians, Guatemalans, and Peruvians are "Americans," too!)

The phrase *I am* _____ reflects a state of being. As such, it is intimately connected to identity.

The Specialized Language of Social Studies

Runaway horses, stampeded cattle, prairie fires, blizzards, heat, sunstroke, Indians, lice, snakes and the pure loneliness of the open plains—all of these and more faced the western pioneers of the 1800's. Certainly there were those who gave up, moving back to the security of the East, but many more stayed and helped build and shape the West one sod shack at a time, one small farm at a time and eventually one town at a time. They traveled forth on horseback, in Conestoga wagons . . . some even walked. For them it wasn't a question of how long it would take, only that it had to be done. And they did it. (American Westward Expansion, 2006, para. 9)

In the passage above, analyzed by Brown (2007), we can observe the complexity of this text for students who may not have knowledge of the westward expansion. In addition, the text is filled with rarely encountered terms, such as *stampeded, prairie fires, blizzards, open plains, western pioneers, sod shack, Conestoga wagons.* New terms like these can overwhelm readers and cause them to misinterpret the passage. The type of grammatical constructions (such as dependent or multiple clauses that connect a series of ideas, concepts, and facts, as in the excerpt above) may cause students to be unable to differentiate main points from supporting details.

This type of complexity is also present in classroom assignments. For example, in middle and high school history classes, students are often expected to write argument papers about a particular issue. This is a difficult genre that requires students to construct the claims, analysis, and evidence *before* they can construct effective arguments (Schleppegrell, 2005). Often, the specific linguistic features (like those for an argument paper) needed for students to successfully access and produce different types of genres are not necessarily taught within the social studies classroom. Yet students are expected to be able to produce comparisons, syntheses, persuasive arguments, analyses, and classifications in the history classroom.

The social studies language register, characterized by an abundance of unfamiliar vocabulary terms, difficult grammatical constructions, and distinctive genres, can present many challenges even to the average native English-speaking student. Thus, for ELLs—even those at advanced levels of language proficiency—the language of social studies can

FIGURE 11.1 Types of Vocabulary in Social Studies

General Academic Vocabulary	Specialized Academic Vocabulary	Technical Academic Vocabulary
(Terms Used in Social Studies and in Other Subjects)	(Terms Associated with Social Studies)	Terms Associated with a Specific Social Studies Topic)
• conflict resolution	• identity crisis	• psychoanalysis
• theory	• human development	• autonomy
• stages	• psychosocial development	• stagnation
• adolescence	• inferiority	• generativity
• maturity	• social pressure	• ego integrity

pose numerous obstacles. More detailed explanations and examples showcasing the uniqueness of the language of social studies are described below. These explanations and examples are organized into sections about vocabulary, grammatical structures, and discourse.

Vocabulary

The social studies register includes a vast amount of words, phrases, and expressions drawn from the social sciences, natural sciences, and the humanities. Each of the more than 10 disciplines covered in social studies has its own set of specialized terminology and concepts that students must understand and be able to use appropriately in order to succeed in this area. Figure 11.1 presents definitions and examples of general, specialized, and technical academic vocabulary terms needed to understand psychologist Erik Erikson's eight stages of human emotional development.

The vocabulary terms in Figure 11.1 pertain to just one short unit on human development. However, the vastness of the field of social studies in terms of disciplines and content suggests that the number of new terms that ELLs encounter in the social studies classroom is extensive. In fact, in a recent study by Eric Dwyer investigating the vocabulary used in textbooks according to grade level, the findings indicated that the increase of social studies vocabulary by grade exceeded that of other content areas (2007, as cited in Cho & Reich, 2008, p. 236).

Another consideration in planning for and successfully teaching social studies vocabulary is that many terms may not have direct translations to other languages. For example, in the Russian language, words like *privacy, challenge, take care,* and *efficiency* have no direct translation. As you might expect, terms in other languages also do not have direct

> ### ⌕Ⓡ RESOURCES
>
> For information about Erik Erikson, visit the Erikson Institute at **http://www.erikson.edu/default/aboutei/ history/erikerikson.aspx**. A 6-minute video about the eight stages of psychosocial development, produced by Ohio State University HDFS 361 class, can be found at **http://www.youtube.com/watch?v=bdPPXGadRAU& feature=player_embedded.**

Stop and Do

Specific content vocabulary • Select two areas below and jot down the academic vocabulary that students need to know in order to participate successfully in the discussion of the corresponding topics:

Anthropology, elementary: understanding time capsules

Archeology, middle school: learning how to think like an archeologist

Economics, elementary: why and how we save

Geography, high school: demographer's challenge: understanding megalopolis

History, middle school: exploring the perils of colonization

Sociology, high school: theory and practice of crime and punishment equivalents in English. In the French the term *malencontreux* is an adjective that means "unfortunate, ill-timed, untimely, and inopportune" all at the same time. Also in French, the terms *gare* and *station* both translate as *station* in English; the former is used only for trains or buses, while the latter is used only for the metro, subway, or underground.

Another challenging aspect about many of the terms and concepts used in social studies, particularly in relation to history, is that words can be culturally situated and may have different meanings for students coming from other countries. A case in point is the term *colony*. For most students born in the United States, the term *colony* is positively associated with the thirteen colonies, independence from Great Britain, and the beginning of the United States. For many immigrant students, however, the terms *colony* and *colonization* are associated with oppression, enslavement, and, in some cases, genocide.

Georges Mounin (1973) states that the problems of translating terms and concepts to other languages become more complex when dealing with sociocultural terms. For example, how can the nonspecific words *brother* and *sister* be translated into Mayan when that language has specific terms for *younger brother* or *older brother*? In another context, while finding words for colors in other languages is not difficult, the *connotations* that different colors have in different languages might make a fully nuanced translation rather tricky. Take, for example, the color red, as in *seeing red* (representing being angry) or *the red light district*. In Russian, the color red connotes beauty and is similar to the way *golden* is used in English. Hence, throughout the years, we have used the directly translated, color-bound phrases *Red Square* and *the Red Army* instead of the more socioculturally contextualized translations of "Golden Square" and "the Golden Army." One final example is the meaning of the color white. In the United States and in many European countries, white is associated with purity and moral goodness. Hence, brides wear white during their wedding. In China, brides wear red because this color is associated with good luck, happiness, and prosperity, and people wear white only when a family member has died. In China, white is associated with weakness, paleness, and a lack of vitality.

Thus, it is not difficult to understand why language is so intertwined with culture. We have all heard that Eskimos have 27 words for *snow* and that the Puyallup Indians in the Northwest have numerous terms for *salmon*. For someone in Florida, snow is that "cold, fluffy, white stuff" that falls on the ground during the winter. For Eskimos, as for skiers, snow may take very different forms and textures that require different labels. And thus, language is culturally bound.

Stop and Think

People living in the northwestern portion of the United States use many synonyms and colloquialisms to refer to rain. Can you list at least six synonyms or phrases to use in place of the word *rain*? (One example is *mist*.)

Some words and phrases have different layers of meaning because of their symbolic nature and emotional charge. Think about the terms *buffalo, swastika, holocaust, Indian reservation, Crusades, Inquisition,* and *conquistador* (M.R. Mason, personal communication, June 28, 2009). For some students, some of these terms may bring a host of feelings and additional layers of meaning.

Finally, another level of difficulty for ELLs in the social studies class is that many of the terms and concepts discussed are highly abstract, and their meanings are difficult to convey by giving a simple explanation or using visuals or illustrations. Some examples are the words *democracy, economy, citizenship, the Harlem Renaissance,* and *capitalism.* Unlike science or math classrooms, social studies classrooms do not often include the use of hands-on experiments or manipulatives.

Stop and Think

How would you help fifth-graders understand the following terms?

abolitionist	primary source/secondary source	debt/credit
urbanization	physical and political boundaries	amendments

Grammatical Features

> *The Non-Intercourse Act of 1809—a watered-down version of Jefferson's embargo aimed solely at Britain and France—was due to expire in 1810. To Madison's dismay, Congress dismantled the embargo completely with a bargaining measure known as Macon's Bill No. 2. While reopening American trade with all the world, Macon's Bill dangled what Congress hoped was an attractive lure.* (Kennedy, Cohen, & Bailey, 2002, p. 228)

In their analysis of this text, Cho and Reich (2008) highlight the challenges faced by students: (1) the need to know the different meanings of discipline-specific words (e.g., *act, bill*); and (2) encountering advanced vocabulary words such as *embargo, dismantle, dangle,* and *lure,* which they will most likely not find in their everyday lives. In addition to the vocabulary, the structure of the sentences tends to be very complex, where relationships of cause and effect are embedded in ways that make them difficult for ELLs to recognize (Cho & Reich, 2008, p. 237).

Other characteristics of textbooks and materials used in social studies classrooms include the use of the passive voice; complex and dense texts; and an abundance of dependent clauses or multiple clauses that connect a series of facts, ideas, and concepts in one long sentence. These and other features make it difficult for ELLs to differentiate main ideas from supporting details.

Cause-and-effect relations, discussed in Chapter 8, are also pervasive in social studies texts. An examination of texts and tasks used in social studies showed that selected linguistic signals cue student to time references, cause and effect, and comparison and contrast in text structures. Such signals

Stop and Think

Using the information about the specific characteristics of social studies vocabulary and grammatical constructions discussed in this chapter, imagine how an ELL student might feel when opening a thick social studies textbook. What predictions can you make about the challenges that ELLs face?

include verb tenses and condition, expressions of time, rhetorical markers (e.g., temporal phrases, conjunctions), and causative words (e.g., *thus, hence*). Observations by Short (1994) in social studies classrooms demonstrate that explicit instruction of these signal words can be very beneficial in improving students' reading and writing skills. See Figure 11.2 for words that signal different types of organizational patterns.

FIGURE 11.2 Words That Signal a Type of Organizational Pattern

Classification	Cause	Effect
various	because	finally
several	due to	as a result
numerous	on account of	thus
another	because	therefore
still others	reason	outcome
furthermore	leads to	consequently
first, second, third, etc.	led to	for this reason
1, 2, 3, etc.	as	hence
also	for the reason that	in order to
one	given that	so

Sequence	Comparison	Contrast
meanwhile	similarly	notwithstanding
initially	both	in spite of
previously	all	conversely
next	by the same token	even though
immediately	likewise	nevertheless
presently	as well as	on the contrary
formerly	in comparison	instead
later	as	despite
after	correspondingly	regardless
first, second, third, etc.	equally	whereas
ultimately	in the same way	although
finally		unlike
		however

Discourse

At the discourse level, we will discuss two specific aspects of the language of social studies: (1) the difficulties presented by social studies textbooks and other kinds of texts for all students, particularly ELLs, and (2) the different genres of language that students need to produce to be successful in the social studies classroom.

1. Difficulties Presented by Social Studies Textbooks and Materials   In most social studies textbooks, facts and details are often condensed. In addition, concrete or anecdotal details, which can help ELLs connect unfamiliar concepts with what they know or have experienced, are often omitted. ELLs' difficulties with reading comprehension are further compounded by textbooks containing a high concentration of new vocabulary or complex sentence patterns.

Recent studies have analyzed the main characteristics of history and social studies textbooks and the difficulties that selected features pose to ELLs when reading these texts (see, for example, Brown, 2002, 2007; Schleppegrell & Achugar, 2003). The following list summarizes the main findings from these studies that may pose challenges to ELLs as they try to crack the textbook code:

- There are few graphic cues.
- There is a less predictable sequence compared with narratives. Thus, it is harder to predict what will happen next.
- Insufficient glossaries cause students to look up terms in dictionaries.
- Expository texts assume that readers have the necessary background knowledge to understand the text, and the texts do not fill in the gaps when readers lack relevant background information.
- Some readers' prior knowledge may be mismatched and could interfere with comprehension of the text.
- Vocabulary in social studies can be highly technical and abstract.
- Written discourse, particularly if it does not include pictorial or graphic material, lacks nonverbal clues to meaning, for example, facial expressions, intonation, or gestures.
- Instantaneous clarification and feedback are not possible, not like they can be in face-to-face communication. Readers of written text must figure out what they are reading without input from the author. Without seeking the assistance of other people, readers must draw on their own

RESOURCES

Nonverbal communication • Guerrero, DeVito, and Hecht (1999) discuss eight basic nonverbal codes: kinesics, physical appearance, olfatics, vocalics, proxemics, haptics, chronemics, and environmental features. For additional information about nonverbal communication, see L. K. Guerrero, J. A. DeVito, and M. L. Hecht (Eds.), *The Nonverbal Communication Reader: Classic and Contemporary Readings*, 2nd Edition, Long Grove, IL: Waveland Press, 1999.

prior knowledge and knowledge of the language and writing conventions in order to construct meaning from the text.

- Few terms, usually no more than 10, are defined per chapter.
- Sidebars, boxes, highlights, and other materials break up the main narrative, causing students to be uncertain about how to approach the text.

2. Students Need to Access and Produce Different Kinds of Written Genres   As discussed above, the field of social studies encompasses several disciplines, each with its own sets of vocabulary, grammatical structures, and discourse features. This range of fields requires that students in social studies classes develop strategies to access and, more important, produce a diversity of genres. Figure 11.3 presents a list of different genres or types of tasks used routinely in social studies classrooms across the country. Each task demands that students produce different kinds of texts, each of which may have different organizational and linguistic features.

As the figure indicates, there is a great variety of text types, all of which create many challenges for students. Due to the diversity of demands in each genre, Schleppegrell (2005) advocates for the explicit teaching of *how* to write in a variety of styles, including writing styles that ask students to define a problem, speculate about alternatives, and reformulate information to support a point. For example, teachers can help students understand the differences among historical account, historical explanation, and argument

FIGURE 11.3   **History and Geography Presentation and Writing Genres**

interviews	historical description	timelines
photo essays	media analyses	map making
timeline captions	written debates	travelogues
editorials	multimedia presentations	simulations
biographies	scenarios	autobiographical accounts
journals	factual explanations	rebuttals
digital maps	panel simulations	electronic portfolios
reports	theses	summaries
charts and tables	online bulletin boards	synopses
historical arguments	essays	personal accounts
diagrams	geographical representations	graphics
visual analysis	explanations	models

FIGURE 11.4 Selected Genres of History

Genre	What It Does	Question It Answers
Historical account	Establishes the sequence of events, with causal reasoning about why things happened	Why did it happen? *(analyze)*
Historical explanation	Defines and evaluates; explains and interprets the factors that led to, or the consequences of, historical events	What brought this about? *Or* What was the result of this? *(explain and interpret)*
Historical Argument	Promotes a position on or interpretation of events	What is your judgment of what happened? *(evaluate)*

Source: Adapted from Helping content area teachers work with academic language: Promoting English language learners' literacy in history by Schleppegrell, M. J. (2005). Reprinted with permission.

by providing students with a comparison of the different accounts, as illustrated in Figure 11.4. This kind of information not only helps students understand the goals and characteristics of each genre, it also provides a model for students to organize information when comparing two or more items.

The final section of this chapter provides selected strategies that have proven useful for teaching specific aspects of social studies content and language.

Strategies for Teaching and Learning Social Studies

Szpara and Ahmad (2007) recommend three broad practices to support ELLs in high school social studies classrooms: (1) developing socially supportive classrooms, (2) teaching of academic skills explicitly; and (3) reducing cognitive load and increasing accessibility of complex content knowledge. We build on these recommendations and extend them by providing very specific strategies to accomplish those goals. Many of these strategies have proven successful not only with high school students but with middle and elementary school students, too.

1. Developing Socially Supportive Classrooms   This section suggests ways in which teachers can create a safe space where ELLs' languages, cultures, and experiences are recognized and affirmed (Nieto, 2000) and where ELLs feel comfortable taking the necessary to learn language and content.

Link the unfamiliar with the familiar by tapping students' previous knowledge   By using KWL charts (with the headings Know, Want to Know, and Learned) or analogies, or discussing concepts and ideas relevant to students' lives, teachers can link students' experiential knowledge with curricular content. For example, a teacher might help ELLs understand the tensions between the American colonies and Great Britain by having students talk about the issues that arise when parents or other adults change the rules.

Use collaborative groups for tackling complex reading materials   By dividing the reading material and assigning each group a section, the reading becomes more manageable for students. Students' responsibilities include reading and understanding their assigned sections and teaching those sections to the rest of the class by using visuals, performances, or realia. In this way, students are not overwhelmed by lengthy or complex texts.

Level the field by making students the teachers and teachers the learners   ELLs have a wide array of experiences that make them experts in some aspects where most native English speakers might have very little knowledge. Think about topics such as long-distance transportation, immigration, world geography, and currency exchange, among many others. Immigrant students may be very knowledgeable in these areas and can shine when they have opportunities to discuss these topics. Teachers can also become learners by attempting to learn students' native languages, geography, currency names and values, and other culture-specific information and customs.

Build on the "funds of knowledge" of students, families, and communities   Throughout this book, we have discussed the importance of building on the knowledge and skills held by ELL students, their families, and the communities in which they reside (Moll, Amanti, Neff, & Gonzalez, 1992; Monzó & Rueda, 2003). When teachers get to know students and their families and communities, they can appreciate the richness of cultural and cognitive resources available to support and enhance meaningful learning. For example, in a fourth- and fifth-grade combined, sheltered classroom, students asked their parents and family to list all the countries they have visited or lived in and to list the languages they spoke. After combining all the information by placing thumbtacks on a world map and listing all the different languages, students and teacher decided to focus on the linguistic diversity that existed in their classroom and the surrounding community. Throughout the school year, the teacher and students invited community members to come and read a book in their native language. Students created an archive of oral and written language samples, explored language families, and found out about the countries in which those languages were spoken. The learning was tremendous, both in terms of the appreciation and validation of the

Funds of Knowledge The term *funds of knowledge* is used by researchers Luis Moll, Cathy Amanti, Deborah Neff, and Norma Gonzalez (2001) "to refer to the historically accumulated and culturally developed bodies of knowledge and skills essential for household or individual functioning and well-being" (p. 133).

community's linguistic diversity and also in terms of students' better understanding of the world's linguistic diversity.

Promote an oral history approach   Oral history projects help students understand that history includes the collection and recording of personal memories as historical documentation. Complex issues can become more accessible when they are developed from students' background and experiences. In working with data obtained from oral histories, students are engaging in many of the historical thinking skills outlined in the U.S. history standards (Wrigley, 2001). Some topics that lend themselves to this kind of approach include dependence and interdependence, the interaction of human beings and their environment, the causes and results of war, resource development and use, scarcity, acculturation, migration, and the impact of economic or technological changes on societies. When students work on oral histories, they enhance their understanding of the past and their own personal experiences. They also enhance their English language proficiency by using their oral skills as they interview and present information and their literacy skills by recording and transcribing oral interviews. Using an oral history approach also promotes parental involvement, native language use in meeting instructional goals, validation of the students' cultures and experiences, and enhancement of self-esteem (Wrigley, 2001).

2. Explicit Teaching of Academic Skills   In this section, we discuss the various ways in which teachers can help students learn the necessary thought processes and academic skills needed to access the texts, tasks, and teacher talk in the social studies classroom.

Offer explicit instruction of learning strategies
Several instructional approaches, such as Cognitive Academic Language Learning Approach (CALLA), Sheltered Instruction Observation Protocol (SIOP), and Specially Designed Academic Instruction of English (SDAIE), focus on explicit instruction of learning strategies for ELLs. For example, teachers should not assume that their students know how to skim or scan reading materials, use a planner, or break tasks into manageable sections. ELLs' prior schooling experiences may not have included these types of academic strategies.

> **R**ESOURCES
>
> Several instructional approaches for English language learners foster content and language learning while pursuing high levels of cognitive development. You may find more information about these well-known approaches such as CALLA (Chamot & O'Malley, 1994, 1996), SIOP (Echevarria & Graves, 2007; Echevarria, Vogt, & Short, 2004), and SDAIE in books, articles, and websites. Go, for example, to http://www.rohac.com/sdaieinfo.htm.

Plan for academic classroom discussions   Because much of what transpires in social studies classrooms takes place via whole-class discussions, English language learners need to be involved and encouraged to practice extended academic talk with their peers and with the teacher. Through effective *academic classroom discussions* (Zwiers, 2009), also called *instructional conversations* (Tharp & Gallimore, 1988), teachers can help students develop skills in answering both factual and higher-order questions and prompt students to elaborate on, justify, or evaluate their own (or a peer's) comments (Short, 2002). Zwiers (2009) also suggests that classroom discussions:

- Allow for repetition of terms, phrases, and grammatical and thinking processes, which is conducive to the acquisition of those terms and processes.
- Encourage students to think quickly, respond, organize their thoughts into sentences, and ask for clarification.
- Allow students to observe how others think and use language to describe their thinking.

Encourage students to practice how to ask questions and request clarifications   One issue for ELLs is that they often do not know how to ask questions or how to request clarification. When teachers ask all the students in the class if they understand the task at hand or the requirements for the homework, it is not uncommon for ELLs to remain quiet or pretend to have no questions even though they might not have understood the directions. Modeling, role playing, planned interviews, a short handout containing four or five sentence or question starters (leveled to the English proficiency level of your ELL students), and small-group discussions can provide ELLs with opportunities to practice what to say in interactive settings where participation is expected. Here are some examples of sentence and question starters:

- "I like how you . . ."
- "I was unclear about . . ."
- "What did . . . mean?"
- "Could you tell me more about . . . ?"

Use deliberate instruction about how to navigate textbooks   In Chapter 9, we discussed some of the problems that ELLs encounter in mathematics textbooks. Social studies textbooks can also pose challenges for ELLs, partly because of the density of the material (that is, high concentrations of information per page). Helping students learn about the different features of a textbook provides many benefits, particularly because many ELLs come from cultures where reading is done from right to left, where the table of contents is in the back of the book, and where textbooks are primarily in black and white and contain few or no illustrations. Figure 11.5 lists many of the features that characterize textbooks in general. Reviewing these textbook features with students may help them become familiar with the text and learn some strategies, such as distinguishing between the main ideas and the supporting details in a portion of text.

FIGURE 11.5 Common Text Features

Organization of text	• Table of contents • Index • Glossary • Page numbers
Organization of ideas	• Synopses • Titles • Headings • Subheadings • Conclusion
Graphical aids	• Illustrations • Photographs • Diagrams • Charts and tables • Maps
Elaboration and emphasis	• Captions • Bold, italicized, or highlighted text • Footnotes • Margin notes
Extension of understanding	Questions

Use graphic organizers   Graphic organizers offer students visual models for organizing, understanding, and applying information regarding terms and concepts and their relationships (Gallavan & Kotler, 2007). The popularity of graphic organizers has increased in recent years because they are useful in helping students understand complex material and manage data before, during, and after reading. Many books, materials, and websites provide a wide array of graphic organizers suitable for any purpose imaginable. This diversity of formats and models allows teachers to keep their students engaged. For examples of how to apply diverse graphic organizers in the social studies classrooms, see Gallavan and Kottler (2007).

3. Reducing Cognitive Load and Increasing Accessibility of Complex Content Knowledge   "Reducing cognitive load" does not mean simplifying the material or "dumbing down the curriculum." On the contrary, the goal is to encourage cognitive complexity by using linguistic simplicity. Suggestions for accomplishing this goal include (1) locating materials in the first language to provide some background knowledge, (2) finding

materials for ELLs on the same topic that are written using simpler language (e.g., some topics in fifth-grade textbooks are similar to those in eighth-grade textbooks but are written in much simpler language), and (3) providing outlines or PowerPoint presentations to further support students' understanding.

Use role play to make abstract concepts concrete   If ELLs are unfamiliar with the concept of *dilemma*, a role play may be created in which students have to make a difficult decision. ELLs do not need to participate to benefit from this activity; observing other students or participating in writing the script can also benefit them.

Preview reading assignments   As discussed in Chapter 9, students can preview reading assignments via summary, outline, or PowerPoint presentation, or they can take the textbook home for review. This affords students excellent opportunities to become familiar with the topics and concepts to be discussed *before* they are introduced by the teacher.

Provide or encourage students to locate materials and information in their native language   Locating materials in the native language that relate to the unit or lesson to be discussed can help students have advance knowledge of the terms, concepts, and content objectives before the lesson is given. For example, when studying geography, students can search for atlases, books, and other materials at their school or local libraries. Many websites offer translations of topics, key vocabulary terms, and materials for social studies classes.

Use cognates with your Spanish-speaking students   There are many cognates (words that are written similarly) in English and Spanish. Figure 11.6 lists examples of cognates pertaining to social studies, particularly history and geography, in English and Spanish. As you can see, your Spanish speakers may know more terminology than you think! As discussed in Chapter 9, cognates are also found in Russian and several other languages, especially European languages.

Conclusion

The field of social studies may present multiple challenges for English language learners because of the diversity of disciplines and topics that may be completely new to them, the

FIGURE 11.6 English–Spanish Cognates in Social Studies

History		Geography	
circumstance	circunstancia	continent	continente
civilization	civilización	globe	globo
clemency	clemencia	dessert	desierto
constitution	constitución	geography	geografía
democracy	democracia	gulfs	golfos
federal	federal	hemisphere	hemisferio
federation	federación	latitude	latitud
legislature	legislatura	longitude	longitud
public sector	sector público	nation	nación
presidency	presidencia	poles	polos
reform	reforma	oceans	océanos
social	social	peninsulas	peninsulas
science	ciencia	reserve	reserva

abstract nature of terms and concepts, the overreliance on textbook reading and teacher lecture, and the culture-specific background knowledge that is required to interpret and contextualize knowledge. When it comes to history, one of the main issues for ELLs is that they do not have the cumulative knowledge that U.S. students have attained through study in previous grade levels. Within social studies, however, a few areas of study, such as world geography, cultural geography, and physical geography, can provide ELLs with opportunities to build on what they know and teachers with opportunities to utilize a variety of instructional supports for enhancing the teaching and learning process. Careful planning and deliberate and explicit instruction regarding vocabulary, grammatical structures, and genres that comprise the language of social studies benefits all students, but particularly English language learners.

─────────────────── • Extensions • ───────────────────

For Reflection

1. *Culturally unfamiliar topics.* As discussed in this chapter, many ELLs may not be familiar with famous people in U.S. history (e.g., Franklin D. Roosevelt), with places and settings of historic importance (e.g., the Oregon Trail), and concepts and topics tied to democracy (e.g., civil rights). Think about other topics and concepts that might be unfamiliar to students who did not grow up in the

United States. What strategies can you use to make these topics more accessible to your ELLs?

For Action

1. *Adapting instruction.* Identify a chapter in a social studies textbook pertaining to your grade level or teaching context. List all the specific terms, concepts, and grammatical structures you think will be difficult for ELLs, particularly those ELLs in the early stages of language proficiency, to understand or use. Select a list of potential strategies for facilitating instruction of those difficult aspects. Make a plan about how you or the teacher can teach those aspects so that all students in the classroom can access and demonstrate knowledge of the chapter you have identified.

2. *Building on ELLs' experiences.* Earlier in the chapter, we discussed that world and physical geography are excellent topics to build on ELLs' background knowledge and experiences. Think about other social studies topics that can be taught by building on what ELLs already know.

2. *Community cultural exploration.* Search for places in your community where ELLs and their families might spend time on evenings and weekends. For example, explore the possibility of attending a religious service in another language; visiting an ethnic market; attending a Sunday language school; or having a meal in a small, family-owned ethnic restaurant. During your visit, note the different resources (e.g., artifacts, communication, traditions) available in that location that could be used in your teaching context.

chapter 12

Putting It All Together

• Key Issues •

1. Every lesson must be accessible to all students.

2. Lessons that focus on content and language, connections to students, engaging tasks, and authentic assessments are more accessible than those that do not.

3. Every lesson can be improved in some way.

$\mathscr{A}$s you read the scenario below, think about how you might explain to your peers the important concepts in this book.

As first-year teacher Sidra Fitzgerald's group of diverse fifth-grade students left her classroom after their science period, Sidra's principal Anita Alaniz entered. Anita was amazed at how animatedly even the ELLs were involved in discussions about the science topic with native English-speaking students as they exited. Anita wanted to know what Sidra did to help her students form such bonds and to be excited about the difficult science concepts. Sidra explained how she helped all her students access the language and content of her curriculum by including the language, connections, focused task elements, and assessments that would help all students achieve. Anita wanted to hear more and assured Sidra that her colleagues would, too. They arranged to have Sidra available at the next teacher working lunch to demonstrate these concepts to her peers.

Background

As we noted in the preface, this book does not address all that teachers need to know about working with diverse learners; there are many great resources that fill this need. Rather, the focus of this text is on the specifics of lesson planning for classrooms with diverse learners. Previous chapters introduced components and ideas that are essential for meeting the needs of diverse learners. This chapter pulls together the information in this text by presenting several lessons and explaining how the pieces fit together to make each lesson more accessible. Because instructional contexts vary, the lessons are necessarily rather generic. Teachers can focus the connections, language objectives, tasks, and assessments in ways that serve the needs of their own classrooms as they implement lessons and experiment with the delivery of carefully planned instruction.

Stop and Think

What strategies and techniques would you use to implement carefully designed lessons? What do your choices depend on?

Understanding the Whole

This text's focus on language objectives, connections, engaging tasks, and authentic assessment doesn't mean that these are the only important parts of the lesson; it does mean that these lesson features need special attention in order to provide content and language access to students. Although lesson structure and content vary from one teacher or program to another, the inclusion of these components can make a big difference in every lesson.

A lesson component checklist was presented in Chapter 7. In this chapter, the checklist is used as a guide to construct, evaluate, and adapt lessons in order to provide a more coherent idea of the overall integration of these components.

Lesson Examples

Creating a New Lesson

The first example in this chapter demonstrates a process for creating a lesson based on the concepts presented in Figure 7.7. It proposes generic steps that illustrate a hypothetical teacher's planning process. A complete lesson is not reproduced here, but the general ideas should be clear.

Step 1: Find and Create the Learning Targets   The national standards note that students of all ages should understand "the people, events, problems, and ideas that were significant in creating the history of their state" (National Center for History in the Schools, 2005). Local standards based on this national standard require that each student:

- Creates and uses a research question to conduct research on an issue or event.
- Understands that there are multiple perspectives and interpretations of historical events.
- Understands the main ideas from an artifact, primary source, or secondary source in order to gather accurate information on an issue or historical event.

A required topic for fourth-graders is "Exploring the Pacific Northwest Prior to Statehood: Whitman Massacre." The teacher can create a variety of content objectives from these general standards and other requirements. She decides that the students will be able to (SWBAT):

- Develop a question to guide an investigation of the Whitman massacre after looking at primary and secondary sources.
- Draw one or more conclusions or state a perspective about the question by referencing two or more sources.
- List two or more sources, including the title, author, type of source, and date of each source. (Adapted from OSPI, http://www.k12.wa.us/assessment/WASL/SocialStudies/BridgingDocuments/Elem08/ElemHistory-DigDeep-CBA.pdf)

To meet these content objectives, students need a variety of language skills. For example, students need to understand vocabulary terms (among them *primary*, *secondary*, *source*, *massacre*); question formation; reading for information; and probably functions such as summarizing, paraphrasing, and writing in complete sentences. Knowing that the students understand how to create complete sentences and questions, the teacher may decide on language objectives such as these:

- SWBAT define and use vocabulary related to the assignment, including *primary*, *secondary*, *source*, and *massacre*.
- SWBAT demonstrate the ability to read for information.

Step 2: Make Initial Connections   In this step, the teacher can develop assessments (as discussed in Chapter 7 on backward design), or develop, in a more linear progression, the anticipatory set that includes connections to students' backgrounds and interests.

The teacher decides to introduce the topic by connecting it to previous lessons on Washington state history (academic connection) and to different views that students have of items and people in their lives, for example, the cafeteria's meatloaf, Britney Spears, other fifth-graders (personal connection). She then links the idea of different perspectives to history and to the idea of primary and secondary sources. In doing so, she also introduces some of the essential vocabulary and has students post it on the classroom word wall. She uses a questioning framework during this section of the lesson so that student input is central to setting up the lesson. She then presents students with the lesson objectives and answers any questions about the procedures of the lesson. To pique the students' interest, she reads the following quote that she has written on the board:

> The Whitmans are regarded by some as pioneer heroes; others see them as white settlers who attempted to impose their religion on the Native Americans and otherwise unjustly intruded. ("Whitman massacre," Wikipedia, 2009)

She discusses with students the impact that these different perceptions might have had on the development of the state of Washington.

Step 3: Create Engaging Tasks The teacher continues to use information that she has collected about and from students to plan the lesson tasks. She knows that some of her students like to work together, while others do better individually. She understands that there is a wide variety in their reading skills and interests and that engaging her learners means providing structured choices. Her task decisions are presented in Figure 12.1.

As you can see from the figure, the teacher has built in choices to engage students, and provided students with reasons to listen (an authentic audience and a variety of products to present) and enough scaffolding that students can do the project on their own or receive help when needed. She has incorporated many modes for students to gain and to express knowledge, making those tasks easier.

Step 4: Assessment The teacher will observe students throughout the lesson, checking informally for understanding as often as needed. In addition, the state school administration has provided a sample rubric to help the teacher measure the final product, and the teacher decides to use it with input from her students on adaptations. She will be sure that the rubric covers all of the objectives and that students are given separate grades for language use and content knowledge. She will also ask the audience to provide feedback as they participate in the presentations. To double-check the results, she will assign interactive homework in which students present perceptions from both sides of the Whitman massacre to a family member and record their family member's opinion. When they present these findings, the teacher will use a checklist to note students' language use and content outcomes.

This assessment plan provides students with practice and review and is ongoing throughout the lesson. Because the teacher discussed it with students at the beginning of the lesson and during its development, it is transparent. In addition, it is fair to ELLs and other students who may have barriers to linguistic expression of the content concepts.

Stop and Do

Use the checklist in Figure 7.7 to evaluate the lesson on the Whitman massacre. What is missing? What was done well? Discuss your findings with the class.

Adapting Lessons

It is not always necessary or desirable to create lessons from scratch. In some instances, teachers are required to use

FIGURE 12.1 Process and Product for the Lesson About the Whitman Massacre

Process	
Instructional groupings	A choice: dyads or individuals.
Modes	Primary and secondary sources that the teacher has gathered include picture books, historical texts, the letters and journals of Narcissa Whitman, a filmstrip.
Task structure	Cooperative: to try to come to an agreement about the massacre.
Time and pacing	In addition to regular class time, students may use some of their sustained silent reading time to review resources. They may also work at home. Product development will be spread over a week, and those students who finish early can either assist others or work on an extension.
Scaffolding	Handout with models of a question, graphic organizer to create their conclusions, and citations for their resources.
Resources and texts	Resources at different levels. Students can check these or find their own.
Teacher's and students' roles	Teacher will help students evaluate their questions and direct them toward appropriate resources; students will choose their resources. Teacher will focus on language objectives with groups that she observes need help or with those groups that ask for it. Students will take the position of an observer, a news reporter, or an artist to create a document that presents their perspective of the Whitman massacre.
Procedural tools	Bookmarked websites will be available; students can use the library and ask questions of the librarian; a film projector will be set up.
Product	
Audience and mode for product	The teacher will invite local community members (historical society) to assess the conclusions reached in each project. Students will have a choice of how to present their projects (in writing, orally, computer-based, etc.). Students will also get to comment on their peers' projects. As they listen, read, or view the product presentations, they will complete a worksheet on the information presented and the sources used. They will then refer to the resources for their homework.

lessons that come ready-made in their commercially prepared text packages. For others, many excellent sites on the Web offer standards-based lesson plans that are indexed according to grade level and content area. Any of these lessons can be adapted to better help students access the lesson content and language. This section presents three examples of lesson adaptations.

Adaptation 1   This first example needs little adaptation. The framework is different than the lesson presented above, but it contains the same basic components. The segments in bold within parentheses point out where the teacher has included the essential components that are not already highlighted, and the adaptations are indicated by italics within parentheses.

Measuring Up

Topic: Measurement Terms

Grades: 6–8

Learning Targets:
Standard:
- Understand both metric and customary systems of measurement.

Content objectives:
- SWBAT identify and classify terms related to measurement.
- SWBAT demonstrate the relationships between terms of measurement.

(*Language objectives*:
- *SWBAT define the terms.*
- *SWBAT write complete sentences about the terms.*)

Lesson Procedure:

- (*Present and discuss the objectives and assessment of the lesson.*)

- Have students brainstorm a list of all the terms they know that relate to measurement. (*Provide a model for them to get started.*) Record their answers in list form on a chart. Students may also write each term on a separate index card. (*Have students define the words on their index cards. Remind them and/or model how to write complete sentences. Also encourage students to draw pictures or add whatever other notes or ideas they need to help them identify the words.*)

- Organize the students in pairs and have them group and label the terms that the class has just brainstormed. (*Provide a spoken and written model of this activity.*)

Adapted from a lesson by Katie Carbone, http://illuminations.nctm.org/LessonDetail.aspx?ID=L509

This helps students establish connections among the various categories of terms. Students can move the cards around on the chart paper as they group the terms. (*To make sure that all students have the opportunity to contribute, group the students based on your knowledge of their skills, abilities, etc.*)

- Have the class reach a consensus on the major categories in which the terms can be grouped and record these categories on a chart. Then ask students to group terms that have common attributes. Students may work in groups or individually to write brief sentences about what they know about the terms (*or categories*). (*Provide scaffolding in the form of a graphic organizer as needed.*)

- As time permits, have a class discussion about the terms the students just brainstormed. Access students' prior knowledge about the relationships between the terms. For example, how does a foot compare to a yard? (**academic connection**) Other questions for students include the following:
  - How are the terms that you listed related to one another? What guidelines did you use to classify your terms?
  - How and when have you used these types of measurement? (**personal/academic connection**)
  - Were any of these terms of measurement new to you? If so, which ones? What did you learn in this lesson about appropriate uses of these terms?

Assessment At this stage of the unit, students should be able to do the following (*and the teacher can observe throughout the lesson whether they seem to*):
- Understand major terms associated with measurement.
- Know how these terms of measurement relate to one another.
- Know how certain measurements are used in the real world.
- Make connections between their own experiences and the words they generated in their brainstorming.

(**Homework** *To add practice and additional assessment, the teacher can ask the students to list all the measurement terms that the family uses at home by brainstorming with family members and listing the results by room, family event (such as dinner or TV watching), or in some other way. Students who speak a language other than English at home can list terms in their first language to share with the class.*)

Evaluation of the Lesson The teacher-author of this lesson notes that the opening activity "allows you to get an idea of what the students know before you delve further into the concepts of the unit. The activity gives you an opportunity to adjust the lesson based on students' strengths and weaknesses. It also gives students an idea of what topics will be covered in upcoming lessons." She adds that "this activity aids in planning and pacing the remainder of this unit. Keep the results from this activity to determine how students can add to or adjust the lists that they created. Students will need to refer again to their brainstormed lists in a future lesson."

Although she made connections at the end of the lesson, the teacher was working throughout the lesson on ideas that the students knew and that diverse students could contribute to. The variety of instructional groupings, the language practice provided in different parts of the task, and the multimodal nature of the activities help all students access the lesson. The small but important adaptations contribute even more to student opportunities for success.

Stop and Do

Use the checklist in Figure 7.7 to evaluate the lesson on measurement terms. What is missing? What was done well? Discuss your findings with the class.

Adaptation 2 This example presents a social studies lesson for kindergarten through Grade 3. It is adapted from the Council for Economic Education (http://www.econedlink.org/lessons/index.php?lesson=EM468&page=teacher). The lesson needs some adjustments to provide access to the content and language for diverse learners. Once again the format is different, but the same components should be present.

A Perfect Pet

Key Economic Concepts:

- Choice
- Decision making
- Economic wants
- Scarcity

Lesson Objectives

SWBAT:

- Identify economic wants of pet owners.
- Use an experience of scarcity when making choices.
- Explain why people have different economic wants.

(Language Objectives:

- *Construct sentences with the formats "I want _____ because _____,"* *and "I would _____ because _____."*
- *Use vocabulary related to the lesson such as economic want, scarcity, and so* *on.)*

Introduction

(Preview the American idea of "pet," helping students understand that not all cultures believe in keeping pets and that some have a distinct aversion to it. Discuss

pets that students have or might want.) (*Prepare students with vocabulary and main ideas from the story and focus on the reason they are reading it.*) Have students read (*and listen to*) the story, "The Perfect Pet" (http://www.storyplace.org/preschool/activities/petsonstory.asp). (*Discuss what students understood from the story, and review as necessary.*) Then discuss the following: "Do you have a dog or know someone else who does? **(personal connection)** If you do, you know that adopting a dog means more than just finding an animal that is cute and cuddly. You have to care for it. Pets depend on their owners to provide the goods and services that keep them healthy and happy. These things are called economic wants." (*Review the term and brainstorm with students what else may be an economic want. Have students write and illustrate the vocabulary in their vocabulary journals or a word wall. Make an* **academic connection** *to previous study and to the current lesson, introducing the objectives, tasks, and assessments.*)

Process

Activity 1 (*Brainstorm vocabulary and ideas that students think may be in the story, and then*) Read to OR have students read the flash activity "Economic Wants of Pet Owners" (http://www.econedlink.org/lessons/popup.php?lesson_number=468&&flash_name=em468_definitions.swf). Use the text and questions in the Think About It section of the student version as the basis for a discussion on economic wants and scarcity. "What things would you want for your pet?" (*Have students brainstorm with a partner before presenting to the class, thus providing extra support for students who may not understand the reading.*)

"Few pet owners have enough money to buy everything they want for their pets. This is called a scarcity problem. Scarcity forces people to make choices." (*Review the term and have students include it in their vocabulary notebooks or word wall.*)

"If you could buy just five of the many things at the pet store for your new dog, what would you buy?" (*Review with the students the grammatical construction used to answer this question and encourage them to use it in their reply.*)

NOTE TO TEACHER: If time allows, you may want to have students write a list or draw pictures of the five items they would choose in response to this question (*using the constructions in the language objectives if possible*). Have several students share their choices with classmates to help illustrate the point that students—and people in general—have different economic wants (*and to provide listening/speaking practice with the language objectives*). Then ask (*students to share with their seat partners*):

- Which of your choices are the same as those of your classmates?
- Why do you think these choices are the same?
- Which of your choices are different?
- Why do you think these choices are different?

Activity 2 (*Make a link between Activity 1 and Activity 2.*) Have students imagine that the girl in the story "A Perfect Pet" picked a fish instead of a dog as her new pet. Direct students to look at the items she wants for her fish, as identified in the

interactive activity (http://www.econedlink.org/lessons/popup.php?lesson_number=
468&&flash_name=em468_dragndrop_v2_save.swf). Announce that, like most
people, the little girl has a scarcity problem. She has only $5.00 to make her pur-
chases. Direct students to choose the items they would purchase with the girl's $5.00.
(*Have students discuss their choices with their seat partners, using the grammatical
constructions in the language objectives.*)

Conclusion

Ask students to summarize the reasons people's choices are not always the same
(*they can write, draw, or record their answers individually or in groups before sharing with the class*). Three factors to be identified include:

1. Our personal preferences—what we like.
2. Our values—what we think is important.
3. Our haves—what we already own or have access to.

Assessment Activity

Have students give reasons for their choices in Activity 2. For younger students, this
may be an oral report. Older students can write sentences or paragraphs citing their
choices and the reasons for their choices. (*During discussions, circulate and observe
students' participation and whether they use the grammatical structures and vocabulary. For interactive homework practice and assessment, have the student explain the
terms* economic want *and* scarcity *to a family member and have them come up with
an example of each to share with the class using the language objectives.*)

Extension Activity

Have students try to unscramble the picture of a dog and dog house in the Pet Puzzle
activity.

Lesson Evaluation

In its original form, this lesson included a variety of modes and a personal connection
to American children, but it lacked scaffolding (particularly for language) and cultural
sensitivity. In addition, very little explicit assessment was included. In the adapted
version, many more instances of scaffolding have been added, language objectives
are addressed throughout, and multiple forms of assessment have been added.

Stop and Do

Use the checklist in Figure 7.7 to evaluate
the lesson on pets. What is still missing?
What was done well? Discuss your findings
with the class.

Adaptation 3   This final example lesson was submitted by
Allen Payton, from Nickajack Elementary School in Smyrna,
Georgia, to the lesson databank at PE Central (http://www
.pecentral.org/lessonideas/ViewLesson.asp?ID=6598). Some
teachers think that content areas such as art and physical education are easier for ELLs because they don't carry as much

linguistic weight, but like science, math, and other content areas, they have their own jargon, genre, and cultural background that diverse students need support for. The terms and format of this lesson are different than those previously presented, but they demonstrate the same basic process of lesson planning.

Zone Ball

Purpose of Activity: The purpose of this activity is for students to learn the fundamental concepts of a zone defense in basketball. In doing so, students should also break the habit of everyone gravitating to the person holding the ball. On the offensive side, students will utilize nonbounce passing skills to share the ball successfully with teammates. Students will also learn how to move without having the ball in their hands.

   (*Language objective*: *SWBAT define the terms* zone, pass, dribble, offense, rebound, *and* defense *and use them appropriately in discussion.*)

Prerequisites: Students should have had practice with passing, shooting, and defensive stance.

Suggested Grade Level: 7–12

Description of Idea: (*Connect the current lesson to previous lessons on basketball and to previous experiences that students have had playing basketball. Ask about problems that their teams have had and if they have any ideas for how to play better. Review the vocabulary, introducing the concept of a zone. Provide models and graphics as the vocabulary and concepts are discussed. Explain the objectives of the lesson and how students will be assessed.*)

   The teacher can set up different types of defenses such as a 2-1-2, a 3-2, or a 2-3 around the basketball goal using the hula hoops. Five to six students will be selected to play defense. Those students will be restricted to either standing inside the hula hoop or have one foot in and one foot out (teacher's choice) until a turnover occurs or a basket is scored. In doing so, students will understand their area in the zone defense. (*Model this and other tasks several times so that students understand.*) The offense must chest-pass the ball to one another without letting the ball touch the ground; there is no dribbling in this activity. The student must freeze when he or she receives a pass and quickly decide who to pass to next. (*Provide practice for students who have not played basketball, and use an understanding of student abilities to create teams.*) Each person on offense must pass the ball at least once before a shot can occur. Encourage students to move around as much as possible and find open space to handle the ball and receive passes. (*Ask students what they are supposed to do, encouraging them to use the focus vocabulary by asking questions [e.g., "Are you allowed to dribble during this activity?"]*).

   Each time the defense tips a pass away and the ball touches the ground, a turnover occurs and players switch: Offense becomes defense, and vice versa.

Each player gets a pass and can shoot; if the ball touches the ground, it is considered a turnover. However, if a student rebounds the ball, he or she can shoot again. (*Take breaks when necessary to review the rules of the activity and reiterate the objectives.*)

Assessment Ideas

If each student passes the ball successfully without the ball touching the ground before shooting, she or he has met the objective.

If the defense stays within its hula hoop space and makes attempts to disrupt the offensive team's passing lanes, it has met the objective.

(*The teacher can use observation throughout the lesson to determine if students understand the vocabulary and concepts. The teacher can use a checklist to note which students have mastered the concepts. In addition, students can take a multi-media quiz in which they match vocabulary terms with pictures or actions.*)

Evaluation of Lesson

Even physical education lessons must have language objectives so that students understand the topic under discussion. For students new to basketball, the rules and ideas might seem very foreign and so need to be addressed with as much scaffolding as possible. Because sports activities often build on previous lessons, it's important to understand whether students have mastered the concepts before continuing with the next set of rules. This lesson shows that *all* teachers are language teachers to some extent.

Stop and Do

Use the checklist in Figure 7.7 to evaluate the lesson on zone defense. What is still missing? What was done well? Discuss your findings with the class.

Guidelines for Creating and Adapting Lessons

In addition to the suggestions throughout this text, two final guidelines can help teachers in their lesson planning. Figure 12.2 summarizes the following guidelines.

Guideline 1: Do Not Reinvent the Wheel

Sometimes teachers need to develop new lessons. In cases where lesson plans are not provided by administration or by commercially produced curricula, websites such as Thinkfinity (www.thinkfinity.org), the International Reading Association/National Council of Teachers of English ReadWriteThink (www.readwritethink.org), and Discovery Education

FIGURE 12.2 Guidelines for Creating and Adapting Lessons

Guideline	Explanation
Do not reinvent the wheel.	Find standards-based lessons from a variety of resources and adapt them for specific contexts.
Share.	Post lesson successes and failures to the Web or share with colleagues in other ways.

(school.discoveryeducation.com) have excellent standards-based lessons in all content areas. Teachers can also share lessons with colleagues and work off the ideas of peers. Using and/or adapting premade lessons can save time and provide effective ideas, as long as the lessons are focused on the needs of the specific students who will participate in them.

Guideline 2: Share

Teachers have the universal goal of student achievement. To meet this goal, information about lessons that are effective and successful (or that are ineffective and useless) should be shared with colleagues. Teachers can post lessons and comments online, at sites such as Lesson Plan Central (http://lessonplancentral.com/); use in-service time to present; or discuss lessons with peers at lunch, in meetings, or during less formal occasions. The chapter-opening scenario provided one such example.

Conclusion

The focus of this chapter was bringing the suggestions and guidelines presented in the rest of this text together in the form of lesson plans. No lesson is perfect, and few work for all students in a class. However, the ideas and lesson components that are outlined in this book are keys to achievement because they provide access for diverse students to the content and language of the lesson.

─────────────── • Extensions • ───────────────

For Reflection

1. *Review the text.* Review the chapters in this book. What did you learn that you didn't know? What else do you need to know in order to serve diverse learners better? Where can you find the information that you need?

2. *Think about sharing.* How can you share some of the ideas you have learned from this text? Who would benefit most from your sharing?

For Action

1. *Create a lesson.* Employing the guidelines, lists, and ideas most useful to you and your current or future students, develop a lesson starting with the standards for your area. Include all the essential components.

2. *Adapt a lesson.* Find a lesson on one of the lesson plan sites recommended in this chapter. Read the lesson carefully, noting where and how each important component is included (or left out). Revise the lesson, changing and adding as necessary to make the lesson more effective.

• Contents •

1. Answers to the common teacher behaviors questions in Figure 3.4.

2. The home-visit brochure mentioned in Chapter 3.

3. A reproducible copy of Figure 7.7.

4. A copy of Figure 7.7 without the criteria inserted in order to support the gradual release of responsibility in lesson planning for teachers.

Behavior	Might be misunderstood	Cultural group(s) that might misunderstand
Sitting with legs crossed with your shoe pointed or shoe sole turned toward your students.	X	Offensive to Arab/Muslim students.
Making the "okay" sign with your thumb and first finger.	X	Brazilians, Germans, Russians, and Greeks may consider this vulgar, and French students may think you are telling them "nothing."
Telling your class to take a "bathroom" break.	X	Any ELL may have trouble with this because they understand that you are telling them to bathe—use the word *toilet* if that's what you mean.
Shaking hands with a parent.	X	In many Arab and/or Muslim cultures, it is inappropriate to touch people of the opposite gender. Check if it is okay before you extend your hand and obligate the parent to respond.
Waving with your whole hand.	X	In many cultures, this means no.
Touching a student on the head, giving a high-five, or patting a student on the back.	X	Indian, Japanese, and other students; particulary Thai for head patting.
Signaling to a student by using one finger.	X	Most Asian students consider this rude and understand that you are angry.
Taking a student's photograph.	X	Many native cultures around the world believe that this steals the subject's soul.

Sources: Adapted from Axtell, R. (Ed.) (1993). *Do's and Taboos Around the World.* New York: John Wiley & Sons; Teacher Taboos, EnglishClub.com, available at http://www.englishclub.com/teaching-tips/teacher-taboos.htm

Making Your First Home Visit:
A Guide for Classroom Teachers

A home visit program can show that the teachers, principal, and school staff are willing to "go more than halfway" to involve all parents in their children's education. Home visits help teachers demonstrate their interest in students' families and understand their students better by seeing them in their home environment.

These visits should not replace parent-teacher conferences or be used to discuss children's progress. When done early, before any school problems can arise, they avoid putting any parents on the defensive and signal that teachers are eager to work with all parents. Teachers who have made home visits say that they build stronger relationships with parents and their children, and improve attendance and achievement.

Planning:

1. If possible, find someone who speaks the home language to schedule the visit. You can also talk with an older sibling who is fairly proficient in English or a district translator or home outreach liaison.

2. You can follow up with a brief written note, with the exact date and time of the scheduled visit, preferably written in the family language.

3. Schedule a home visit a week to 10 days in advance. Be sure to communicate the purpose of your visit and approximately how long the visit will last (30 to 45 minutes).

4. Ask another adult to accompany you to the first home visit, preferably someone who speaks the language of the family or a teacher of a sibling.

5. Learn a few words in the first language, even if it's only *hello* or *thank you*. This shows you care enough to make the effort and may help break the ice.

6. Learn the names of family members.

7. Be on time. While some cultures do not mind a late arrival, this is not true for all.

8. Some parents may be familiar and comfortable with home visits, having experienced them in their countries of origin. Some may not be familiar or comfortable with the idea.

9. If parents have difficulty scheduling a time to meet with you, be aware that some parents work two or more jobs in order to provide for their families.

10. Begin making home visits prior to the start date of school. This may help to lower the anxiety level of your ELL students and will help you become aware of your students' English language proficiency levels.

11. Dress appropriately.

12. To gain the most benefit from a family visit experience, consider the following:
    a. Parents and family members know the children very well.
    b. Personal sharing may be appropriate at times.
    c. Observing and listening can lead to insights, as can asking and answering questions.

Arrival:

1. Be aware of (look for) cultural expectations in the home. For example, in some cultures it is expected that people entering the home remove their shoes and walk about the home in socks or in special footwear provided by the host.
2. If you're nervous, remember: The family you are visiting is also probably nervous.
3. Remember that in many cultures, teachers are more highly respected than they are in the United States. It is a significant event to host a teacher at home.
4. Don't be afraid to look foolish or silly while trying to bridge the language gap. Try drawing pictures or acting out what you mean.
5. Make eye contact as appropriate for the cultural background of the host family.
6. Do not take notes or record your conversation with the family. This can be perceived as rude or threatening.
7. Conversation starters: (a) How are schools in _____ (country of origin)? (b) Please tell me about _____ (siblings or other family members). Can you talk about your home town? While you want to do more listening than talking, you can also talk about how school works in the United States, your classroom's curriculum, or teacher expectations, among other topics.
8. Do not talk about negative topics.
9. Understand that some parts of the home are "public spaces," while others may be private. After all, do you want strangers wandering around your bedroom?
10. Don't impose your own values on what you see in the home. Try to view the host home through the lens of those living there. What do they see? How do they view their home?

Departure:

1. Lay the groundwork for future visits and/or other types of contact.
2. Provide information so that parents can contact you, if desired.

Post Visit:

1. Take a few moments *away* from the student's home to write down a quick summary of the visit.

Source: Prepared by Gisela Ernst-Slavit and Michele Mason and used with permission.

MY LESSON TOPIC: _____

Lesson Component	Criteria	Element	Implementation
Objectives	• Tied to standards • Tied to content objectives • Based on student needs • Measurable • Presented to students	Content Language	
Connections	• Based on student interests, needs, backgrounds, abilities • Tie current topic and tasks to past lessons • Tie current topic to personal lives • Tie lesson tasks to personal lives • Assessed for relevancy, accuracy with students	Personal Academic Instructional	
Tasks	• Address both content and language objectives • Engaging • Authentic • Relevant • Multimodal • Explicit and implicit • Break language down as necessary • Culturally responsive • Learner-centered and/or -produced • Focus on process and product • Provide students with reasons to listen	Instructional groupings Audience Modes Task structure Time and pacing Scaffolding Resources/texts Teacher/student roles Procedural tools	
Assessment	• Ongoing • Authentic • Multiple measures • Provides practice and review • Transparent to all participants • Relevant, engaging, and interactive	Traditional Alternative Homework	

My Lesson Topic: _____

Lesson component	Element	Implementation
Objectives	Content	
	Language	
Connections	Personal	
	Academic	
	Instructional	
Tasks	Instructional groupings	
	Audience	
	Modes	
	Task structure	
	Time and pacing	
	Scaffolding	
	Resources/texts	
	Teacher/student roles	
	Procedural tools	
Assessment	Traditional	
	Alternative	
	Homework	

Source: Copyright Egbert and Ernst-Slavit. Reproducible for classroom use.

references

Allen, J. (2008). Family partnerships that count. *Educational Leadership, 66*(1), 22–27.

American Westward Expansion. (2006). Retrieved September 27, 2009, from http://www.americanwest.com/pages/wexpansi.htm

Anzaldúa, G. (1987). *Borderlands/La frontera: The new mestiza*. San Francisco, CA: Aunt Lute Books.

August, D., & Hakuta, K. (Eds.). (1998). *Educating language minority children*. Washington, DC: National Academy Press.

Bailey, A.L. (Ed.). (2006). *The language demands of school: Putting academic English to the test*. Princeton, NJ: Yale University Press.

Bartolomé, L.I. (1998). *The misteaching of academic discourses*. Boulder, CO: Westview Press.

Biancarosa, G., & Snow, C. (2006). *Reading Next— A vision for action and research in middle and high school literacy* (2nd ed.). Washington, DC: Alliance for Excellence Education.

Bloome, D., & Paul, P. V. (2006). The issue (introduction). *Theory into Practice, 45*(4), 293–295.

Boswell, L. A., Copley, J., Gyles, R., Jackson, A. L., Manfre, E. Gillespie, J. G., Reynosa, M. A., Shaw, J., Stiff, L., & Thompson, C. (2001). *Math central*. Boston, MA: Houghton Mifflin.

Brown, C. L. (2002). Supporting English language learners in content-reading. *Reading Improvement, 44*(1), 32–39.

Brown, C. L. (2007). Strategies for making social studies texts more comprehensible for English-language learners. *The Social Studies, 98*(5), 185–188.

Bruner, J. S. (1961). The act of discovery. *Harvard Educational Review, 31*(1), 21–32.

Bulgren, J. A., Lenz, B. K., Deshler, D. D., & Schumaker, J. B. (1995).The Cue-Do-Review Sequence. Available at http://www.onlineacademy.org/modules/a304/lesson/lesson_2/xpages/a304c2_40700.html

Burke, K. (1994). *How to assess authentic learning*. Arlington Heights, IL: IRI/Skylight Training and Publishing, Inc.

Carle, E. (1969). *The very hungry caterpillar*. New York: Collins Publishers.

Carrasquillo, A. L., & Rodríguez, V. (2005). Integrating language and science learning. In P. Richard-Amato & M. A. Snow (Eds.), *Academic success for English language learners: Strategies for K–12 mainstream teachers* (pp. 436–454). White Plains, NY: Longman, Pearson.

Center for Research on Education, Diversity & Excellence (CREDE). (1998). *Developing language proficiency and connecting to students' lives: Two standards for effective teaching*. Occasional Reports. Santa Cruz, CA: University of California.

Chamot, A. U., & O'Malley, J. M. (1994). *The CALLA handbook: Implementing the cognitive academic language learning approach*. New York: Longman.

Chamot, A. U., & O'Malley, J. M. (1996). The cognitive academic language learning approach: A model for linguistically diverse classrooms. *The Elementary School Journal, 96*(3), 259–273.

Chao, C. (2008). [[Title of Chao's work.]]In J. Egbert & E. Hanson-Smith (Eds). *CALL environments: Research, practice, and critical issues* (pp. 000–000). Alexandria, VA: TESOL, Inc.

Chapman, C., & King, R. (2005). *Differentiated assessment strategies: One tool doesn't fit all*. Thousand Oaks, CA: Corwin Press.

Cho, S., & Reich, G. A. (2008). New immigrants, new challenges: High school social studies teachers and English language learner instruction. *The Social Studies, 99*(6), 235–242.

Christen, W., & Murphy, T. (1991). Increasing comprehension by activating prior knowledge. *ERIC Digest*. Available at www.ericdigests.org/pre-9219/prior.htm

Clifford, R. (2008). Our biggest challenge. *Foreign Language Annals, 41*(2), 197.

Cloud, N., Genesee, F., & Hamayan, E. (2000). *Dual language instruction: A handbook for enriched education*. Boston: Heinle & Heinle.

Crawford, J., & Krashen, S. (2007). *English learners in American classrooms: 101 questions, 101 answers*. New York: Scholastic.

Csikszentmihalyi, M. (1990). Literacy and intrinsic motivation. *Daedalus, 119*, 115–140.

Cummins, J. (1981). The role of primary language development in promoting educational success for language minority students. In California State Department of Education, *Schooling and language minority students: A theoretical framework* (pp. 3–49). Los Angeles: California State University,

Los Angeles, Evaluation, Dissemination, and Assessment Center.

Cummins, J. (1984). *Bilingualism and special education: Issues in assessment and pedagogy.* Clevedon, England: Multilingual Matters.

Cummins, J. (2005). Teaching the language of academic success: A framework for school-based language policies. In California State Department of Education, *Schooling and language minority students: A theoretico-practical framework* (3rd ed., pp. 3–32). Los Angeles: California State University Evaluation, Dissemination, and Assessment Center

Dale, T. C., & Cuevas, G. J. (1992). Integrating mathematics and language learning. In P. Richard-Amato & A. Snow (Eds.), *The multicultural classroom: Readings for content area teachers.* New York: Addison-Wesley.

Dhority, L., & Jensen, E. (1998). *Joyful fluency: Brain-compatible second language acquisition.* Thousand Oaks, CA: Corwin/Sage.

Echevarria, J., & Graves, A. (2007). *Sheltered content instruction: Teaching English language learners with diverse abilities* (3rd ed.). Boston, MA: Pearson Allyn and Bacon.

Echevarria, J., Vogt, M., & Short, D. (2008). *Making content comprehensible for English learners.* Boston, MA: Pearson/Allyn & Bacon.

Edelsky, C. (1990). *With literacy and justice for all: Rethinking the social in language and education.* London: The Falmer Press.

Edelsky, C., Hudelson, S., Altwerger, B., Flores, B., Barkin, F., Jilbert, K. (1983). Semilingualism and language deficit. *Applied Linguistics, 4*(1), 1–22.

Egbert, J. (2007). Asking useful questions: Goals, engagement, and differentiation in technology-enhanced language learning. *Teaching English with Technology, 7*(1), n.p. Available at http://www.iatefl.org.pl/call/j_article27.htm

Egbert, J., & Salsbury, T. (in press). Out of complacency and into action: An exploration of professional development experiences in school/home literacy engagement. *Teaching Education.*

Epstein, J., Sanders, M., Simon, B., Salinas, K., Jansorn, N., & Van Voorhis, F. (2002). *School, family, and community partnerships: Your handbook for action* (2nd ed.). Thousand Oaks, CA: Corwin Press.

Epstein, J., Simon, B., & Salinas, K. (1997). Involving parents in homework in the middle grades. *Phi Delta Kappa Research Bulletin.*

Epstein, J., & Van Voorhis, F. (2001). More than minutes: Teachers' roles in designing homework. *Educational Psychologist, 36,* 181–194.

Ernst-Slavit, G., Mason, M. R., & Wenger, K. J. (April 2009). Academic language, tricky words, and everyday language: Implications for teaching English language learners. Paper presented at the American Educational Research Association (AERA) annual conference, San Diego, CA.

Ernst-Slavit, G., & Mulhern, M. (2003, September/October). Bilingual books: Promoting literacy and biliteracy in the second-language and mainstream classroom. *Reading Online, 7*(2). Available at http://www.readingonline.org/articles/art_index.asp?HREF=ernst-slavit/index.html

Ernst-Slavit, G., & Slavit, D. (2007). Educational reform, mathematics, and diverse learners: Meeting the needs of all students. *Multicultural Education, 14*(4), 20–27.

Fathman, A. K., Quinn, M. E., & Kessler, C. (1992*). Teaching science to English learners, Grades 4–8.* NCBE Program Information Guide Series, Number 11. Washington, DC: National Clearinghouse for Bilingual Education.

Fisher, D., & Frey, N. (2008). *Improving adolescent literacy: Content area strategies at work* (2nd ed.). Upper Saddle River, NJ: Pearson/Merrill.

Fisher, D., Rothenberg, C., & Frey, N. (2007). *Language learners in the English classroom.* Urbana, IL: National Council of Teachers of English.

Gallavan, N. P., & Kottler, E. (2007). Eight types of graphic organizers for empowering social studies students and teachers. *The Social Studies, 98*(3), 117–123.

Gee, J. P. (1990). *Sociolinguistics and literacies: Ideology in discourses.* London: Falmer Press.

Gee, J. P. (1992). Reading. *Journal of Urban and Cultural Studies, 2*(2), 65–77.

Gersten, T., Baker, S. K., Shanahan, T., Linan-Thompson, S., Collins, P., & Scarcella, R. (2007). *Effective literacy and English language instruction for English learners in the elementary grades: A practice guide* (NCEE 2007-4011). Washington, DC: National Center for Education Evaluation and Regional Assistance, Institute of Education Sciences, U.S. Department of Education. Available at http://ies.ed.gov/ncee/wwc/pdf/practiceguides/20074011.pdf

Gottlieb, M. (2006). *Assessing English language learners: Bridges from language proficiency to academic achievement.* Thousand Oaks, CA: Corwin Press.

Gottlieb, M. (2007). Assessing the language of mathematics. In S. Irujo & A. Ragan, *Academic language notebook: The language of math assessment handbook.* Haverhill, MA: Course Crafters Publishing.

Gottlieb, M., Cranley, M. E., & Oliver, A. R. (2007). *The CAN DO Descriptors for WIDA's levels of English language proficiency.* Madison, WI: WIDA Consortium. Available at http://www.wida.us/standards/elp.aspx.

Gottlieb, M., Katz, A., & Ernst-Slavit, G. (2009). *Paper to practice: Using the TESOL English language proficiency standards in PreK–12 Classrooms.* Alexandria, VA: Teachers of English to Speakers of Other Languages.

Graham, S., & Perin, D. (2007). *Writing next: Effective strategies to improve writing of adolescents in middle and high schools: A report to Carnegie Corporation of New York.* Washington, DC: Alliance for Excellent Education.

Guthrie, J. T., Schafer, W. D., & Huang, C. (2001). Benefits of opportunity to read and balanced reading instruction for reading achievement and engagement: A policy analysis of state NAEP in Maryland. *Journal of Educational Research, 94*(3), 145–162.

Halliday, M. A. K. (1993). Towards a language-based theory of learning. *Linguistics and Education 5*(2), 93–116.

Hargett, G. (1998). Assessment in ESL and bilingual education: A hot topics paper. NWREL's Comprehensive Center, Region X. Available at http://www.nwrac.org/pub/hot/assessment.html

Ioannou-Georgiou, S., & Pavlou, P. (2003). *Assessing young learners.* New York, NY: Oxford University Press.

Irujo, S. (2007, March/April). Teaching math to English language learners: Can research help? *The ELL Outlook.* Available at http://www.coursecrafters.com/ELL-Outlook/2007/mar_apr/ELLOutlookITIArticle1.htm

Kern, R. (2000). *Literacy and language teaching.* New York: Oxford University Press.

Kinsella, K. (1997). Moving from comprehensible input to "learning to learn" in content-based instruction. In M. A. Snow & D. B. Brinton (Eds.), *The content-based classroom: Perspectives on integrating language and content* (pp. 46–68). White Plains, NY: Longman.

Krashen, S. (1981). *Second language acquisition and second language learning.* Oxford, UK: Pergamon Press.

Kreeft-Peyton, J. (2000). *Dialogue journals: Interactive writing to develop language and literacy.* CAELA.

Available at http://www.cal.org/caela/esl_resources/digests/Dialogue_Journals.html

Larson, E. Boswell, L. A., Kanold, T. D., and Stiff, L. (2007). *Mathematics concepts and skills, course 2.* Boston, MA: McDougal Littell.

Lee, O., & Fradd, S. H. (1998). Science for all, including students from non-English-speaking-language backgrounds. *Educational Researcher, 27*(4), 12–21.

Lemke, J. (1990). *Talking science: Language, learning, and values.* Norwood, NJ: Ablex.

Lewis, B. (2008a). Activating prior knowledge. Available at http://k6educators.about.com/od/education glossary/g/gactiveprknow.htm

Lewis, B. (2008b). Lesson plan step #2—Anticipatory sets. Available at k6educators.about.com/od/lessonplanheadquarters/g/anticipatoryset.htm

Long, M. (2001). Focus on form: A design feature in language teaching methodology. In C. Candlin, C. Candlin, & N. Mercer (Eds.), *English language teaching in its social context* (ch. 10, pp. 000–000). London: Taylor and Francis.

MacSwan, J., & Rolstad, K. (2003). Linguistic diversity, schooling, and social class: Rethinking our conception of language proficiency in language minority education. In C. B. Paulston & R. Tucker (Eds.), *Sociolinguistics: The essential readings* (pp. 329–340). Oxford: Blackwell.

MacSwan, J., & Rolstad, K. (2006). How language tests mislead us about children's abilities: Implications for special education placements. *Teachers College Record, 108*(11), 2304–2328.

Mansor, N. (2007, March). Collaborative learning via email discussion: Strategies for ESL writing classroom. *The Internet TESL Journal, 13*(3).

Martin, J. R. (2002). Writing history: Construing time and value in discourses of the past. In M. J. Schleppegrell & M. Cecilia Colombi (Eds.), *Developing advanced literacy in first and second languages: Meaning with power* (pp. 87–118). Mahwah, NJ: Lawrence Erlbaum.

Mastropieri, M. A., & Scruggs, T. E. (1998). Enhancing school success with mnemonic strategies. *Intervention in School and Clinic, 33,* 201–208.

National Center for History in the Schools. (2005). Overview of K–4 content standards. Available at http://www.sscnet.ucla.edu/nchs/standards/standardsk-4.html

National Council for the Social Studies. (n.d.). *Curriculum standards for social studies:*

I. Introduction. Retrieved October 10, 2009, from http://www.socialstudies.org/standards/

McKenzie, J. (1998, September). Grazing the Net: Raising a generation of free range students. *Phi Delta Kappan, 80*(1), 26–31. Online version available at http://fno.org/text/grazing.html

McKenzie, J. (1997). A questioning toolkit. *From Now On, 7*(3). Available at http://www.fno.org/nov97/toolkit.html

McLaughlin, B., & McLeod, B. (1966, June). *Educating all our students: Improving education for children from culturally and linguistically diverse backgrounds* (Vol. 1). Santa Cruz, CA, and Washington, DC: National Center for Research on Cultural Diversity and Second Language Learning.

Meltzer, J., & Hamann, E. (2004). *Meeting the literacy development needs of adolescent English language learners through content area learning. Part one: Focus on motivation and engagement.* Providence, RI: The Brown University Education Alliance/Northeast and Islands Regional Education Laboratory.

Moje, E. B., Ciechanowski, K. M., Kramer, K., Ellis, L., Carrillo, R., & Collazo, T. (2004). Working toward third space in content area literacy: An examination of everyday funds of knowledge and discourse. *Reading Research Quarterly, 39*(1), 38–70.

Moll, L., Amanti, C., Neff, D., &Gonzalez, N. (2001). Funds of knowledge for teaching: Using a qualitative approach to connect homes and classrooms. *Theory Into Practice, 31*(2), 132–141.

Monzó, L. D., & Rueda, R. S. (2003). Shaping education through diverse funds of knowledge: A look at one Latina paraeducator's lived experiences, beliefs, and teaching practice. *Anthropology & Education Quarterly, 34*(1), 72–95.

Morrison, T. (1987). *Beloved.* New York: Alfred Knopf.

Mounin, G. (1963). *Les problèmes théoretiques de la traduction.* Paris: Gallimard.

Murray, B. (1999). Connecting course content with students' lives. *The Monitor Online, 30*(11). Available at www.apa.org/monitor/dec99/ed2.html

National Center for History in the Schools. (2005). *Overview of K–4 content standards.* Available at http://www.sscnet.ucla.edu/nchs/standards/standardsk-4.html

National Council of Teachers of English/International Reading Association Standards. (2006). *Standards for the English language arts.* Available at http://www.ncte.org/standards

National Council of Teachers of Mathematics. (1989). *Curriculum and evaluation standards for school mathematics.* Reston, VA: Author.

National Council of Teachers of Mathematics. (1991). *Professional standards for teaching mathematics.* Reston, VA: Author.

National Research Council. (1996). *National science education standards.* Washington, DC: National Academy Press.

Nieto, S. (2000). *Affirming diversity: The sociopolitical context of multicultural education* (3rd ed.). New York: Longman.

North Central Regional Education Laboratory. (1995). *Critical issue: Building on prior knowledge and meaningful student context/cultures.* Available at http://www.ncrel.org/sdrs/areas/issues/students/learning/lr100.htm

Norton, B. (1997). Language, identity, and the ownership of English. *TESOL Quarterly 31*(3), 409–430.

Oh, J. (2005). Connecting learning with students' interests and daily lives with project assignment: "It is my project." *Proceedings of the 2005 American Society for Engineering Education Annual Conference and Exposition.* Available at www.aaee.com.au/conferences/papers/2005/Paper/Paper253.pdf

O'Loughlin, J., & Haynes, J. (1998–2004).*Organizing and assessing in the content area class.* Available from www.everythingESL.net

O'Malley, M., & Pierce, L. (1996). *Authentic assessment for English language learners: Practical approaches for teachers.* White Plains, NY: Addison-Wesley/Pearson.

Paulsen, G. (1999). *Hatchet.* New York: Aladdin Paperbacks.

Peregoy, S., & Boyle, O. (2004). *Reading, writing and learning in ESL: A resource book for K–12 teachers* (4th ed.). Boston, MA: Pearson/Allyn & Bacon.

Perez, B. (2004). *Sociocultural contexts of language and literacy.* Mahwah, NJ: Lawrence Erlbaum.

Pike, K. L. (1982). *Linguistic concepts: An introduction to Tagmemics.* Lincoln, NE: University of Nebraska Press.

Prensky, M. (2007). New issues, new answers: Changing paradigms. *Educational Technology, 47*(4), 64.

Robertson, K. (2007). Connect students' background knowledge to content in the ELL classroom. Available at http://www.colorincolorado.org/article/20827

Roseberry, A., McIntyre, E., & Gonzalez, N. (2001). Connecting students' cultures to instruction. In

E. McIntyre, A. Roseberry, & N. Gonzalez (Eds.), *Classroom diversity: Connecting curriculum to students' lives*. Portsmouth, NH: Heinemann.

Rowe, M. (1972). *Wait-time and rewards as instructional variables, their influence in language, logic, and fate control*. Paper presented at the National Association for Research in Science Teaching, Chicago, IL, ED 061 103.

Salinas, C., Fránquiz, M. E., & Guberman, S. (2006). Introducing historical thinking to second language learners: Exploring what students know and what they want to know. *The Social Studies, 97*(5), 203–207.

Salinas, C., Fránquiz, M. E., & Reidel, M. (2008). Teaching world geography to late-arrival immigrant students: Highlighting practice and content. *The Social Studies, 99*(2), 71–76.

Saville-Troike, M. (1978). *A guide to culture in the classroom*. Rosslyn, VA: National Clearinghouse for Bilingual Education.

Scarcella, R. (2003). *Accelerating academic English: A focus on English language learners*. Oakland, CA: Regents of the University of California.

Scarcella, R., & Rumberger, R. W. (2000, Summer). Academic English key to long term success in school. *University of California Linguistic Minority Research Institute Newsletter, 9*(4), 1–2. Available from the UC LMRI website at http://lmri.ucsb.edu/publications/newsletters/index.php

Schleppegrell, M. J. (2004). *The language of schooling: A functional linguistics perspective*. Mahwah, NJ: Lawrence Erlbaum.

Schleppegrell, M. J. (2005). *Helping content area teachers work with academic language: Promoting English language learners' literacy in history*. Final Report for Individual Research Grant Award #03-03CY-061G-D. Davis, CA: University of California Linguistic Minority Research Institute. Retrieved April 14, 2008, from http://www.lmri .ucsb.edu/research/lmri-grants/database/index .php?title=&pi=Schleppegrell&keyword=&sort=yearDesc&Submit=Search

Schleppegrell, M., & Achugar, M. (2003). Learning language and learning history: A functional linguistics approach. *TESOL Journal, 12*(2), 21–27.

Simich-Dudgeon, C., & Egbert, J. (2000). Science as a second language. Verbal interactive strategies help English language learners develop academic vocabulary. *The Science Teacher, 67*(3), 28–32.

Skemp, R. R. (1987). *The psychology of learning mathematics*. Hillsdale, NJ: Lawrence Erlbaum.

Slavit, D., & Ernst-Slavit, G. (2007). Teaching mathematics and English to English language learners simultaneously. *Middle School Journal, 39*(2), 4–11.

Smith, M. K. (2003). Learning theory. *The Encyclopedia of Informal Education*. Available at http://www.infed .org/biblio/b-learn.htm

Snow, C. (2005). From literacy to learning: Catherine Snow on vocabulary, comprehension, and the achievement gap. *Harvard Education Letter,* July/August. Available at http://www.edletter.org/current/snow.shtml

Spencer, B., & Guillaume, A. (2009). *35 strategies for developing content area vocabulary*. Boston, MA: Pearson/Allyn & Bacon.

Stoddart, T., Pinal, A., Latzke, M., & Canaday, D. (2002). Integrating inquiry science and language development for English language learners. *Journal of Research in Science Teaching, 39*(8), 664–687.

Strangman, N., & Hall, T. (2004). Background knowledge. Wakefield, MA: National Center on Accessing the General Curriculum. Available at http://www.cast.org/publications/ncac/ncac_backknowledge.html

Szpara, M.Y., & Ahmad, I. (2007). Supporting English-language learners in social studies class: Results from a study of high school teachers. *The Social Studies, 98*(5), 189–195.

Taboada, A., & Guthrie, J. (2006). Contributions of student questioning and prior knowledge to construction of knowledge from reading information text. *Journal of Literacy Research, 38*(1), 1–35.

Teachers of English to Speakers of Other Languages, Inc. (2006). *PreK–12 English language proficiency standards*. Alexandria, VA: Author.

The Writing Center. (2007). University of North Carolina. Available at http://www.unc.edu/depts/wcweb/handouts/sciences.html

Van Voorhis, F. (2001). Interactive science homework: An experiment in home and school connections. *NASSP Bulletin, 85,* 20–32.

Vygotsky, L. (1986). *Thought and language*. Boston: MIT Press.

Wiggins, G., & McTighe, J. (1998). *Understanding by design*. Upper Saddle River, NJ: Prentice Hall/Pearson.

Wong-Fillmore, L. & Snow, C. (2000). *What teachers need to know about language*. Washington, D.C. Clearinghouse on Languages and Linguistics. Available at http://faculty.tamu-commerce.edu/jthompson/Resources/FillmoreSnow2000.pdf

Wrigley, P. (2001). *The help! kit: A resource guide for secondary teachers of migrant English language learners.* Oneonta, NY: Eastern Stream Center on Resources and Training (ESCORT), State University of New York.

Young, T. A. (1990). The dialogue journal: Empowering ESL students. *Writing Notebook: Creative Word Processing in the Classroom, 8*(1), 16–17.

Ziori, E., & Dienes, Z. (2008). How does prior knowledge affect implicit and explicit concept learning? *Quarterly Journal of Experimental Psychology, 61*(4), 601–624.

Zwiers, J. (2008). *Building academic language: Essential practices for content classrooms.* San Francisco, CA: Jossey-Bass.

Achugar, M., 169
Ahmad, I., 171
Amanti, C., 40, 172
Anzaldúa, G., 161
August, D., 32
Axtell, R., 194

Bailey, A. L., 12, 167
Bartolomé, L. I., 11, 15
Biancarosa, G., 146
Bloome, D., 140
Boyle, O., 39, 46, 48, 82
Brophy, J., 80
Brown, C. L., 164, 169
Bruner, J., 80
Bulgren, J. A., 73
Burke, K., 91

Carbone, K., 184
Carrasquillo, A. L., 108
Chamot, A. U., 173
Chao, C., 92
Chapman, C., 100
Cho, S., 165, 167
Christen, W., 68
Clifford, R., 68
Cloud, N., 20
Crawford, J., 55
Csikszentmihalyi, M., 80
Cuevas, G.J., 128
Cummins, J., 6, 11, 12, 13, 14, 15, 16

Dale, T. C., 128
Deshler, D. D., 73
DeVito, J. A., 169
Dhority, L., 80
Dienes, Z., 68
Dwyer, E., 165

Echevarria, J., 39, 58, 68, 100, 173
Edelsky, C., 15
Egbert, J., 80, 81, 96, 98, 114, 198
Epstein, J., 96
Ernst-Slavit, G., 4, 10, 32, 33, 34,
    109, 123, 124, 126, 129, 133,
    196, 198

Fathman, A. K., 131
Fisher, D., 147, 149
Fradd, S. H., 107
Fránquiz, M. E., 161, 162
Frey, N., 147, 149

Gallavan, N. P., 175
Gee, J. P., 11, 15
Genesee, F., 20
Gonzalez, N., 40
Gottlieb, M., 4, 10, 11, 109, 124
Graham, S., 149
Graves, A., 173
Guerrero, L. K., 169
Guthrie, J. T., 68, 80

Hakuta, K., 32
Hall, T., 72, 84
Halliday, M. A. K., 4
Hamman, E., 80, 84
Hamayan, E., 20
Hecht, M. L., 169
Huang, C., 80
Hymes, D., 30

Ioannou-Georgiou, S., 91
Irujo, S., 130

Jensen, E., 80

Katz, A., 4, 10, 109
Kern, R., 20
Kessler, C., 131
King, R., 100
Kotler, E., 175
Krashen, S., 55, 131
Kreeft-Peyton, J., 43

Latzke, M., 109
Lee, O., 107
Lemke, J., 108, 126
Lenz, B. K., 73
Lewis, B., 68, 74
Long, M., 55
Lopez, J., 40

Mason, M. R., 129, 166, 196
Mastropieri, M. A., 152
McIntyre, E., 40, 52
McKenzie, J., 84
McLaughlin, B., 123
McLeod, B., 123
McSwan, J., 15
McTighe, J., 91
Meltzer, J., 80, 84
Moll, L., 40, 172
Monzó, L. D., 172

Mounin, G., 166
Mulhern, M., 33, 34
Murphy, T., 68
Murray, B., 85

Neff, D., 40, 172
Nieto, S., 171
Norton, B., 32

Oh, J., 85
O'Malley, J. M., 173
O'Malley, M., 91

Paul, P. V., 140
Pavlou, P., 91
Peregoy, S., 39, 46, 48, 82
Perez, B., 68
Perin, D., 149
Peyton, J., 43
Pierce, L., 91
Pike, K. L., 28
Pinal, A., 109
Prensky, M., 84

Quinn, M. E., 131

Reich, G. A., 165, 167
Reidel, M., 161, 162
Robertson, K., 50
Rodriguez, V., 108
Rolstad, K., 15
Roseberry, A., 40
Rothenberg, C., 147, 149
Rueda, R. S., 172
Rumberger, R., 12

Salinas, C., 161, 162
Salinas, K., 96
Salsbury, T., 96, 98
Saville-Troike, M., 39, 44, 46, 49, 50, 51, 52, 53
Scarcella, R., 8, 12, 15, 110
Schleppegrell, M. J., 12, 164, 169, 170, 171
Scruggs, T. E., 152
Shafer, W. D., 80
Short, D., 39, 58, 68, 100, 168, 173
Simich-Dudgeon, C., 114
Simon, B., 96
Skemp, R. R., 124
Slavit, D., 32, 123, 124, 126, 133
Smith, M. K., 81
Snow, C., 126, 146, 150

Staton, J., 43
Stoddart, T., 109
Strangman, N., 72
Szpara, M. Y., 171

Taboada, A., 68
Tomlinson, C., 84

VanVoorhis, F., 96
Vogt, M., 39, 58, 68, 100, 173
Vygotsky, L., 80

Wiggins, G., 91
Wong-Fillmore, L., 126
Wrigley, P., 173

Young, T. A., 43

Ziori, E., 68
Zwiers, J., 108, 109, 113, 128, 173, 174

subject index

Academic background. *See* Educational background
Academic classroom discussions, 173
Academic connections, 69, 71, 185, 187
Academic English, 12
Academic language, 4, 8–11
  dimensions of, 9
  discourse, 8, 9, 11
  emphasis on, 142
  grammatical construction, 8, 9
  social *versus*, 11–12, 13
  vocabulary, 8, 9
Accuracy, in language, 13
Acquisition, of English, 24
Activities, objectives *versus*, 56
Additive bilingualism, 142
Adolescent literacy, improving, 145
Alternative assessment, 93
  rubrics, 95
  student roles in, 95–96
  traditional *versus*, 94
American Council of Teachers of Foreign Languages (ACTFL), 28
Anticipatory sets, for connections, 75
Articles, grammatical, 155
Aspects, of social language, 6–8
Assessment, 182
  alternative, 93
  definition of, 91
  formal, 41
  formative, 41
  grades and, 99–100
  guidelines for, 92, 99–100
  homework and, 96, 98–99
  informal, 41, 45
  of language needs, 45
  of lessons, 100–102
  purposes of, 92–94
  scenarios about, 90
  of student process and product, 94–96
  of student strengths and needs, 38–52
  summative, 41
  traditional classroom, 92
  traditional *versus* alternative, 94
  transparency, 99
  understanding, 91–94
Autonomy, 87
Auxiliaries, 155

Background knowledge
  social studies and, 173
  techniques for building, 72–74
Backgrounds
  content, 46–47
  cultural, 48–51

gathering information on, 43–45
student, 55–56, 67–68
Basic interpersonal communication skills (BICS), 2, 12–15, 44
  critiques of, 15–16
  Cummin's quadrants, 14
  language of school and, 16–17
Behaviors, teacher, 49, 193–94
Bilingual books, 33
  strategies for use of, 34
Bilingual buddies, 33
Bridging English language proficiency, 27

CAN DO descriptors, 28, 44
  for reading and writing, 29
Cause and effect technique, 116–17
  vocabulary, 117
Cognates, 133–34, 151
  social studies and, 176, 177
  vocabulary instruction and, 151
Cognitive Academic Language Learning Approach (CALLA), 173
Cognitive academic language proficiency (CALP), 2, 12–15, 44
  critiques of, 15–16
  language of school and, 16–17
Cognitive demands, 13
Cognitive load, reducing, 175–76
Collaborative groups, 172
Collaborative writing, 148
Common European Framework of Reference for Languages: Learning, Teaching, Assessment, 28
Communication
  anticipatory sets for, 75
  barriers to, 50
Communicative competence, 28–35
  definition of, 30
  discourse, 31
  elements of, 30–32
  grammatical, 30
  linguistic, 30
  sociolinguistic, 31
  strategic, 31, 32
Compare and contrast technique, 114–15
  vocabulary, 116
Complex noun phrases, 113
Connections
  academic, 68, 71, 85, 185
  anticipatory sets for, 75
  content, 68
  guidelines for making, 76
  initial, 181–82
  instructional, 68
  integrating, 74–75

pedagogical, 68, 85
personal, 68–70, 185, 187
principles for, 86
specific to common, 77–78
transferring to students' lives, 76
types of, 69
understanding, 68–71
Content
  integration of, 62–63
  social studies, 161
Content backgrounds, discovering, 46–47
Content connection, 68
Content knowledge, comprehension techniques, 48
Content objectives, 56–57
  language objectives *versus,* 58
Content-specific language, 12
Conversations, as data collection technique, 44
Cooperative learning, 134
Core-Plus Mathematics, 16
Cue-Do-Review, 72
Cultural background, 48–51
Cultural facts, integrating, 86
Cultural knowledge, 49
Culturally relevant literacy practices, 141–42
Culture
  connections with, 76
  definition of, 40
  native, 32–33

Decontextualization, 62
Decontextualized language, 15
Developing English language proficiency, 26
Dialog journals, 43, 44, 50, 51
Differentiation, 84
Direct instruction, 72
Discourse, 8, 9, 11
  competencies, 31
  examples, across content areas, 11
  language arts, 156–57
  language objectives, 59
  mathematics, 128–30
  science, 113–14
  social studies, 169–71
Domains, language, 21–22

Economics, lesson, 186–88
Education, science, 107–8
Educational background
  of students, 39–41
  understanding, 45–46
Elementary grades, literacy practices for ELLs in, 141–49
Emerging English language proficiency, 25–26

Engagement, 80–81
English
  academic, 12
  acquisition of, 24
  social, 4
English as a second language (ESL), 3, 43
  scenarios about, 55
English language learners (ELL), 3, 7, 19, 80
  asking questions, 174
  challenges in language arts, 137–38
  challenges in mathematics, 121–22, 130–31
  challenges in science, 106–7, 109, 110
  challenges in social studies, 160
  example of, 38–39
  grades and, 99
  grammatical features for, 154
  homework and, 96, 98
  literacy practices for, 141–49
  native language and, 32
  organizational and study skills for, 134–35
  problematic mathematics vocabulary for, 127
  reading instruction for, 146–47
  scenario about, 54–55
  social studies and, 160
  social studies textbooks and, 169–70
  writing instruction for, 147–49
English language proficiency (ELP), 22–23
  bridging, 27
  developing, 26
  emerging, 25–26
  expanding, 27
  levels, 23–27
  stages of, 25–27
  standards, 24
  starting, 25
Evaluation, 91
Expanding English language proficiency, 27

Far transfer, 68
Field trips, 72–73
Formal assessment, 41
Formative assessment, 41
Funds of knowledge, 40, 172

General academic vocabulary, 9
Genres, writing, 170–71
  history and geography, 170, 171
Goals, objectives *versus*, 56
Grades, 99–100
Grammar, 9
  examples of, by content area, 10
  language objectives, 59
  science, 113
Grammatical competencies, 30, 31
Grammatical constructions, 8
Grammatical features
  of language arts, 153–54
  of mathematics, 128
  of social studies, 167–68

Grammatical metaphor, 113
Graphic organizers, 73, 131
  social studies, 175
Graphs, creating, 130
Greek roots, 117–18, 119
A Guide to Culture in the Classroom
  (Saville-Troike), 50

Hands-on experience, 72–73
Heterogeneous groups, 82
Home/school connections, 50
Home visit, guide for teachers, 195–96
Homework, 96, 98–99
  interactive assignments, 96, 98
Homogeneous groups, 82
Hybrid test questions, 94, 95

Idiomatic expressions/idioms, 152, 154, 155
Inclusive teaching, 40
Individualized education plan (IEP), 46
Informal assessment, 41, 45
Instructional connections, 68
Instructional conversations, 174
Instructional groupings, 82
Instructional strategies, 63
Instructional videos, 72
Interactive homework, 96, 98
Interactive journals, 138
Interest Inventory WebQuest, 47, 48
International Reading Association (IRA),
  139, 190
Interviews, as assessment, 93

Journals
  as assessment, 93
  dialog, 43, 44, 50, 51
  interactive, 138
  personal vocabulary, 150

Key word method, 151
Knowledge
  background, 72–74
  content, 46–47
  cultural, 48–49
  funds of, 40, 172
  range of, 13
KWL chart, 47
KWLS chart, 47, 48, 51

Language
  about, 5
  academic, 4, 8–11
  breaking down, 63
  content-specific, 12
  decontextualized, 15
  functions, 13, 58, 109, 154
  integration of, 62–63

  of language arts, 137–58
  of mathematics, 121–36
  native, 32–33
  needs, determining, 59
  perspectives on, 142
  proficiencies, 4
  of school, 2–17
  of science, 106–20
  social, 4, 6–8
  of social studies, 159–78
  social *versus* academic, 11–12
  through, 5
  types of learning, 5
  use of, 5
Language arts
  anticipatory sets for, 75
  challenges for ELL in, 137–38
  discourse, 11, 156–57
  domains, 139–40
  grammatical features of, 10, 152–54
  language functions, 154
  language of, 137–58
  literacy demands, 139–40
  literacy practices for ELLs, 141–49
  multiple literacies, 140
  sentence starters for conversations, 155–56
  vocabulary, 10, 150–52, 153
  writing instruction, 147–49
Language Assessment Scales (LAS), 43
Language domains, 13, 21–22
  listening, 21
  productive, 21
  reading, 21
  receptive, 21
  speaking, 22
  writing, 22
Language instruction, techniques, 63
Language learning strategies, 59
Language needs, assessment of, 45
Language objectives, 57–60
  constructing, 58–59
  content objectives *versus*, 58
  development process, 61
  features of, 60
  guidelines for meeting, 64
  sample, 60
  teaching, 62–64
Language proficiency, 19–35
  defined, 20–21
  native, 32
Language-rich environment, 141
Latin roots, 117–18, 119
Learning, social studies strategies, 171–76
Learning objectives, 56
Learning targets, 180–81
Lesson-component checklist, 101
Lessons
  adapting, 182, 184–89
  assessing, 100–102
  components, 97

creating new, 180–82
economics, example, 186–88
examples, 96, 98–99, 180–90
guidelines for creating and adapting, 190–91
measurement, example, 184–86
multisensory, 130
physical education, 189–90
Limited English proficient (LEP), 3
Limited English speaker (LES), 3
Linguistic competencies, 30
Linguistic features
in early stages, 24
in later stages, 24
Listening, 21
stages in ELP, 25–27
Literacy
culturally relevant practices, 141–42
demands, meeting, 139–40
improving adolescent, 145
improving elementary, 141–42
meaningful, 141
prereading strategies, 142

Mathematics
anticipatory sets for, 75
applying skills in real world, 123
atmosphere, creating, 135
challenges for ELL in, 121–22, 129–30
cognates in, 133–34
cooperative learning, 134
discourse, 128–30
discourse across, 11
grammatical features of, 10, 128
instructional formats and supports,
130–31
interaction opportunities in, 134
issues with word problems, 129
language of, 121–36
multiple meaning key words, 131
nonlinguistic representation, 126
organizational and study skills, 134–35
preview and review, 132–33
reform, 123–24
register, 125
representations and computing methods, 125
specialized language of, 124–30
speech modification, 131–32
strategies for learning and talking, 130–35
vocabulary, 10, 125–27, 131
Meaningful literacy, 141
Measurable verbs, 57
Measurement, lesson, 184–86
Modes, 82
Moving questions, 44
Multiple literacies, 140
Multisensory lessons, 130

National Council for the Social Studies
(NCSS), 159, 161, 163

National Council of Teachers of Mathematics
(NCTM), 123, 124
National Councils of Teachers of English
(NCTE), 139, 190
National Research Council (NRC), 107
National Science Education Standards, 107
National Standards for the English Language
Arts, 139
Native culture
mathematics and, 133–34
role of, 32–33
Native language
in classroom, 33
cognates and, 133–34
role of, 32–33
Needs, student, 41–51
guidelines for understanding, 51–52
Negation, acquisition of, 24
New math, 123–24
Nominalization, 109
Non-English speaker (NES), 3
Non-native speakers (NNS), 3

Objectives
activities *versus,* 56
content, 56–57
definition of, 56
goals *versus,* 56
language, 56, 57–60
learning, 56
standards *versus,* 56
tasks *versus,* 56
understanding, 56–61
Observation, as assessment, 93
Oral history approach, 173
Organizational skills, teaching, 134–35

Pedagogical connections, 68, 85
techniques for making, 85
Personal connections, 68–70, 185, 187
creating, 69
Personal histories, 71
Physical education lesson, 189–90
Plurals, 155
Portfolios, as assessment, 93
*PreK-12 English Language Proficiency
Standards,* 23
Prereading strategies, 142
Preteaching, vocabulary, 72
Preview and review, in mathematics,
132–33
Prewriting, 148
Primary language
clusters, 33
development, 33
Process writing, 148
Productive language, 21–22
speaking, 22
writing, 22

Proficiency
English language, 22–23
language, 4, 20–21
levels, 23–27
*Putting the Pieces Together: Comprehensive
School-Linked Strategies for Children*
(NCREL), 43

Reading, 21
CAN DO descriptors for, 29
instruction for ELLs, 146
stages in ELP, 25–27
strategies, for intermediate, 143, 145
strategies for beginning, 143, 144
*Reading Next: A Vision for Action and Research
for Middle and High School Literacy*
(Biancarosa and Snow), 146
Receptive language, 21
listening, 21
reading, 21
Register, 5
Risk-taking atmosphere, in mathematics, 135
Root words, 117–18, 119
vocabulary instruction and, 150
Rubrics, 95
online makers, 96

Scaffolding, 55, 67, 83
sentence starters for conversations,
155–56
School
language of, 2–17
strategies, 46
School Climate Survey, 46
School Strategies Scale, 46
Science
anticipatory sets for, 75
cause and effect, 116–17
challenges for ELL in, 106–7, 109, 110
compare and contrast, 114–15
discourse, 11, 113–14
education, 107–8
grammatical features of, 10, 113
Greek and Latin roots, 117–18, 119
language, 106–20
specialized language of, 108–14
strategies for learning and talking, 114–19
vocabulary, 10, 110–12
Scientific inquiry, 107–8
language of, 114
sentence starters for, 115
Second language learner, 3
Sentence starters
for scaffolding conversations, 155–56
for scientific inquiry, 115
Sentence structure, 154
Sheltered Instruction Observation Protocol
(SIOP), 68, 100, 173
Social English, 4

Social language, 6–8
  academic *versus*, 11–12, 13
  everyday aspects of, 6
  instructional aspects of, 8
  intercultural aspects of, 7
Social studies
  background on, 161–63
  challenges for ELLs in, 160
  cognates and, 176, 177
  content, 161
  discourse, 11, 169–71
  grammatical features of, 10, 167–68
  language of, 159–78
  oral history approach, 173
  specialized language of, 163–71
  strategies for teaching and learning,
    171–76
  supportive classrooms, 171
  textbooks and materials, 169–70
  vocabulary, 10, 164–67
Sociolinguistic competencies, 31
Speaking, 21, 22
  stages in ELP, 25–27
Specialized academic vocabulary, 9
Specially Designed Academic Instruction
  of English (SDAIE), 173
Specific content vocabulary, 165
Speech, modifying for ELLs, 131–32
Standardized tests, 43
Standards, 57
  ELP, 24
  NCTE/IRA, 139
  objectives *versus*, 56
Starting English language proficiency, 25
Strategic competencies, 31, 32
Strategies
  mathematics, 130–35
  prereading, 142
  reading, for beginning readers, 143, 144
  reading, for intermediate readers, 143, 145
  science, 114–19
  teaching vocabulary, 150–53
  vocabulary trading, 152
  writing, 149
Strengths
  guidelines for understanding, 51–52
  of students, 41–51
Students
  assessing strengths and needs, 38–52
  background, 55–56, 67–68
  collecting general information about,
    41–43

  connections to lives, 76
  educational background of, 39–41
  gathering information on backgrounds,
    43–45
  guidelines for understanding strengths
    and needs, 51–52
  role in alternative assessments, 95–96
  strengths and needs, 41–51
  techniques for data collection, 44
Study skills, teaching, 134–35
Subject-verb agreement, 154
Summative assessment, 41
Survey, 44
Sustained institutional support, 11
Syntactic ambiguity, 113
Syntax, 9

Table, 131
Task process, 81
  elements of, 82
  instructional groupings, 82
  modes, 82
  procedural tools, 84
  resources/texts, 83
  scaffolding, 83
  task structure, 82
  teacher/student roles, 83–84
  time and pacing, 82–83
Task product, 81
  audience, 84
  elements of, 84–85
  modes, 84–85
Tasks
  designing engaging, 79–88, 182
  elements of, 81–85
  guidelines for designing, 85–88
  objectives *versus*, 56
  for students, 87
  understanding, 80–85
Task structure, 82
Taxonomy, 108
Teacher behaviors, 49, 193–94
Teachers of English to Speakers
  of Other Languages (TESOL),
    20, 23, 112
Teaching
  language objectives, 62–64
  organizational and study skills, 134–35
  social studies, 171–76
  vocabulary, 72
Technical academic vocabulary, 9

Testwiseness, 92
Text features, 175
Text sets, 83
Theoretical orientation, 141
Time order, 113
Traditional classroom assessment, 92
  adapting, 94–95
  alternative *versus*, 94
Transparency, in assessment, 99

Venn diagrams, 115, 116
Verbs
  measurable, 57
  phrases, 154
  tense, 154
Vocabulary, 8, 9
  cause and effect, 117
  compare and contrast, 116
  examples of, 10
  general academic, 9
  language arts, 150–52, 153
  language objectives, 58
  mathematics, 125–27, 131
  preteaching and reinforcing, 72
  science, 110–12
  signaling organizational pattern, 168
  social studies, 164–67
  specialized academic, 9
  specific content, 165
  teaching strategies, 72, 150–53
  technical academic, 9
  trading strategies, 152
  types of, 10

Wait-time, 132
Wall-write, 42, 44
Word choice, 155
Word games, 151
Word maps, 151
Word problems, issues with, 129
World-Class Instructional Design and
  Assessment (WIDA), 28, 35
Writing, 21, 22
  CAN DO descriptors for, 29
  collaborative, 148
  for content learning, 149
  genres, 170–71
  instruction for ELLs, 147–49
  process, 148
  stages in ELP, 25–27
  strategies, 149